D1479543

# CIS Access 2013
## Exploring Microsoft® Office 2013

Camden County College

Taken from:
*Exploring Microsoft® Access 2013: Introductory*
Series Editor Mary Anne Poatsy
Krebs | Cameron
Series Created by Dr. Robert T. Grauer

Cover Art: Courtesy of Photodisc/Getty Images.

Taken from:

*Exploring Microsoft® Access 2013: Introductory*
by Mary Anne Poatsy, Cynthia Krebs, Eric Cameron, and Dr. Robert T. Grauer
Copyright © 2014 by Pearson Education, Inc.
Upper Saddle River, New Jersey 07458

This special edition published in cooperation with Pearson Learning Solutions.

All trademarks, service marks, registered trademarks, and registered service marks are the property of their respective owners and are used herein for identification purposes only.

Pearson Learning Solutions, 501 Boylston Street, Suite 900, Boston, MA 02116
A Pearson Education Company
www.pearsoned.com

Printed in the United States of America

3 4 5 6 7 8 9 10 V0ZV 17 16 15

000200010271905634

RD

ISBN 10: 1-269-94367-7
ISBN 13: 978-1-269-94367-3

# Dedications

For my husband, Ted, who unselfishly continues to take on more than his share to support me throughout the process; and for my children, Laura, Carolyn, and Teddy, whose encouragement and love have been inspiring.

**Mary Anne Poatsy**

To my students—you continue to inspire me. Thank you for all you have taught me and shared with me.

**Cynthia Krebs**

I dedicate this book to my fiancée, Anny, for encouraging me throughout the writing process and for being the person she is, to Sonny, to Drs. Hubey, Boyno, Bredlau, and Deremer at Montclair State University for educating and inspiring me, and to my students, who I hope will inspire others someday.

**Eric Cameron**

# About the Authors

## Mary Anne Poatsy, Series Editor

Mary Anne is a senior faculty member at Montgomery County Community College, teaching various computer application and concepts courses in face-to-face and online environments. She holds a B.A. in Psychology and Education from Mount Holyoke College and an M.B.A. in Finance from Northwestern University's Kellogg Graduate School of Management.

Mary Anne has more than 12 years of educational experience. She is currently adjunct faculty at Gwynedd-Mercy College and Montgomery County Community College. She has also taught at Bucks County Community College and Muhlenberg College, as well as conducted personal training. Before teaching, she was Vice President at Shearson Lehman in the Municipal Bond Investment Banking Department.

## Cynthia Krebs, Access Author

Cynthia Krebs is the Director of Business and Marketing Education at Utah Valley University. She is a professor in the Information Systems and Technology Department at Utah Valley University (UVU). In 2008, she received the UVU College of Technology and Computing Scholar Award. She has also received the School of Business Faculty Excellence Award twice during her tenure at UVU. Cynthia teaches the Methods of Teaching Digital Media class to future teachers, as well as classes in basic computer proficiency, business proficiency applications, and business graphics.

Cynthia is active in the Utah Business and Computer Education Association, the Western Business Education Association, the National Business Education Association, and the Utah Association of Career and Technical Educators. She was awarded the WBEA Outstanding Educator at the University Level in 2009. Cynthia has written multiple texts on Microsoft Office software, consulted with government and business, and has presented extensively at the local, regional, and national levels to professional and business organizations.

Cynthia lives by a peaceful creek in Springville, Utah. When she isn't teaching or writing, she enjoys spending time with her children, spoiling her grandchildren Ava, Bode, Solee, and Morgan. She loves traveling and reading.

## Eric Cameron, Access Author

Eric holds a M.S. in computer science and a B.S. degree in Computer Science with minors in Mathematics and Physics, both from Montclair State University. He is a tenured Assistant Professor at Passaic County Community College, where he has taught in the Computer and Information Sciences department since 2001. Eric is also the author of the *Your Office: Getting Started with Web 2.0* and *Your Office: Getting Started with Windows 8* textbooks. Eric maintains a professional blog at profcameron.blogspot.com.

## Rebecca Lawson, Office Fundamentals Author

Rebecca Lawson is a professor in the Computer Information Technologies program at Lansing Community College. She coordinates the curriculum, develops the instructional materials, and teaches for the E-Business curriculum. She also serves as the Online Faculty Coordinator at the Center for Teaching Excellence at LCC. In that role, she develops and facilitates online workshops for faculty learning to teach online. Her major areas of interest include online curriculum quality assurance, the review and development of printed and online instructional materials, the assessment of computer and Internet literacy skill levels to facilitate student retention, and the use of social networking tools to support learning in blended and online learning environments.

## Dr. Robert T. Grauer, Creator of the Exploring Series

Bob Grauer is an Associate Professor in the Department of Computer Information Systems at the University of Miami, where he is a multiple winner of the Outstanding Teaching Award in the School of Business, most recently in 2009. He has written numerous COBOL texts and is the vision behind the Exploring Office series, with more than three million books in print. His work has been translated into three foreign languages and is used in all aspects of higher education at both national and international levels. Bob Grauer has consulted for several major corporations including IBM and American Express. He received his Ph.D. in Operations Research in 1972 from the Polytechnic Institute of Brooklyn.

# Brief Contents

# Contents

## Microsoft Office Access 2013

### CHAPTER ONE Introduction to Access: Finding Your Way Through an Access Database 1

### CHAPTER TWO Tables and Queries in Relational Databases: Designing Databases and Extracting Data 59

# Acknowledgments

The Exploring team would like to acknowledge and thank all the reviewers who helped us throughout the years by providing us with their invaluable comments, suggestions, and constructive criticism.

We'd like to especially thank our Focus Group attendees and User Diary Reviewers for this edition:

Stephen Z. Jourdan
Auburn University at Montgomery

Ann Rovetto
Horry-Georgetown Technical College

Jacqueline D. Lawson
Henry Ford Community College

Diane L. Smith
Henry Ford Community College

Sven Aelterman
Troy University

Suzanne M. Jeska
County College of Morris

Susan N. Dozier
Tidewater Community College

Robert G. Phipps Jr.
West Virginia University

Mike Michaelson
Palomar College

Mary Beth Tarver
Northwestern State University

Alexandre C. Probst
Colorado Christian University

Phil Nielson
Salt Lake Community College

Carolyn Barren
Macomb Community College

Sue A. McCrory
Missouri State University

Lucy Parakhovnik
California State University, Northridge

Jakie Brown Jr.
Stevenson University

Craig J. Peterson
American InterContinental University

Terry Ray Rigsby
Hill College

Biswadip Ghosh
Metropolitan State University of Denver

Cheryl Sypniewski
Macomb Community College

Lynn Keane
University of South Carolina

Sheila Gionfriddo
Luzerne College

Dick Hewer
Ferris State College

Carolyn Borne
Louisiana State University

Sumathy Chandrashekar
Salisbury University

Laura Marcoulides
Fullerton College

Don Riggs
SUNY Schenectady County Community College

Gary McFall
Purdue University

James Powers
University of Southern Indiana

James Brown
Central Washington University

Brian Powell
West Virginia University

Sherry Lenhart
Terra Community College

Chen Zhang
Bryant University

Nikia Robinson
Indian River State University

Jill Young
Southeast Missouri State University

Debra Hoffman
Southeast Missouri State University

Tommy Lu
Delaware Technical Community College

Mimi Spain
Southern Maine Community College

We'd like to thank everyone who has been involved in reviewing and providing their feedback, including for our previous editions:

Adriana Lumpkin
Midland College

Alan S. Abrahams
Virginia Tech

Ali Berrached
University of Houston–Downtown

Allen Alexander
Delaware Technical & Community College

Andrea Marchese
Maritime College, State University of New York

Andrew Blitz
Broward College; Edison State College

Angel Norman
University of Tennessee, Knoxville

Angela Clark
University of South Alabama

Ann Rovetto
Horry-Georgetown Technical College

Astrid Todd
Guilford Technical Community College

Audrey Gillant
Maritime College, State University of New York

Barbara Stover
Marion Technical College

Barbara Tollinger
Sinclair Community College

Ben Brahim Taha
Auburn University

Beverly Amer
Northern Arizona University

Beverly Fite
Amarillo College

Bonita Volker
Tidewater Community College

Bonnie Homan
San Francisco State University

Brad West
Sinclair Community College

Brian Powell
West Virginia University

Carol Buser
Owens Community College

Carol Roberts
University of Maine

Carolyn Barren
Macomb Community College

Cathy Poyner
Truman State University

Charles Hodgson
Delgado Community College

Cheri Higgins
Illinois State University

Cheryl Hinds
Norfolk State University

Chris Robinson
Northwest State Community College

Cindy Herbert
Metropolitan Community College–Longview

Dana Hooper
University of Alabama

Dana Johnson
North Dakota State University

Daniela Marghitu
Auburn University

David Noel
University of Central Oklahoma

David Pulis
Maritime College, State University of New York

David Thornton
Jacksonville State University

Dawn Medlin
Appalachian State University

Debby Keen
University of Kentucky

Debra Chapman
University of South Alabama

Derrick Huang
Florida Atlantic University

Diana Baran
Henry Ford Community College

Diane Cassidy
The University of North Carolina at Charlotte

Diane Smith
Henry Ford Community College

Don Danner
San Francisco State University

Don Hoggan
Solano College

Doncho Petkov
Eastern Connecticut State University

Donna Ehrhart
State University of New York at Brockport

Elaine Crable
Xavier University

Elizabeth Duett
Delgado Community College

Erhan Uskup
Houston Community College–Northwest

Eric Martin
University of Tennessee

Erika Nadas
Wilbur Wright College

Floyd Winters
Manatee Community College

Frank Lucente
Westmoreland County Community College

G. Jan Wilms
Union University

Gail Cope
Sinclair Community College

Gary DeLorenzo
California University of Pennsylvania

Gary Garrison
Belmont University

George Cassidy
Sussex County Community College

Gerald Braun
Xavier University

Gerald Burgess
Western New Mexico University

Gladys Swindler
Fort Hays State University

Heith Hennel
Valencia Community College

Henry Rudzinski
Central Connecticut State University

Irene Joos
La Roche College

Iwona Rusin
Baker College; Davenport University

J. Roberto Guzman
San Diego Mesa College

Jan Wilms
Union University

Jane Stam
Onondaga Community College

Janet Bringhurst
Utah State University

Jeanette Dix
Ivy Tech Community College

Jennifer Day
Sinclair Community College

Jill Canine
Ivy Tech Community College

Jim Chaffee
The University of Iowa Tippie College of Business

Joanne Lazirko
University of Wisconsin–Milwaukee

Jodi Milliner
Kansas State University

John Hollenbeck
Blue Ridge Community College

John Seydel
Arkansas State University

Judith A. Scheeren
Westmoreland County Community College

Judith Brown
The University of Memphis

Juliana Cypert
Tarrant County College

Kamaljeet Sanghera
George Mason University

Karen Priestly
Northern Virginia Community College

Karen Ravan
Spartanburg Community College

Kathleen Brenan
Ashland University

Ken Busbee
Houston Community College

Kent Foster
Winthrop University

Kevin Anderson
Solano Community College

Kim Wright
The University of Alabama

Kristen Hockman
University of Missouri–Columbia

Kristi Smith
Allegany College of Maryland

Laura McManamon
University of Dayton

Leanne Chun
Leeward Community College

Lee McClain
Western Washington University

Linda D. Collins
Mesa Community College

Linda Johnsonius
Murray State University

Linda Lau
Longwood University

Linda Theus
Jackson State Community College

Linda Williams
Marion Technical College

Lisa Miller
University of Central Oklahoma

Lister Horn
Pensacola Junior College

Lixin Tao
Pace University

Loraine Miller
Cayuga Community College

Lori Kielty
Central Florida Community College

Lorna Wells
Salt Lake Community College

Lorraine Sauchin
Duquesne University

Lucy Parakhovnik (Parker)
California State University, Northridge

Lynn Mancini
Delaware Technical Community College

Mackinzee Escamilla
South Plains College

Marcia Welch
Highline Community College

Margaret McManus
Northwest Florida State College

Margaret Warrick
Allan Hancock College

Marilyn Hibbert
Salt Lake Community College

Mark Choman
Luzerne County Community College

Mary Duncan
University of Missouri–St. Louis

Melissa Nemeth
Indiana University-Purdue University
Indianapolis

Melody Alexander
Ball State University

Michael Douglas
University of Arkansas at Little Rock

Michael Dunklebarger
Alamance Community College

Michael G. Skaff
College of the Sequoias

Michele Budnovitch
Pennsylvania College of Technology

Mike Jochen
East Stroudsburg University

Mike Scroggins
Missouri State University

Muhammed Badamas
Morgan State University

NaLisa Brown
University of the Ozarks

Nancy Grant
Community College of Allegheny
County–South Campus

Nanette Lareau
University of Arkansas Community
College–Morrilton

Pam Brune
Chattanooga State Community College

Pam Uhlenkamp
Iowa Central Community College

Patrick Smith
Marshall Community and Technical College

Paul Addison
Ivy Tech Community College

Paula Ruby
Arkansas State University

Peggy Burrus
Red Rocks Community College

Peter Ross
SUNY Albany

Philip H. Nielson
Salt Lake Community College

Ralph Hooper
University of Alabama

Ranette Halverson
Midwestern State University

Richard Blamer
John Carroll University

Richard Cacace
Pensacola Junior College

Richard Hewer
Ferris State University

Rob Murray
Ivy Tech Community College

Robert Dušek
Northern Virginia Community College

Robert Sindt
Johnson County Community College

Robert Warren
Delgado Community College

Rocky Belcher
Sinclair Community College

Roger Pick
University of Missouri at Kansas City

Ronnie Creel
Troy University

Rosalie Westerberg
Clover Park Technical College

Ruth Neal
Navarro College

Sandra Thomas
Troy University

Sheila Gionfriddo
Luzerne County Community College

Sherrie Geitgey
Northwest State Community College

Sophia Wilberscheid
Indian River State College

Sophie Lee
California State University,
Long Beach

Stacy Johnson
Iowa Central Community College

Stephanie Kramer
Northwest State Community College

Stephen Jourdan
Auburn University Montgomery

Steven Schwarz
Raritan Valley Community College

Sue McCrory
Missouri State University

Susan Fuschetto
Cerritos College

Susan Medlin
UNC Charlotte

Suzan Spitzberg
Oakton Community College

Sven Aelterman
Troy University

Sylvia Brown
Midland College

Tanya Patrick
Clackamas Community College

Terri Holly
Indian River State College

Thomas Rienzo
Western Michigan University

Tina Johnson
Midwestern State University

Tommy Lu
Delaware Technical and Community College

Troy S. Cash
NorthWest Arkansas Community College

Vicki Robertson
Southwest Tennessee Community

Weifeng Chen
California University of Pennsylvania

Wes Anthony
Houston Community College

William Ayen
University of Colorado at Colorado Springs

Wilma Andrews
Virginia Commonwealth University

Yvonne Galusha
University of Iowa

Special thanks to our development and technical team:

Barbara Stover

Cheryl Slavick

Elizabeth Lockley

Heather Hetzler

Jennifer Lynn

Joyce Nielsen

Linda Pogue

Lisa Bucki

Lori Damanti

Mara Zebest

Susan Fry

# Preface

## The Exploring Series and You

Exploring is Pearson's Office Application series that requires students like you to think "beyond the point and click." In this edition, we have worked to restructure the Exploring experience around the way you, today's modern student, actually use your resources.

The goal of Exploring is, as it has always been, to go further than teaching just the steps to accomplish a task—the series provides the theoretical foundation for you to understand when and why to apply a skill.

As a result, you achieve a deeper understanding of each application and can apply this critical thinking beyond Office and the classroom.

You are practical students, focused on what you need to do to be successful in this course and beyond, and want to be as efficient as possible. Exploring has evolved to meet you where you are and help you achieve success efficiently. Pearson has paid attention to the habits of students today, how you get information, how you are motivated to do well in class, and what your future goals look like. We asked you and your peers for acceptance of new tools we designed to address these points, and you responded with a resounding "YES!"

## Here Is What We Learned About You

**You are goal-oriented.** You want a good grade in this course—so we rethought how Exploring works so that you can learn the how and why behind the skills in this course to be successful now. You also want to be successful in your future career—so we used motivating case studies to show relevance of these skills to your future careers and incorporated Soft Skills, Collaboration, and Analysis Cases in this edition to set you up for success in the future.

**You read, prepare, and study differently than students used to.** You use textbooks like a tool—you want to easily identify what you need to know and learn it efficiently. We have added key features such as Step Icons, Hands-On Exercise Videos, and tracked everything via page numbers that allow you to navigate the content efficiently, making the concepts accessible and creating a map to success for you to follow.

**You go to college now with a different set of skills than students did five years ago.** The new edition of Exploring moves you beyond the basics of the software at a faster pace, without sacrificing coverage of the fundamental skills that you need to know. This ensures that you will be engaged from page 1 to the end of the book.

**You and your peers have diverse learning styles.** With this in mind, we broadened our definition of "student resources" to include Compass, an online skill database; movable Student Reference cards; Hands-On Exercise videos to provide a secondary lecture-like option of review; Soft Skills video exercises to illustrate important non-technical skills; and the most powerful online homework and assessment tool around with a direct 1:1 content match with the Exploring Series, MyITLab. Exploring will be accessible to all students, regardless of learning style.

## Providing You with a Map to Success to Move Beyond the Point and Click

All of these changes and additions will provide you with an easy and efficient path to follow to be successful in this course, regardless of your learning style or any existing knowledge you have at the outset. Our goal is to keep you more engaged in both the hands-on and conceptual sides, helping you to achieve a higher level of understanding that will guarantee you success in this course and in your future career. In addition to the vision and experience of the series creator, Robert T. Grauer, we have assembled a tremendously talented team of Office Applications authors who have devoted themselves to teaching you the ins and outs of Microsoft Word, Excel, Access, and PowerPoint. Led in this edition by series editor Mary Anne Poatsy, the whole team is equally dedicated to providing you with a **map to success** to support the Exploring mission of **moving you beyond the point and click**.

# Key Features

- **White Pages/Yellow Pages** clearly distinguish the theory (white pages) from the skills covered in the Hands-On Exercises (yellow pages) so students always know what they are supposed to be doing.

- **Enhanced Objective Mapping** enables students to follow a directed path through each chapter, from the objectives list at the chapter opener through the exercises in the end of chapter.
  - **Objectives List:** This provides a simple list of key objectives covered in the chapter. This includes page numbers so students can skip between objectives where they feel they need the most help.
  - **Step Icons:** These icons appear in the white pages and reference the step numbers in the Hands-On Exercises, providing a correlation between the two so students can easily find conceptual help when they are working hands-on and need a refresher.
  - **Quick Concepts Check:** A series of questions that appear briefly at the end of each white page section. These questions cover the most essential concepts in the white pages required for students to be successful in working the Hands-On Exercises. Page numbers are included for easy reference to help students locate the answers.
  - **Chapter Objectives Review:** Appears toward the end of the chapter and reviews all important concepts throughout the chapter. Newly designed in an easy-to-read bulleted format.

- **Key Terms Matching:** A new exercise that requires students to match key terms to their definitions. This requires students to work actively with this important vocabulary and prove conceptual understanding.

- **Case Study** presents a scenario for the chapter, creating a story that ties the Hands-On Exercises together.

Watch the Video for this Hands-On Exercise!

- **Hands-On Exercise Videos** are tied to each Hands-On Exercise and walk students through the steps of the exercise while weaving in conceptual information related to the Case Study and the objectives as a whole.

- **End-of-Chapter Exercises** offer instructors several options for assessment. Each chapter has approximately 12–15 exercises ranging from multiple choice questions to open-ended projects. Newly included in this is a Key Terms Matching exercise of approximately 20 questions, as well as a Collaboration Case and Soft Skills Case for every chapter.

ANALYSIS CASE
CREATIVE CASE

- **Enhanced Mid-Level Exercises** include a **Creative Case** (for PowerPoint and Word), which allows students some flexibility and creativity, not being bound by a definitive solution, and an **Analysis Case** (for Excel and Access), which requires students to interpret the data they are using to answer an analytic question, as well as **Discover Steps**, which encourage students to use Help or to problem-solve to accomplish a task.

MyITLab®
HOE1 Training

MyITLab®
Grader

- **MyITLab** provides an auto-graded homework, tutorial, and assessment solution that is built to match the book content exactly. Every Hands-On Exercise is available as a simulation training. Every Capstone Exercise and most Mid-Level Exercises are available as live-in-the-application Grader projects. Icons are included throughout the text to denote which exercises are included.

# Instructor Resources

The Instructor's Resource Center, available at www.pearsonhighered.com, includes the following:

- **Instructor Manual** provides an overview of all available resources as well as student data and solution files for every exercise.

- **Solution Files with Scorecards** assist with grading the Hands-On Exercises and end-of-chapter exercises.

- **Prepared Exams** allow instructors to assess all skills covered in a chapter with a single project.

- **Rubrics** for Mid-Level Creative Cases and Beyond the Classroom Cases in Microsoft® Word format enable instructors to customize the assignments for their classes.

- **PowerPoint® Presentations** with notes for each chapter are included for out-of-class study or review.

- **Lesson Plans** provide a detailed blueprint to achieve chapter learning objectives and outcomes.

- **Objectives Lists** map chapter objectives to Hands-On Exercises and end-of-chapter exercises.

- **Multiple Choice and Key Terms Matching Answer Keys**

- **Test Bank** provides objective-based questions for every chapter.

- **Grader Projects** textual versions of auto-graded assignments for Grader.

- **Additional Projects** provide more assignment options for instructors.

- **Syllabus Templates**

- **Scripted Lectures** offer an in-class lecture guide for instructors to mirror the Hands-On Exercises.

- **Assignment Sheet**

- **File Guide**

# Student Resources

## Companion Web Site

www.pearsonhighered.com/exploring offers expanded IT resources and self-student tools for students to use for each chapter, including:

- Online Chapter Review
- Web Resources
- Glossary
- Student Data Files
- Chapter Objectives Review

In addition, the Companion Web Site is now the site for Premium Media, including the videos for the Exploring Series:

- Hands-On Exercise Videos*
- Audio PPTs*
- Soft Skills Exercise Videos*

*Access code required for these premium resources.

## Student Reference Cards

A two-sided card for each application provides students with a visual summary of information and tips specific to each application.

Access

# Introduction to Access

## Finding Your Way Through an Access Database

Yuri Arcurs/Shutterstock

## OBJECTIVES  AFTER YOU READ THIS CHAPTER, YOU WILL BE ABLE TO:

1. Understand database fundamentals p. 2

2. Use an existing database p. 9

3. Sort table data on one or multiple fields p. 20

4. Create, modify, and remove filters p. 21

5. Know when to use Access or Excel to manage data p. 29

6. Understand relational power p. 30

7. Create a database p. 37

## CASE STUDY | Managing a Business in the Global Economy

Northwind Traders* is an international gourmet food distributor that imports and exports specialty foods from around the world. Northwind's products include meats, seafood, dairy products, beverages, and produce. Keeping track of customers, vendors, orders, and inventory is a critical task. The owners of Northwind have just purchased an order-processing database created with Microsoft Office Access 2013 to help manage their customers, suppliers, products, and orders.

You have been hired to learn, use, and manage the database. Northwind's owners are willing to provide training about their business and Access. They expect the learning process to take about three months. After three months, your job will be to support the order-processing team as well as to provide detail and summary reports to the sales force as needed. Your new job at Northwind Traders will be a challenge, but it is also a good opportunity to make a great contribution to a global company. Are you up to the task?

*Northwind Traders was created by the Microsoft Access Team as a sample database for Access 2003. Access 2013 does not include a sample database, so you will use a modified version of Northwind Traders. The names of companies, products, people, characters, and/or data are fictitious.

# Databases Are Everywhere!

A *database* is a collection of data organized as meaningful information that can be accessed, managed, stored, queried, sorted, and reported. You probably participate in data collection and are exposed to databases on a regular basis. For example, your community college or university uses a database to store registration data. When you enrolled at your institution, you created a profile that was saved in a database. When you registered for this course, your data was entered into a database. If you have a bank account, have a Social Security card, have a medical history, or have booked a flight with an airline, your information is stored in a record in a database.

If you use the Internet, you probably use databases often because the Internet can provide you with easy access to databases. For example, when you shop online or check your bank statement online, you connect to a database. Even when you type a search phrase into Google and click Search, you are using Google's massive database with all of its stored Web page references and keywords. Look for something on Amazon, and you are searching Amazon's database to find a product that you might want to buy. Need a new driver for golfing? Log on to Amazon, search for "golf clubs driver" (see Figure 1.1), and find the right driver with your preferred loft, hand orientation, flex, shaft material, and price range. All of this information is stored in Amazon's products database.

**FIGURE 1.1** Amazon Web Site
Photo: Copyright © 2013 Amazon .com, Inc.

Organizations rely on data to conduct daily operations, regardless of whether the organization exists as a profit or not-for-profit environment. Organizations maintain data about their customers, employees, orders, volunteers, activities, and facilities. Organizations maintain data about their customers, employees, orders, volunteers, activities, and facilities, and this data needs to be stored, organized, and made available for analysis. *Data* and *information* are two terms that are often used interchangeably. However, when it comes to databases, the two terms mean different things. *Data* is what is entered into a database. *Information* is the finished product that is produced by the database. Data is converted to information by selecting, calculating, sorting, or summarizing records. Decisions in an organization are usually based on information produced by a database, rather than raw data.

In this section, you will learn the fundamentals of organizing data in a database, explore what Access database objects are and what their purpose is, and examine the Access interface.

## Understanding Database Fundamentals

People use databases to store collections of data. A *database management system (DBMS)* is a software system that provides the tools needed to create, maintain, and use a database. Database management systems make it possible to access and control data and display the information in a variety of formats such as lists, forms, and reports. *Access* is the database management system included in the Office 2013 Professional suite and the Office 2013 Professional Academic suite. Access is a valuable decision-making tool that many organizations are using. Advanced Access users and software developers can even use Microsoft Access to develop software applications for specific solutions to the needs of organizations. For example, a health organization uses Access to track and understand disease reports.

## Organize Information in a Database and Recognize Access Objects

STEP 2 » An Access database is a structured collection of *objects*, the main components that are created and used to make the database function. The main object types in an Access database are listed below and discussed in the following paragraphs.

- Tables
- Forms
- Queries
- Reports
- Macros
- Modules

The objects that make up an Access database are available from the *Navigation Pane*. The Navigation Pane is an Access interface element that organizes and lists the database objects in an Access database. You will learn about the object types and their benefits in the remainder of this section. Later you will learn to create and use these objects.

The foundation of every database is a *table*, the object in which data, such as a person's name or a product number, is stored. The other objects in a database are based on one or more underlying tables. To understand how an Access database works and how to use Access effectively, you should learn the structure of a table. Tables organize data into columns and rows. Columns display a *field*, the smallest data element of a table. For example, in the Northwind database, a table containing information about customers would include a Customer ID field. Another field would contain the Company Name. Fields may be required or optional—a contact name may be required, for example, but a contact title may be optional.

Each row in a table contains a *record*, a complete set of all the fields (data elements) about one person, place, event, or concept. A customer record, for example, would contain all of the fields about a single customer, including the Customer ID, the Company Name, Contact Name, Contact Title, Address, City, etc. Figure 1.2 shows the Northwind database with the Customers table selected in the Navigation Pane. The Customers table is open and shows the records of Northwind customers in the table rows. Each record contains multiple fields, with the field name displaying at the top of each column.

**FIGURE 1.2** Customers Table

A *form* is an object that gives a user a way of entering and modifying data in databases. Forms enable you to enter, modify, or delete table data. They enable you to manipulate data in the same manner that you would in a table. The difference is that you can create a form that will limit the user to viewing only one record at a time. This helps the user to focus on the data being entered or modified and also provides for more reliable data entry. As an Access user, you will add, delete, and edit records in Form view. As the Access designer, you will create and edit the form structure.

A *query* is a question that you ask about the data in your database. For example, how many of our customers live in Boston? The answer is shown in the query results. A query can be used to display only records that meet certain conditions and only the fields that you require. In addition to helping you find and retrieve data that meets the conditions that you specify, you can use a query to update or delete records and to perform predefined or custom calculations with your data.

A *report* contains professional-looking formatted information from underlying tables or queries. Reports enable you to print the information in your database and are an effective way to present database information. You have control over the size and appearance of everything in a report. Access provides different views for designing, modifying, and running reports.

Two other object types, macros and modules, are used less frequently unless you are a power Access user. A *macro* object is a stored series of commands that carry out an action. You can create a macro to automate simple tasks by selecting an action from a list of macro actions. A *module* is similar to a macro, as it is an object that adds functionality to a database, but modules are written using the VBA (Visual Basic for Applications) programming language.

Figure 1.3 displays the different object types in Access with the foundation object—the table—in the center of the illustration. The purpose each object serves is explained underneath the object name. The flow of information between objects is indicated by single arrowhead arrows if the flow is one direction only. Two arrowhead arrows indicate that the flow goes both directions. For example, you can use forms to view, add, delete, or modify data from tables.

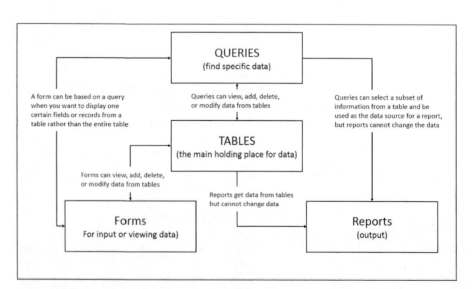

**FIGURE 1.3** Object Types and Flow of Information

## Examine the Access Interface

While Access includes the standard elements of the Microsoft Office applications interface such as the title bar, the Ribbon, the Home tab, the Backstage view, and scroll bars, it also includes elements unique to Access.

The Access Ribbon has five tabs that will always display, as well as contextual tabs that appear only when particular objects are open. The File tab leads to the Backstage view, which gives you access to a variety of database tools such as Save, Save As, Compact and Repair, Backup Database, and Print. The Home tab, the default Access tab, contains basic editing functions, such as cut and paste, filtering, find and replace, and most formatting actions. This tab also contains the features that enable you to work with record creation and deletion, totals, and spelling.

The Create tab contains all the tools used to create new objects in a database whereas the External Data tab contains all of the operations used to facilitate data import and export. Finally, the Database Tools tab contains the feature that enables users to create relationships between tables and enables use of the more advanced features of Access, such as setting relationships between tables, analyzing a table or query, and migrating data to SharePoint.

On the left side of the screen, you will see the Navigation Pane. The Navigation Pane organizes and lists all of the objects that are needed to make the current database function. You can open any object by double-clicking the object's name in the list. You can also open an object by right-clicking the object name and selecting Open from the shortcut menu. Right-clicking provides other options, such as renaming the object, cutting the object, and copying the object.

Most databases contain multiple tables, queries, forms, and reports. By default, the objects display in groups by object type in the Navigation Pane. If you wish, you can collapse the contents of an object group by clicking the group heading or the double arrows to the right of the group heading. To expand the contents of an object group that has been hidden, click the heading again or click the double arrows to the right of the group heading again. If you wish to change the way objects are grouped in the Navigation Pane, click the list arrow on the Navigation Pane title bar and select your preferred configuration of the available options.

By default, Access uses a Tabbed Documents interface. That means that each object that is open has its own tab beneath the Ribbon and to the right of the Navigation Pane. You can switch between open objects by clicking a tab to make that object active. Figure 1.4 shows the Access interface for the Northwind Traders database, which was introduced in the Case Study at the beginning of the chapter. The Navigation Pane is grouped by object type. The Tables and Reports groups in the Navigation Pane are expanded. The Table Tools contextual tab displays because the Employees table is open. The Employees table shows the records for nine employees. The employee records contain multiple fields about each employee, including the employee's Last Name, First Name, Hire Date, Region, and so on. Occasionally a field does not contain a value for a particular record. For example, one of the employees, Nancy Davolio, has not been assigned a title yet. The value of that field is missing. Access shows a blank cell when data is missing.

Customized title bar

Click to change Navigation Pane configuration

Navigation Pane

Table group expanded to show all objects

Click to expand Queries list

Shutter Bar Open/Close button

Click to collapse Reports group

Employees table is open

Navigation bar showing nine records in Employees table

**FIGURE 1.4** Access Interface

## Explore Access Views

Access provides two different ways to view a table: the Datasheet view and the Design view. To switch between views:

- Click the HOME tab and click View in the Views group to toggle between the current view and the previous view.
- Click the HOME tab, click the View arrow in the Views group, and then select the view you want to use.
- Right-click the object tab and select the view you want to use.
- Right-click the object in the Navigation Pane and select the view you want to use.
- Click one of the view shortcuts in the lower-right corner of the Access window.

The *Datasheet view* is a grid containing fields (columns) and records (rows), similar to an Excel spreadsheet. You can view, add, edit, and delete records in the Datasheet view. Figure 1.5 shows the Datasheet view for the Northwind Customers table. Each row contains a record for a specific customer. Click the *record selector* at the beginning of a row to select the record. Each column represents a field or one attribute about a customer. Click the *field selector*, or column heading, to select a column.

**FIGURE 1.5** Customers Table in Datasheet View

The navigation bar at the bottom of Figure 1.5 shows that the Customers table has 91 records and that record number 9 is the current record. The vertical scroll bar on the right side of the window displays only when the table contains more records than can appear in the window at one time. Similarly, the horizontal scroll bar at the bottom of the window displays only when the table contains more fields than can appear in the window at one time.

The pencil symbol to the left of Record 9 indicates that the data in that record is being edited and that changes have not yet been saved. The pencil symbol disappears when you move to another record. It is important to understand that Access saves data automatically as soon as you move from one record to another. This may seem counterintuitive at first because other Office applications, such as Word and Excel, do not save changes and additions automatically.

Figure 1.6 shows the navigation buttons on the *navigation bar* that you use to move through the records in a table, query, or form. The buttons enable you to go to the first record, the previous record, the next record, or the last record. The button with the yellow asterisk is used to add a new (blank) record. You can also type a number directly into the current record field, and Access will take you to that record. Finally, the navigation bar enables you to find a record based on a single word. Type the word in the search box, and Access will locate the first record that contains the word.

**FIGURE 1.6** Navigation Buttons

You can also use the Find command in the Find group on the Home tab to locate specific records within a table, form, or query. You can search for a single field or the entire record, match all or part of the selected field(s), move forward or back in a table, or specify a case-sensitive search. The Replace command can be used to substitute one value for another. Select Replace All if you want Access to automatically search for and replace every instance of a value without first checking with you. Be careful when using the Replace All option for global replacement, however, because unintended replacements are possible.

The **Design view** gives you a detailed view of the table's structure and is used to create and modify a table's design by specifying the fields it will contain, the fields' data types, and their associated properties. Data types define the type of data that will be stored in a field, such as short text, long text, numeric, currency, etc. For example, if you need to store the hire date of an employee, you would enter the field name Hire Date and select the Date/Time data type. The *field properties* define the characteristics of the fields in more detail. For example, for the field Hire Date, you could set a field property that requires a Short Date format.

Figure 1.7 shows the Design view for the Customers table. In the top portion, each row contains the field names, the data type, and an optional description for each field in the table. In the bottom portion, the Field Properties pane contains the properties (details) for each field. Click on a field, and the properties for that field will be displayed in the bottom portion of the Design view window.

Figure 1.7 also shows the primary key. The **primary key** is the field (or combination of fields) that uniquely identifies each record in a table. The CustomerID field is the primary key in the Customers table; it ensures that each record in the table can be distinguished from every other record. It also helps prevent the occurrence of duplicate records. Primary key fields may be numbers, letters, or a combination of both. In Figure 1.7, the primary key has an **AutoNumber** data type (a number that is generated by Access and is automatically incremented each time a record is added). Another example of a primary key is an automatically generated Employee ID.

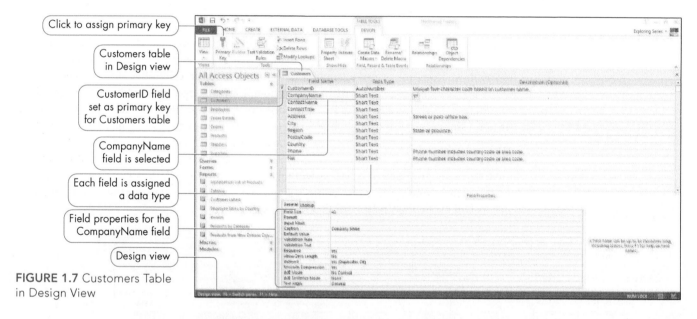

**FIGURE 1.7** Customers Table in Design View

## Open an Access File and Work with Content Security

STEP 1 ▶▶ When Access is first launched, the Backstage view displays. The left side of the view provides a list of databases you have recently used. Beneath the list of recently used databases is the Open Other Files option. Click Open Other Files to access the Open options. You will see a list of the places your account allows you to open a file from: a recent location, your SkyDrive account, your computer, or from any additional places you have added to your Places list. You can also add a new place by clicking the *Add a Place* option. If you select your SkyDrive or another place and the desired database is not in the recent list, you will need to click Browse to open the Open dialog box. Then you can locate and select the database and click Open.

If you are currently using Access and wish to open another database, do the following:

1. Click the FILE tab.
2. Click Open in Backstage view to access Open options.
3. Select the place where the database is stored.

4. Click Browse to open the Open dialog box.
5. Locate and select the database and click Open.

If you open a database from a location you have not designated as a trusted location or open a database that does not have a digital signature from a publisher you can trust, Access will display a message bar immediately below the Ribbon. The message bar displays a security warning designed to prevent you from opening a database that may contain harmful code that can be hidden in macros or VBA modules. Click the Enable Content button if you trust the database's source—it becomes a trusted location. After you click Enable Content, Access closes the database and reopens the file to enable the content. Access also adds the database to its list of trusted documents so you will not see the security message again. All content from this publisher and associated with this book can be trusted.

# Using an Existing Database

Databases must be carefully managed to keep information accurate. Records need to be edited when changes occur and when new records are added, and records may need to be deleted on occasion. All of these processes are easily accomplished using Access. Managing a database also requires that you understand when data is saved and when you need to use the Save commands.

## Understand the Difference Between Working in Storage and Memory

STEP 3 ≫ The way Access performs its save function is different from the other Microsoft Office applications. Word, Excel, and PowerPoint all work primarily from memory. In those applications, your work is not automatically saved to your storage location. You must save your work. This could be catastrophic if you are working with a PowerPoint presentation and you forget to save it. If the power is lost, you may lose your presentation. Access, on the other hand, works primarily from storage. As you enter and update the data in an Access database, the changes are automatically saved to the storage location you specified when you saved the database. If a power failure occurs, you will lose only the changes to the record that you are currently editing.

When you make a change to a record's content in an Access table (for example, changing a customer's cell phone number), Access saves your changes as soon as you move the insertion point to a different record. However, you are required to save after you modify the design of a table, a query, a form, or a report. When you modify an object's design, such as widening a field display on the Customers form, and then close it, Access will prompt you with the message "Do you want to save changes to the design of form 'Customers'?" Click Yes to save your changes.

Also in Access, you can click Undo to reverse the most recent change (the phone number you just modified) to a single record immediately after making changes to that record. However, unlike other Office programs that enable multiple Undo steps, you cannot use Undo to reverse multiple edits in Access.

With an Access database file, several users can work in the same file at the same time. Databases are often located on company servers, making it easy to have multiple users working in the same database at the same time. As long as multiple users do not attempt to change the same record at the same time, Access will let these users access the database simultaneously. So one person can be adding records to the Customers table while another can be creating a query based on the Products table. Two users can even work on the same table as long as they are not working on the same record.

## Add, Edit, and Delete Records

**STEP 4 »** To add a new record, click New in the Records group on the Home tab or click *New (blank) record* on the navigation bar. In a table, you can also click the first column of the blank row beneath the last record. As soon as you begin typing, the asterisk record indicator changes to a pencil icon to show that you are in editing mode. Press Tab to move to the next column so that you can enter the data for the next field. Pressing Tab in the last column in the record saves the record and moves the insertion point to the next record. You can also press Shift+Enter at any time in the record to save the record. The easiest way to save the record is to press the up or down arrow on your keyboard, which moves you to another record. As soon as you move to another record Access automatically saves the changes to the record you created or changed.

To edit a record, tab to the field you want to modify and type the new data. When you start typing, you erase all existing data in the field because the entire field is selected. You can switch to Edit mode by pressing F2. In Edit mode, you will not automatically delete all the data in the field. Instead, you can position your insertion point and make the changes you want.

## REFERENCE — Keyboard Shortcuts for Entering Data

| Keystroke | Result |
|---|---|
| Up arrow (↑) | Moves insertion point up one row. |
| Down arrow (↓) | Moves insertion point down one row. |
| Left arrow (←) | Moves insertion point left one field in the same row. |
| Right arrow (→) | Moves insertion point right one field in the same row. |
| Tab or Enter | Moves insertion point right one field in the same row. |
| Shift+Tab | Moves insertion point left one field in the same row. |
| Home | Moves insertion point to the first field in the current row. |
| End | Moves insertion point to the last field in the current row. |
| Page Up | Moves insertion point up one screen. |
| Page Down | Moves insertion point down one screen. |
| Ctrl+Home | Moves insertion point to the first field in the first row. |
| Ctrl+End | Moves insertion point to the last field in the last row. |
| Esc | Cancels any changes made in the current field while in Edit mode. |
| Ctrl+Z | Reverses the last edit. |
| Ctrl+semicolon (;) | Enters the current date. |
| Ctrl+Alt+Spacebar | Enters the default value of a field. |
| Ctrl+single quote | Enters the value from the same field in the previous record. |
| Ctrl+plus sign (+) | Moves to a new record row. |
| Ctrl+minus sign (−) | Deletes the current record. |

**STEP 5 »** To delete a record, click the row selector for the record you want to delete and click Delete in the Records group on the Home tab. You can also delete a selected record by pressing Delete on the keyboard, or by right-clicking the row selector and selecting Delete Record from the shortcut menu.

**TIP** **Deleting Records**

Be careful about deleting records in a database. Deleting a record may result in the deletion of records in a related table. That information may be critical to the organization. For example, deleting an inactive customer may seem like a good idea, but if you delete the customer it could impact your order history.

## Save As, Compact and Repair, and Back Up Access Files

**STEP 6** The Backstage view gives you access to the Save As command. When you click the Save As command, you can choose the file type you want to save: the database or the current object. Having the option of saving the entire database or just a component of it distinguishes Access from Word, Excel, and PowerPoint. Those applications have only one thing being saved—the primary document, workbook, or presentation. Save Database As enables you to select whether you want to save the database in the default database format (Access 2007–2013 file format), in one of the earlier Access formats, or as a template. Save Object As enables you to make a copy of the current Access object or publish a copy of the object as a PDF or XPS file. A PDF or XPS file looks the same on most computers because these file types preserve the object's formatting. PDF and XPS files also have a small file size. You can also click Save on the Quick Access Toolbar to save an active object—clicking Save on the Quick Access Toolbar does not save the database.

To help you manage your database so that it operates efficiently and securely, Access provides two utilities to help protect the data within a database: *Compact and Repair*, which reduces the size of the database, and *Back Up Database*, which creates a duplicate copy of the database.

Databases have a tendency to expand with everyday use and may become corrupt, so Access provides the *Compact and Repair Database* utility. Entering data, creating queries, running reports, and adding and deleting objects will all cause a database file to expand. This growth may increase storage requirements and may also impact database performance. When you run the Compact and Repair utility, it creates a new database file behind the scenes and copies all the objects from the original database into the new one. As it copies the objects into the new file, Access removes temporary objects and unclaimed space due to deleted objects, which results in a smaller database file. *Compact and Repair* will also defragment a fragmented database file if needed. When the utility is finished copying the data, it deletes the original file and renames the new one with the same name as the original. This utility can also be used to repair a corrupt database. In most cases, only a small amount of data—the last record modified—will be lost during the repair process. You should compact your database every day. To compact and repair an open database, do the following:

1. Close all open objects in the database.
2. Click the FILE tab.
3. Click *Compact and Repair Database* in the Info options.

As an alternative, you can click the Database Tools tab and click *Compact and Repair Database* in the Tools group.

**TIP** **Automatic Compact**

You can have Access compact the open database each time you close it by using the *Compact and Close* option. To use this option, click File to open the Backstage view. Click Options and click Current Database. In the *Options for the current database* pane, click the *Compact on Close* check box under Application Options. Click OK.

The Back Up Database utility makes a copy of the entire database to protect your database from loss or damage. Imagine what would happen to a firm that loses the orders placed but not shipped, a charity that loses the list of donor contributions, or a hospital that loses the digital records of its patients. Making backups is especially important when you have multiple users working with the database. When you use the Back Up Database utility, Access provides a file name for the backup that uses the same file name as the database you are backing up, an underscore, and the current date. This makes it easy for you to keep track of databases by the date they were created. To back up a database, do the following:

1. Click the FILE tab and click Save As.
2. Click Save Database As under File Types, if necessary.
3. Click Back Up Database under the Advanced group.
4. Click Save As. Revise the location and file name if you want to change either and click Save.

In Hands-On Exercise 1, you will work with the Northwind Traders database discussed in the Case Study at the beginning of the chapter. You open the database and examine the interface and Access views, organize information, work with records, and save, compact, repair, and back up the database.

*Quick Concepts*

1. Name the six objects in an Access database and briefly describe the purpose of each. *p. 3*
2. What is the difference between Datasheet view and Design view in a table? *p. 6*
3. What is meant by the statement "Access works from storage"? *p. 9*
4. What is the purpose of the *Compact and Repair* utility? *p. 11*

# Hands-On Exercises

## 1 Databases Are Everywhere!

Northwind purchases food items from suppliers around the world and sells them to restaurants and specialty food shops. Northwind depends on the data stored in its Access database to process orders and make daily decisions. In your new position with Northwind Traders, you need to spend time getting familiar with the Access database. You will open Northwind's database, examine the Access interface, review the existing objects in the database, and explore Access views. You will add, edit, and delete records using both tables and forms. Finally, you will compact and repair, and back up the database.

**Skills covered:** Open an Access File and Work with Content Security • Examine the Access Interface, Explore Access Views, Organize Information in a Database, and Recognize Access Objects and Edit a Record and Understand the Difference Between Working in Storage and Memory • Add a Record • Delete a Record • Save As, Compact and Repair, and Back Up the Database

### STEP 1 ➤ OPEN AN ACCESS FILE AND WORK WITH CONTENT SECURITY

This exercise introduces you to the Northwind Traders database. You will use this database to learn the fundamentals of working with database files. Refer to Figure 1.8 as you complete Step 1.

**FIGURE 1.8** Message Bar Displaying Security Warning

a. Open Access, click **Open Other Files**, click **Computer**, and then click **Browse**. Navigate to the folder location designated by your instructor. Click *a01h1Traders* and click **Open**.

b. Click the **FILE tab**, click **Save As**, click **Save Database As**, and then verify *Access Database* is selected under *Database File Types*. Click **Save As** and save the file as **a01h1Traders_LastFirst**.

   When you save files, use your last and first names. For example, as the Access author, I would save my database as *a01h1traders_KrebsCynthia*. The Security Warning message bar appears below the Ribbon, indicating that some database content is disabled.

c. Click **Enable Content** on the Security Warning message bar.

   When you open an Access file from the student files associated with this book, you will need to enable the content. You may be confident of the trustworthiness of the files for this book. Keep the database open for the rest of the exercise.

### STEP 2 ➤ EXAMINE THE ACCESS INTERFACE, EXPLORE ACCESS VIEWS, ORGANIZE INFORMATION IN A DATABASE, AND RECOGNIZE ACCESS OBJECTS

Now that you have opened Northwind Traders, you examine the Navigation Pane, objects, and views to become familiar with these fundamental Access features. Refer to Figure 1.9 as you complete Step 2.

Step e: Tabs showing open table objects

Step a: Expanded Tables group

Step f: Shutter Bar Open/Close button

Step h: Collapsed Forms group

Step g: Expanded Reports group

**FIGURE 1.9** Access Navigation Pane and Open Objects

a. Scroll through the Navigation Pane and note the Access objects listed under each expanded group.

The Tables group and the Forms group are expanded, displaying all of the tables and forms objects. The Queries, Reports, Macros, and Modules groups are collapsed so that the objects in those groups are not displayed.

b. Right-click the **Customers table** in the Navigation Pane and select **Open**.

The Customers table opens. The Customers tab displays below the Ribbon indicating the table object is open. The data contained in the table displays. Each customer's record displays on a table row. The columns of the table display the fields that comprise the records. You are viewing the table in Datasheet view.

c. Click **View** in the Views group on the HOME tab.

The view of the Customers table switches to Design view. The top portion of the view displays each field that comprises a customer record, the field's data type, and an optional description of what the field should contain. The bottom portion of the view displays the field properties (attributes) for the selected field.

d. Click **View** in the Views group on the HOME tab again.

Because View is a toggle button, your view returns to the Datasheet view, which resembles an Excel worksheet.

e. Double-click **Employees** in the Navigation Pane Tables group and double-click **Products** in the same location.

The tabs for three table objects display below the Ribbon: Customers, Employees, and Products.

f. Click the **Shutter Bar Open/Close button** on the title bar of the Navigation Pane to contract the Navigation Pane. Click the button again to expand the Navigation Pane.

The Shutter Bar Open/Close button toggles to allow you to view more in the open object window, or to enable you to view your database objects.

g. Scroll down in the Navigation Pane and click **Reports**.

The Reports group expands, and all report objects display.

h. Click the arrows to the right of Forms in the Navigation Pane.

The Forms group collapses and individual form objects no longer display.

# STEP 3 ≫ EDIT A RECORD AND UNDERSTAND THE DIFFERENCE BETWEEN WORKING IN STORAGE AND MEMORY

You need to learn to edit the data in the Northwind database, because data can change. For example, employees will change their address and phone numbers when they move, and customers will change their order data from time to time. Refer to Figure 1.10 as you complete Step 3.

Step h: Undo
Step a: Active Employees table
Step c: Pencil indicates the change has not been saved
Step b: Replace *Peacock* with your last name
Step i: Click the Close button to close the Employees table

**FIGURE 1.10** Edit the Employees Table

a. Click the **Employees tab** to activate the Employees table.

b. Click the **Last Name field** in the fourth row. Double-click **Peacock**; the entire name highlights. Type your last name to replace *Peacock*.

   Your last name replaces Peacock. For example, as the Access author, my last name, Krebs, replaces Peacock.

c. Press **Tab** to move to the next field in the fourth row. Replace *Margaret* with your first name and press **Tab**.

   Your first name replaces Margaret. For example, as the Access author, my first name, Cynthia, replaces Margaret. You have made changes to two fields in the same record. The pencil symbol in the row selector box indicates that the record has not yet been saved.

d. Click **Undo** on the Quick Access Toolbar.

   Your first and last names revert back to *Margaret Peacock* because you have not yet left the record.

e. Type your first and last names again to replace *Margaret Peacock*. Press **Tab**.

   You should now be in the title field and your title, *Sales Representative*, is selected. The record has not been saved, as indicated by the pencil symbol in the row selector box.

f. Click anywhere in the third row where Janet Leverling's data is stored.

   The pencil symbol disappears, indicating your changes have been saved.

g. Click the **Address field** in the first record, Nancy Davolio's record. Select the entire address and then type **4004 East Morningside Dr**. Click anywhere on the second record, Andrew Fuller's record.

h. Click **Undo**.

   Nancy Davolio's address reverts back to 507- 20th Ave. E. However, the Undo command is now faded. You can no longer undo the change that you made replacing Margaret Peacock's name with your own.

**i.** Click the **Close (X) button** at the top of the table to close the Employees table.

The Employees table closes. You are not prompted to save your changes; they have already been saved for you because Access works in storage, not memory. If you reopen the Employees table, you will see your name in place of Margaret Peacock's name.

> **TROUBLESHOOTING:** If you click the Close (X) button on the title bar at the top right of the window and accidentally close the database, locate the file and double-click it to reopen the file.

# STEP 4 ≫ ADD A RECORD

You need to add new products to the Northwind database because the company is adding a new line of products. Refer to Figure 1.11 as you complete Step 4.

Step f: Click Find to locate a specific record

Step c: Forms group expanded

Step i: Type the new product information

Step h: Click New (blank) record to create a new record

Step e: Navigation (buttons)

**FIGURE 1.11** Newly Created Record in the Products Form

**a.** Right-click the **Customers tab** and click **Close All**.

**b.** Click the **Tables group** in the Navigation Pane to collapse it and collapse the **Reports group**.

**c.** Click the **Forms group** in the Navigation Pane to expand the list of available forms.

**d.** Double-click the **Products form** to open it.

**e.** Locate the navigation buttons at the bottom of the Access window. Practice moving from one record to the next. Click **Next record** and click **Last record**; click **Previous record** and click **First record**.

**f.** Click **Find** in the Find group on the HOME tab, type **Grandma** in the **Find What box**, click the **Match arrow**, and then select **Any Part of Field**. Click **Find Next**.

You should see the data for Grandma's Boysenberry Spread. Selecting the Any Part of the Field option will return a match even if it is contained in the middle of a word.

**g.** Close the Find dialog box.

**h.** Click **New (blank) record** on the navigation bar.

i. Enter the following information for a new product.

| Field Name | Value to Type |
|---|---|
| Product Name | *Your name's* Pecan Pie |
| Supplier | Grandma Kelly's Homestead (click the arrow to select from the list of Suppliers) |
| Category | Confections (click the arrow to select from the list of Categories) |
| Quantity Per Unit | 1 |
| Unit Price | 15.00 |
| Units in Stock | 18 |
| Units on Order | 50 |
| Reorder Level | 20 |
| Discontinued | No (leave the check box unchecked) |

As soon as you begin typing in the product name box, Access assigns a Product ID, in this case 78, to the record. The Product ID is used as the primary key in the Products table.

j. Click anywhere on the Pecan Pie record you just entered. Click the **FILE tab**, click **Print**, and then click **Print Preview**.

The first four records display in the Print Preview.

k. Click **Last Page** in the navigation bar and click **Previous Page** to show the new record you entered.

The beginning of the Pecan Pie record is now visible. The record continues on the next page.

l. Click **Close Print Preview** in the Close Preview group.

m. Close the Products form.

## STEP 5 ≫ DELETE A RECORD

To help you understand how Access stores data, you verify that the new product is in the Products table. You also attempt to delete a record. Refer to Figure 1.12 as you complete Step 5.

**FIGURE 1.12** Deleting a Record with Related Records

a. Click the **Forms group** in the Navigation Pane to collapse it and expand the **Tables group**.

b. Double-click the **Products table** to open it.

c. Click **Last record** in the navigation bar.

The Pecan Pie record you entered in the Products form is listed as the last record in the Products table. The Products form was created from the Products table. Your newly created record, Pecan Pie, is stored in the Products table even though you added it using the form.

**d.** Navigate to the fifth record in the table, *Chef Anton's Gumbo Mix*.

**e.** Use the horizontal scroll bar to scroll right until you see the Discontinued field.

The check mark in the Discontinued check box tells you that this product has been discontinued.

**f.** Click the **row selector** to the left of the fifth record.

The row highlights with a red-colored border to show that it is selected.

**g.** Click **Delete** in the Records group and read the error message.

The error message that displays tells you that you cannot delete this record because the table 'Order Details' has related records. (Customers ordered this product in the past.) Even though the product is now discontinued and no stock remains, it cannot be deleted from the Products table because related records exist in the Order Detail table.

**h.** Click **OK**.

**i.** Navigate to the last record and click the **row selector** to highlight the entire row.

**j.** Click **Delete** in the Records group. Read the warning.

The warning box that appears tells you that this action cannot be undone. Although this product can be deleted because it was just entered and no orders were created for it, you do not want to delete the record.

**k.** Click **No**. You do not want to delete this record. Close the Products table.

> **TROUBLESHOOTING:** If you clicked Yes and deleted the record, return to Step i. Reenter the information for this record. You will need it later in the lesson.

## STEP 6 ⟫ SAVE AS, COMPACT AND REPAIR, AND BACK UP THE DATABASE

You will protect the Northwind Traders database by using the two built-in Access utilities—Compact and Repair and Back Up Database. Refer to Figure 1.13 as you complete Step 6.

**FIGURE 1.13** Back Up Database Utility

**a.** Click the **FILE tab** to open the Backstage view.

**b.** Click Compact & Repair Database.

Using the *Compact and Repair* utility helps improve the performance of your database.

c. Click the **FILE tab**, click **Save As**, and then click **Save Database As** under *File Types*, if necessary.

d. Double-click **Back Up Database** under the Advanced group to open the **Save As** dialog box.

   The backup utility assigns the default name by adding a date to your file name.

e. Verify the *Save in* folder displays the location where you want your file saved and click **Save**.

   You just created a backup of the database after completing Hands-On Exercise 1. The original database *a01h1traders_LastFirst* remains onscreen.

f. Keep the database open if you plan to continue with Hands-On Exercise 2. If not, close the database and exit Access.

# Sorts and Filters

Access provides you with many tools that you can use to change the order of information and to identify and extract only the data needed at the moment. For example, you might need to display information by customer name in alphabetical order. Or you might need to know which suppliers are located in New Orleans or which customers have outstanding orders that were placed in the last seven days. You might use that information to identify possible disruptions to product deliveries or customers who may need a telephone call to let them know the status of their orders.

In this section, you will learn how to sort information and to isolate records in a table based on certain criteria.

## Sorting Table Data on One or Multiple Fields

You can change the order of information by sorting one or more fields. A *sort* lists records in a specific sequence, such as alphabetically by last name or by ascending EmployeeID. To sort a table on one criteria, do the following:

**STEP 4 ⟫**
1. Click in the field that you want to use to sort the records.
2. Click Ascending or Descending in the Sort & Filter group on the HOME tab.

*Ascending* sorts a list of text data in alphabetical order or a numeric list in lowest to highest order. *Descending* sorts a list of text data in reverse alphabetical order or a numeric list in highest to lowest order. Figure 1.14 shows the Customers table for a bank sorted in ascending order by state.

Click Ascending to apply an A–Z sort

Click Remove Sort to undo the A–Z sort

Customers sorted in ascending order by State

**FIGURE 1.14** Customers Table Sorted by State

Access can sort records by more than one field. Access sorts multiple criteria by first sorting the column on the left. The column immediately to the right of that column is sorted next. Because of this, you must arrange your columns in this order. To move a column, select the column and hold down the left mouse button. A heavy black bar appears to the left of the column. Drag the column to the position where you want it for the multiple sort.

# Creating, Modifying, and Removing Filters

In Hands-On Exercise 1, you added Pecan Pie to the Products table with a category of Confections, but you also saw many other products. Suppose you wanted to see a list of just the products in the Confections category. To obtain this list, you would open the Products table in Datasheet view and create a filter. A *filter* displays a subset of records based on specified criteria. A *criterion* (or criteria, plural) is a number, a text phrase, or an expression used to select records from a table. Therefore, to view a list of all Confections, you would need to filter the Category field of the Products table using Confections as the criterion.

You can use filters to analyze data quickly. Applying a filter does not delete any records; filters only *hide* records that do not match the criteria. Two types of filters are discussed in this section: *Filter by Selection* and *Filter by Form*.

## Use, Modify, and Remove a Filter

*Filter by Selection* displays only the records that match a criterion you select. To use *Filter by Selection*, do the following:

STEP 1 »
1. Click in any field that contains the criterion on which you want to filter.
2. Click Selection in the Sort & Filter group on the HOME tab.
3. Select *Equals "criterion"* from the list of options.

Figure 1.15 displays a Customers table with 10 records. The records in the table are displayed in sequence according to the CustomerID, which is also the primary key (the field or combination of fields that uniquely identifies a record). The navigation bar at the bottom indicates that the active record is the first row in the table. *Owner* in the Job Title field is selected.

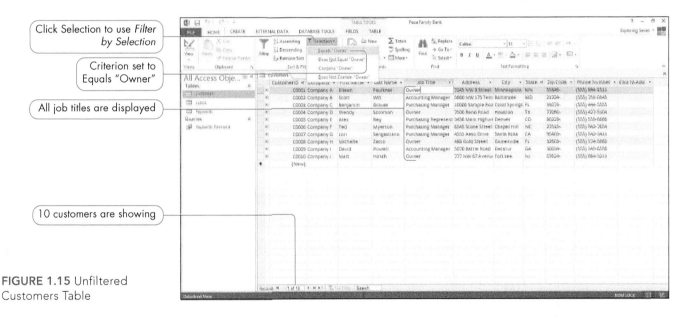

- Click Selection to use *Filter by Selection*
- Criterion set to Equals "Owner"
- All job titles are displayed
- 10 customers are showing

**FIGURE 1.15** Unfiltered Customers Table

Figure 1.16 displays a filtered view of the Customers table, showing records with the job title *Owner*. The navigation bar shows that this is a filtered list containing 4 records matching the criteria. (The Customers table still contains the original 10 records, but only 4 records are visible with the filter applied.)

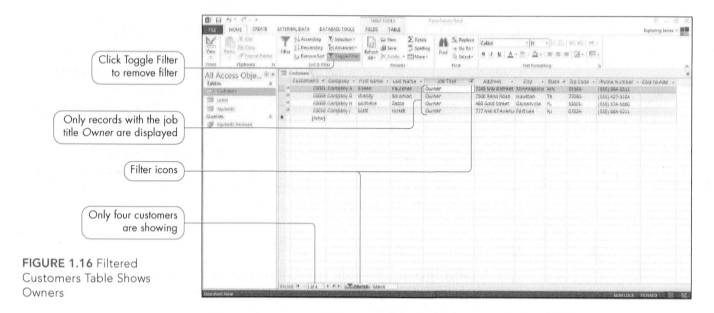

Click Toggle Filter to remove filter

Only records with the job title *Owner* are displayed

Filter icons

Only four customers are showing

**FIGURE 1.16** Filtered Customers Table Shows Owners

*Filter by Form* is a more versatile method of selecting data because it enables you to display table records based on multiple criteria. When you use *Filter by Form*, all of the records are hidden and Access creates a blank form in a design grid. You see only field names with an arrow in the first field. Click on other fields and an arrow displays. Click an arrow and a list opens for you to use to specify your criterion. You can specify as many criteria as you need. When you apply the filter, Access displays the records that meet your criteria.

**STEP 3** ❯❯

An advantage of using this filter method is that you can specify AND and OR logical operators. If you use the AND operator, a record is included in the results if all the criteria are true. If you use the OR operator, a record is included if at least one criterion is true. Another advantage of *Filter by Form* is that you can use a comparison operator. A *comparison operator* is used to evaluate the relationship between two quantities. For example, a comparison operator can determine if quantities are equal or not equal. If they are not equal, a comparison operator determines which one is greater than the other. Comparison operator symbols include: equal (=), not equal (<>), greater than (>), less than (<), greater than or equal to (>=), and less than or equal to (<=). To use *Filter by Form*, do the following:

1. Click Advanced in the Sort & Filter group on the HOME tab.
2. Click *Filter by Form*.
3. Click in the field you want to use as a criterion. Click the arrow to select the criterion from existing data.
4. Add additional criterion and comparison operators as needed.
5. Click Toggle Filter in the Sort & Filter group on the HOME tab to apply the filter.

In Figure 1.17, the Northwind Traders Products table is open. *Filter by Form* is set to select products with an inventory (Units in Stock) level greater than 30 (>30).

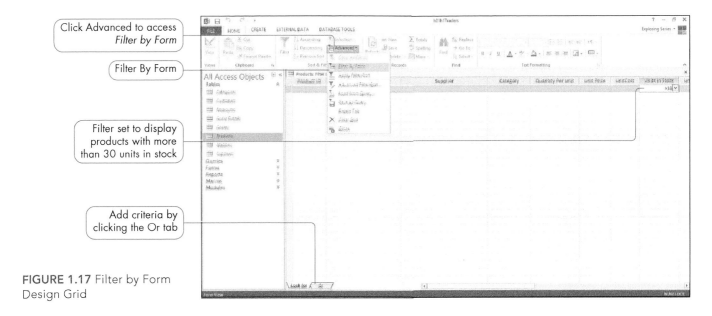

Click Advanced to access *Filter by Form*

Filter By Form

Filter set to display products with more than 30 units in stock

Add criteria by clicking the Or tab

**FIGURE 1.17** Filter by Form Design Grid

The sort and filter operations can be done in any order; that is, you can sort a table first and apply a filter. Conversely, you can filter a table first to show only selected records and sort the filtered table to display the records in a certain order. It does not matter which operation is performed first.

You can also filter the table further by applying a second, third, or more criteria. For example, in the Products table shown in Figure 1.17, you can apply *Filter by Form* by clicking in the Supplier cell, selecting Exotic Liquids from the list, and then applying the filter. Then you could click Beverages and apply *Filter by Selection* to display all the beverages supplied by Exotic Liquids. You can also click Toggle Filter at any time to remove all filters and display all the records in the table. Filters are a temporary method for examining table data. If you close the filtered table and reopen it, the filter will be removed and all of the records will be restored.

---

## TIP   Use Undo After Applying a Filter by Selection

You can apply one *Filter by Selection* to a table, and then a second, and then a third to display certain records based on three criteria. If you click Toggle Filter, all three filters will be removed. What if you only want the last filter removed? Click Undo to remove only the last filter. Click Undo again and remove the second-to-last filter. This feature will help you apply and remove multiple filters, one at a time.

---

*Quick Concepts*

1. What are the benefits of sorting the records in a table? *p. 20*

2. What is the purpose of creating a filter? *p. 21*

3. What is the difference between *Filter by Selection* and *Filter by Form*? *pp. 21–22*

4. What is a comparison operator and how is it used in a filter? *p. 22*

Watch the Video
for this Hands-
On Exercise!

MyITLab®
HOE2 Training

# 2 Sorts and Filters

The sales manager at Northwind Traders needs quick answers to her questions about customer orders. You use the Access database to filter tables to answer these questions, then sort the records based on the manager's needs.

**Skills covered:** Use Filter by Selection with an Equal Condition • Use Filter by Selection with a Contains Condition • Use Filter by Form with a Comparison Operator • Sort a Table

## STEP 1 >> USE FILTER BY SELECTION WITH AN EQUAL CONDITION

The sales manager asks for a list of customers who live in London. You use *Filter by Selection* with an equal condition to locate these customers. Refer to Figure 1.18 as you complete Step 1.

Step d: Click Selection

Step e: Select Equals "London"

Step c: Select London

Step e: Six customers match the criteria

**FIGURE 1.18** Customers Table Filtered for London Records

a. Open the *a01h1traders_LastFirst* database if you closed it after the last Hands-On Exercise and save it as **a01h2Traders_LastFirst**, changing *h1* to *h2*.

> **TROUBLESHOOTING:** If you make any major mistakes in this exercise, you can close the file, open *a01h1Traders_LastFirst* again, and then start this exercise over.

b. Double-click the **Customers table** in the Navigation Pane under *Tables*, navigate to record 4, and then replace *Thomas Hardy* with your name in the Contact Name field.

c. Scroll right until the City field is visible. The fourth record has a value of *London* in the City field. Click the field to select it.

d. Click **Selection** in the Sort & Filter group on the HOME tab.

e. Select **Equals "London"** from the menu. Note that six customers were located.

The navigation bar display shows that six records that meet the *London* criterion are available. The other records in the Customers table are hidden. The Filtered icon also displays on the navigation bar, indicating that the Customers table has been filtered.

**f.** Click **Toggle Filter** in the Sort & Filter group to remove the filter.

**g.** Click **Toggle Filter** again to reset the filter. Leave the Customers table open for the next step.

## STEP 2 ≫ USE FILTER BY SELECTION WITH A CONTAINS CONDITION

The sales manager asks you to narrow the list of London customers so that it displays only Sales Representatives. To accomplish this task, you add a second layer of filtering using the *Filter by Selection* feature. Refer to Figure 1.19 as you complete Step 2.

**FIGURE 1.19** Customers in London with the Contact Title *Sales Representative*

**a.** Click in any field in the Contact Title column that contains the value *Sales Representative*.

**b.** Click **Selection** in the Sort & Filter group and click **Contains "Sales Representative"**. Locate your name in the filtered table. Compare your results to those shown in Figure 1.19.

Three records match the criteria you set. You have applied a second layer of filtering to the customers in London. The second layer further restricts the display to only those customers who have the words *Sales Representative* contained in their titles.

> **TROUBLESHOOTING:** If you do not see the record for Victoria Ashworth, you selected *Equals "Sales Representative"* instead of *Contains "Sales Representative"*. Repeat steps a and b, making sure you select *Contains "Sales Representative"*.

**c.** Close the Customers table. Click **Yes** if a dialog box asks if you want to save the design changes to the Customers table.

## STEP 3 ≫ USE FILTER BY FORM WITH A COMPARISON OPERATOR

You are asked to provide a list of records that do not match just one set of criteria. You are asked to provide a list of all extended prices less than $50 for a specific sales representative. Use *Filter by Form* to provide the information when two or more criteria are needed. You also preview the results in Print Preview to see how the list would print. Refer to Figure 1.20 as you complete Step 3.

Step i: Enter <50 for the ExtendedPrice criteria

Step d: Click Advanced to select Filter by Form

Steps f–h: Select your first and last names

**FIGURE 1.20** Filter by Form Selection Criteria

a. Click the **Tables group** in the Navigation Pane to collapse the listed tables.

b. Click the **Queries group** in the Navigation Pane to expand the list of available queries.

c. Locate and double-click the **Order Details Extended query** to open it.

This query contains information about orders. It has fields containing information about the sales person, the Order ID, the product name, the unit price, quantity ordered, the discount given, and an extended price. The extended price is a field used to total order information.

d. Click **Advanced** in the Sort & Filter group and select **Filter by Form** from the list.

All of the records are now hidden, and you see only field names and an arrow in the first field. Although you are applying *Filter by Form* to a query, you can use the same process as applying *Filter by Form* to a table. You are able to enter more than one criterion using *Filter by Form*.

e. Click in the first row under the First Name field, if necessary.

An arrow appears at the right of the box.

f. Click the **First Name arrow**.

A list of all available first names appears. Your name should be on the list. Figure 1.20 shows *Cynthia Krebs*, which replaced Margaret Peacock in Hands-On Exercise 1.

> **TROUBLESHOOTING:** If you do not see your name and you do see Margaret on the list, you probably skipped steps in Hands-On Exercise 1. Close the query without saving changes, return to the first Hands-On Exercise, and then rework it, making sure not to omit any steps. Then you can return to this location and work the remainder of this Hands-On Exercise.

g. Select your first name from the list.

h. Click in the first row under the Last Name field to reveal the arrow. Locate and select your last name by clicking it.

i. Scroll right until you see the Extended Price field. Click in the first row under the Extended Price field and type **<50**.

This will select all of the items that you ordered where the total was under $50. You ignore the arrow and type the expression needed.

j. Click **Toggle Filter** in the Sort & Filter group.

You have specified which records to include and have executed the filtering by clicking Toggle Filter. You should have 31 records that match the criteria you specified.

k. Click the **FILE tab**, click **Print**, and then click **Print Preview**.

You instructed Access to preview the filtered query results. The preview displays the query title as a heading. The current filter is applied, as well as page numbers.

l. Click **Close Print Preview** in the Close Preview group.

m. Close the Order Details Extended query. Click **Yes** if a dialog box asks if you want to save your changes.

# TIP | Deleting Filter by Form Criterion

While working with *Filter by Selection* or *Filter by Form*, you may inadvertently save a filter. To view a saved filter, open the table or query that you suspect may have a saved filter. Click Advanced in the Sort & Filter group and click *Filter by Form*. If criteria appear in the form, then a filter has been saved. To delete a saved filter, toggle the filter, click Advanced, and then click Close All Filters. Close and save the table or query.

## STEP 4 >> SORT A TABLE

The Sales Manager is pleased with your work; however, she would like some of the information to appear in a different order. You will now sort the records in the Customers table using the manager's new criteria. Refer to Figure 1.21 as you complete Step 4.

Step i and j: Records are sorted by Country, then City

Step c: Shutter Bar Open/Close button

Steps i and j: Click Ascending to sort by Country, then City

**FIGURE 1.21** Customers Table Sorted by Country, Then City

a. Click the **Queries group** in the Navigation Pane to collapse the listed queries.

b. Click the **Tables group** in the Navigation Pane to expand the list of available tables and double-click the **Customers table** to open it.

   This table contains information about customers. The table is sorted in alphabetical order by Company Name.

c. Click the **Shutter Bar Open/Close button** in the Navigation Pane to close the Navigation Pane.

   It will be easier to locate fields in the Customer table if the Navigation Pane is closed.

d. Click any field in the Customer ID column, the first field in the table. Click **Descending** in the Sort & Filter group on the HOME tab.

   Sorting in descending order on a character field produces a reverse alphabetical order.

e. Scroll right until you can see both the Country and City fields.

f. Click the **Country column heading**.

   The entire column is selected.

g. Click the **Country column heading** again and hold down the **left mouse button**.

   A thick dark blue line displays on the left edge of the Country field.

**h.** Check to make sure that you see the thick blue line. Drag the **Country field** to the left until the thick black line moves between the City and Region fields. Release the mouse and the Country field position moves to the right of the City field.

You moved the Country field next to the City field so that you can easily sort the table based on both fields. In order to sort by two or more fields, they need to be placed adjacent to each other.

**i.** Click any city name in the City field and click **Ascending** in the Sort & Filter group.

The City field displays the cities in alphabetical order.

**j.** Click any country name in the Country field and click **Ascending**.

The countries are sorted in alphabetical order. The cities within each country also are sorted alphabetically. For example, the customer in Graz, Austria, is listed before the customer in Salzburg, Austria.

**k.** Close the Customers table. Click **Yes** to save the changes to the design of the table.

**l.** Click the **Shutter Bar Open/Close button** in the Navigation Pane to open the Navigation Pane.

**m.** Click the **FILE tab** to open the Backstage view and click **Compact & Repair Database**.

**n.** Click the **FILE tab**, click **Save As**, and then click **Save Database As** in File Types, if necessary.

**o.** Double-click **Back Up Database** under the Advanced group to open the Save As dialog box.

**p.** Verify the *Save in* folder displays the location where you want your file saved and click **Save**.

**q.** Close the database and submit based on your instructor's directions. Leave Access open if you plan to continue with Hands-On Exercise 3. If not, exit Access.

# Access Versus Excel, and Relational Databases

Both Access and Excel contain powerful tools that enable you to extract the information you need and arrange it in a way that makes it easy to analyze. An important part of becoming a proficient Office user is learning which of these applications to use to accomplish a task.

In this section, you will learn how to decide whether to use Access or Excel by examining the distinct advantages of each application. Ideally, the type of data and the type of functionality you require should determine which program will work best.

## Knowing When to Use Access or Excel to Manage Data

You are probably familiar with working in an Excel spreadsheet. You type the column headings, enter the data, perhaps add a formula or two, and then add totals to the bottom. Once the data has been entered, you can apply a filter, sort the data, or start all over—similar to what you learned to do in Access with filters. It is true that you can accomplish many of the same tasks using either Excel or Access. Although the two programs have much in common, they each have distinct advantages. How do you choose whether to use Access or Excel? The choice you make may ultimately depend on how well you know Access. Users who know Excel only are more likely to use a spreadsheet even if a database would be better. When database features are used in Excel, they are generally used on data that is in one table. When the data is better suited to be on two or more tables, then using Access is preferable. Learning how to use Access will be beneficial to you because it will enable you to work more efficiently with large groups of data.

### Select the Software to Use

A contact list (for example, name, address, phone number) created in Excel may serve your needs just fine in the beginning. Each time you enter a new contact, you can add another row to the bottom of your worksheet. You can sort the list by last name for easier look-up of names. In Excel, you can easily move an entire column, insert a new column, or copy and paste data from one cell to another. This is the "ease of use" characteristic of Excel.

If you need to expand the information in Excel to keep track of each time you contacted someone on your contact list, you may need an additional worksheet. This additional sheet would only list the contacts whom you have contacted and some information about the nature of the contact. Which contact was it? When was the contact made? Was it a phone contact or a face-to-face meeting? As you track these entries, your worksheet will contain a reference to the first worksheet using the contact name.

If a contact is deleted on the first worksheet, that contact's information will still remain on the second worksheet, unless someone remembers to remove it. Similarly, information could be added about a contact on the second worksheet without the contact being officially entered into the first worksheet. As the quantity and complexity of the data increase, the need to organize your data logically also increases.

Access provides built-in tools to help organize data better than Excel. One tool that helps Access organize data is the ability to create relationships between tables. A *relationship* is a connection between two tables using a field that is common to the two tables. The benefit of a relationship is the ability to efficiently combine data from related tables for the purpose of creating queries, forms, and reports. Relationships are the reason Access is referred to as a relational database.

## Use Access

STEP 1 » Use Access to manage data when you:

- Require multiple related tables to store your data.
- Have a large amount of data.
- Need to connect to and retrieve data from external databases, such as Microsoft SQL Server.
- Need to group, sort, and total data based on various parameters.
- Have an application that requires multiple users to connect to one data source at the same time.

## Use Excel

Use Excel to manage data when you:

- Need only one worksheet to handle all of your data.
- Have mostly numeric data—for example, you need to maintain an expense statement.
- Require subtotals and totals in your worksheet.
- Want to primarily run a series of "what if" scenarios on your data.
- Need to create complex charts and/or graphs.

# Understanding Relational Power

In the previous section, we compared Excel worksheets to Access relational databases. Access has the ability to create relationships between two tables, whereas Excel does not. Access is known as a *relational database management system* (RDBMS); using an RDBMS, you can manage groups of data (tables) and set rules (relationships) between tables. When relational databases are designed properly, users can easily combine data from multiple tables to create queries, forms, and reports.

Good database design begins with grouping data into the correct tables. This practice, known as *normalization*, will take time to learn, but over time you will begin to understand the fundamentals. The design of a relational database management system is illustrated in Figure 1.22, which shows the table design of the Northwind Traders database. The tables have been created, the field names have been added, and the data types have been set. The diagram shows the relationships that were created between tables using *join lines*. Join lines enable you to create a relationship between two tables using a common field. Figure 1.22 also shows the join lines between related tables as a series of lines connecting common fields. For example, the Suppliers table is joined to the Products table using the common field SupplierID. If you examine some of the connections, you will see that the EmployeeID is linked to the Orders table by a join line. This means that you can produce a report displaying all orders for a customer and the employee who entered the order. The Orders table is joined to the Order Details table where the OrderID is the common field. The Products table is joined to the Order Details table where the ProductID is the common field. These table connections enable you to query the database for information stored in multiple tables. This feature gives the manager the ability to ask questions like "How many different beverages were shipped last week?" or "What was the total revenue generated from seafood orders last year?"

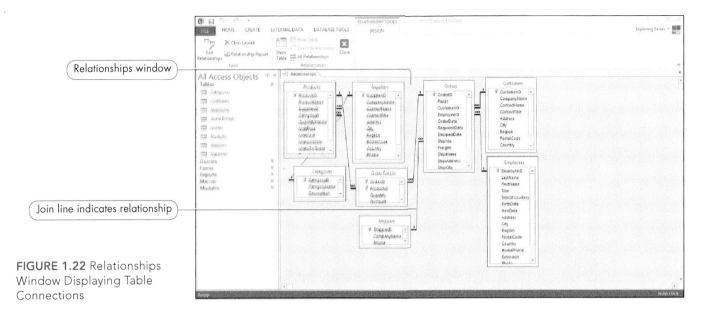

Relationships window

Join line indicates relationship

**FIGURE 1.22** Relationships Window Displaying Table Connections

## Use the Relationships Window

Relationships are set in the Relationships window by the database developer after the tables have been created but before any sample data is entered. The most common method of connecting two tables is to connect the primary key from one table to the foreign key of another. A *foreign key* is a field in one table that is also the primary key of another table. In the previous figure, Figure 1.22, the SupplierID (primary key) in the Suppliers table is joined to the SupplierID (foreign key) in the Products table. Remember, a primary key is a field that uniquely identifies each record in a table.

To create a relationship between two tables, follow these guidelines:

1. Click Relationships in the Relationships group on the DATABASE TOOLS tab.
2. Add the two tables that you want to join together to the Relationships window.
3. Drag the common field (e.g., SupplierID) from the primary table (e.g., Suppliers) onto the common field (e.g., SupplierID) of the related table (e.g., Products). The data types of the common fields must be the same.
4. Check the Enforce Referential Integrity check box.
5. Close the Relationships window.

**STEP 2»**   **View Join Lines**

Databases with many tables with relationships may make it difficult to see the join lines between tables. Tables may be repositioned to make it easier to see the join lines. To reposition a table, drag the table by its table name to the new position.

## Enforce Referential Integrity

**STEP 3»** Enforce referential integrity is one of three options you can select when setting a table relationship. When *enforce referential integrity* is checked, Access ensures that data cannot be entered into a related table unless it first exists in the primary table. For example, in Figure 1.22 you cannot enter a product into the Products table using a SupplierID that does not exist in the Suppliers table. This rule ensures the integrity of the data in the database and improves overall data accuracy. Referential integrity also prohibits users from deleting a record in one table if it has records in related tables.

In Hands-on Exercise 3, you examine the strengths of Access and Excel in more detail so that you can better determine when to use which application to complete a given task. You will also explore relationships between tables and learn about the power of relational data.

## TIP Create Sample Data

When learning database skills, starting with a smaller set of sample data prior to entering all company records can be helpful. A small amount of data gives you the ability to check the tables and quickly see if your results are correct. Even though the data amounts are small, as you test the database tables and relationships, the results will prove useful as you work with larger data sets.

*Quick* Concepts

1. How can you determine when to use Access or Excel to manage data? *p. 29*

2. Explain the term RDBMS. *p. 30*

3. What is the purpose of a join line? *p. 30*

# Hands-On Exercises

 Watch the Video for this Hands-On Exercise!

## 3 Access Versus Excel, and Relational Databases

In this exercise, you review the relationships set in the Northwind Traders database. This will help you learn more about the overall design of the database. Examining the relationships will also help you understand why Access rather than Excel is used by Northwind Traders for data management.

**Skills covered:** Know When to Use Access or Excel to Manage Data • Use the Relationships Window, Use Filter by Form with a Comparison Operator, and Reapply a Saved Filter • Enforce Referential Integrity

---

### STEP 1 >> KNOW WHEN TO USE ACCESS OR EXCEL TO MANAGE DATA

In this exercise, you examine the connections between the tables in the Northwind Traders database and review the reasons that Access was selected as the application for this data. Refer to Figure 1.23 as you complete Step 1.

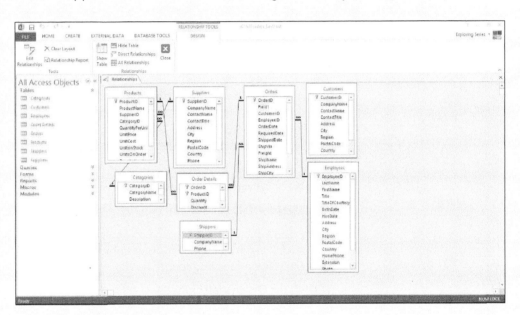

**FIGURE 1.23** Relationships Window for the Northwind Database

a. Open the *a01h2Traders_LastFirst* database if you closed it after the last Hands-On Exercise and save it as **a01h3Traders_LastFirst**, changing *h2* to *h3*.

b. Click the **DATABASE TOOLS tab** and click **Relationships** in the Relationships group.

c. Examine the join lines showing the relationships that connect the various tables. For example, the Orders table is connected to the Order Details table.

Examining the number of tables in a database and their relationships is a good way to determine whether you need to use Excel or Access for your data. Because this data needs more than one table, involves a large amount of connected data, needs to group, sort, and total data based on various parameters, and needs to allow multiple users to connect to one data source at the same time, it is better to manipulate this data using Access rather than using Excel.

Use the Relationships window to move tables to make the join lines easier to view. To reinforce your filter skills, use *Filter by Form* to solve more complex questions about the Northwind data. After you retrieve the records, save the *Filter by Form* specifications so that you can reapply the filter later. Refer to Figure 1.24 as you complete Step 2.

**FIGURE 1.24** Query Results with Your Name and Extended Price >$2,000

a. Reposition the Shippers table beneath the Orders table by dragging it to the right by its table name. Reposition the Categories table beneath the Order Details table by dragging it to the right by its table name.

   Tables may be repositioned to make it easier to see the join lines creating the relationships.

b. Click **Show Table** in the Relationships group on the RELATIONSHIPS TOOLS DESIGN tab.

   The Show Table dialog box opens. It shows you the eight tables that are available in the database. If you look in the Relationships window, you will see that all eight tables are open in the relationships diagram.

c. Click the **Queries tab** in the Show Table dialog box.

   All of the queries created from the tables in the database are listed in the Show Table dialog box. You could add all of the queries to the Relationships window. Things might become cluttered, but you could tell at a glance from where the queries get their information.

d. Close the Show Table dialog box.

e. Click the **Shutter Bar Open/Close button** in the Navigation Pane to open the Navigation Pane, if necessary.

f. Click **All Access Objects** on the Navigation Pane and click **Tables and Related Views**.

   You now see each table and all the queries, forms, and reports that are based on each table. If a query is created using more than one table, it appears multiple times in the Navigation Pane.

g. Close the Relationships window. Save the changes to the design. Click **All Tables** on the Navigation Pane and click **Object Type**.

h. Collapse the Tables group in the Navigation Pane, expand the **Queries** group, and then double-click the **Order Details Extended query**.

i. Click **Advanced** in the Sort & Filter group, select **Filter by Form**, click in the first row under the Last Name field, and then select your last name.

**j.** Scroll right (or press **Tab**) until the Extended Price field is visible. Click in the first row in the Extended Price field and type **>2000**.

The Extended Price field shows the purchased amount for each item ordered. If an item sold for $15 and a customer ordered 10, the Extended Price would display $150.

**k.** Click **Toggle Filter** in the Sort & Filter group. Examine the filtered results.

Your comparison operator, >2000, identified 18 items ordered where the extended price exceeded $2,000.

**l.** Close the Order Details Extended query by clicking the **Close (X) button**. Click **Yes** to save changes.

**m.** Open the Order Details Extended query again.

The filter disengages when you close and reopen the object. However, because you opted to save the changes before closing, the filter has been stored with the query. You may reapply the filter at any time by clicking the Toggle Filter command (until the next filter replaces the current one).

**n.** Click **Toggle Filter** in the Sort & Filter group. Compare your results to Figure 1.24.

**o.** Save and close the query.

## STEP 3 ≫ ENFORCE REFERENTIAL INTEGRITY

You need an additional relationship created between the Orders table and the Customers table. You create the relationship and enforce referential integrity. Refer to Figure 1.25 as you complete Step 3.

**FIGURE 1.25** Relationship Created Between Orders Table and Customers Table

**a.** Click the **DATABASE TOOLS tab** and click **Relationships** in the Relationships group.

**b.** Locate the CustomerID field in the Orders table and drag it to the CustomerID field (primary key) in the Customers table.

The Edit Relationships dialog box opens. It shows that the Table/Query is from the Customers table and the related Table/Query comes from the Orders table. The relationship type is displayed at the bottom of the dialog box and indicates that this will be a One-To-Many relationship.

**c.** Click **Enforce Referential Integrity**.

Access will now ensure that data cannot be entered into the related table (Orders) unless it first exists in the primary table (Customers).

**d.** Click **Create**.

A join line displays between the Orders and Customers tables.

**e.** Click the **FILE tab** and click **Compact & Repair Database**. Click **Yes** if asked if you want to save changes to the layout of Relationships.

**f.** Click the **FILE tab**, click **Save As**, and then click **Save Database As** under *File Types* if necessary. Double-click **Back Up Database** in the Advanced group to open the Save As dialog box.

**g.** Verify the *Save in* folder displays the location where you want your backup file saved and click **Save**.

A duplicate copy of the database is saved with the default file name that is the original file name followed by the current date.

**h.** Exit Access.

# Access Database Creation

Now that you have examined the fundamentals of an Access database and explored the power of relational databases, it is time to create one! In this section, you explore the benefits of creating a database using each of the methods discussed in the next section.

## Creating a Database

When you first start Access, the Backstage view opens and provides you with three methods for creating a new database. These methods are:

- Creating a custom Web app
- Creating a blank desktop database
- Creating a database from a template

Creating a **custom Web app** enables you to create a database that you can build and then use and share with others through the Web. Creating a blank desktop database lets you create a database specific to your needs. Rather than starting from scratch by creating a blank desktop database, you may want to use a template to create a new database. An Access **template** is a predefined database that includes professionally designed tables, forms, reports, and other objects that you can use to jumpstart the creation of your database.

Figure 1.26 shows the options for creating a custom Web app, a blank desktop database, and multiple templates from which you can select the method for which you want to create a database.

**FIGURE 1.26** Backstage View with Database Creation Options

## Create a Web Application Using a Template

Creating a Web app (application) is new in Access 2013. An Access Web app is a new type of database that lets you build a browser-based database application— you can create a database in the cloud that you and others can access and use simultaneously. This requires that you use a host server such as SharePoint (a Web application platform developed by Microsoft) or Office 365 (a cloud service edition of SharePoint).

To create a Web app, click *Custom web app* in the Backstage view, give your app a name, and then choose a location. Once you click Create, a blank database opens. You then create the tables that will serve as the foundation of your database. The easiest way to add a table is to use the Access library of Table Templates. Each of the templates in the library includes tables, fields, and views that you will need to create an app. Some templates also include related tables.

As an alternative to creating a Web app from scratch, you can select a Web app template from the Backstage view. These templates are fully functional Web databases. Click one of the Web app template tiles and an introduction screen appears that previews the datasheet, provides a description of the purpose of the datasheet, lets you know the download size of the database, and even displays how users like you have rated the database. You give the app a name and select the Web location where the app is to be saved. Finally, you create the app. When you have completed the database, click Launch App in the View group on the Home tab. You can then use it and share it on the Web. Figure 1.27 shows the introduction screen for the Asset tracking template. This template requires SharePoint so that you can share content with others.

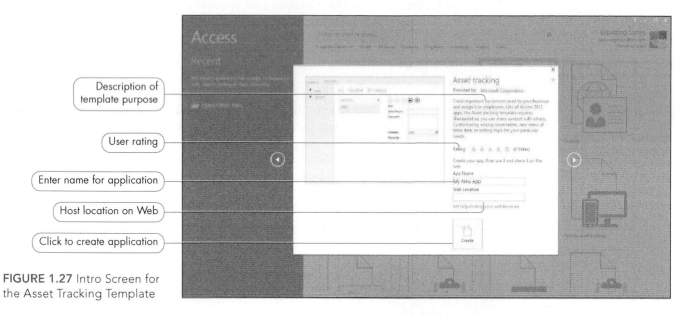

Description of template purpose

User rating

Enter name for application

Host location on Web

Click to create application

**FIGURE 1.27** Intro Screen for the Asset Tracking Template

## Create a Blank Desktop Database

To create a blank desktop database specific to your needs, click *Blank desktop database* in the Backstage view. Access opens to a blank table in Datasheet view where you can add data. You can refine the table in Design view. You would then create additional tables and objects as necessary. To create a blank desktop database, do the following:

1. Open Access or click the FILE tab to open the Backstage view and click New.
2. Click the *Blank desktop* database tile.
3. Enter the file name for the file in the text box, click the Browse button to navigate to the folder where you want to store the database file, and then click OK.
4. Click Create.
5. Enter data in the empty table that displays.

## Create a Desktop Database Using a Template

Using a template to start a database saves you a great deal of creation time. Working with a template can also help a new Access user become familiar with database design. Templates are available from the Backstage view, where you can select from a variety of templates or search online for more templates.

Access also provides templates for desktop use. To create a desktop database from a template, do the following:

**STEP 1 ≫**
1. Open Access or click the FILE tab to open the Backstage view and click New.
2. Click the database template you want to use.
3. Enter the file name for the file in the text box, click the Browse button to navigate to the folder where you want to store the database file, and then click OK.

4. Click Create to download the template.
5. Open the database and click Enable Content in the Security Warning message bar if you trust the source of the database.

Once the database is open, you may see a Getting Started page that includes links you can use to learn more about the database. A new Access user can gain valuable information by watching any associated videos and clicking provided hyperlinks. When finished reviewing the learning materials, close the Getting Started page to view the database. Figure 1.28 displays the Getting Started page included with the *Desktop task management* template. Two videos are provided to aid you in using and modifying the database. Because this database contains a Contacts table, there is a hyperlink to a wizard that will import contacts from Microsoft Outlook (if you use Microsoft Outlook). Links are available that will connect you with experts, enable you to get free advice from a forum, and get more help from Microsoft .com. The Getting Started page also includes a button you can click to open a survey that provides feedback to Microsoft. Close the Getting Started page to return to the database.

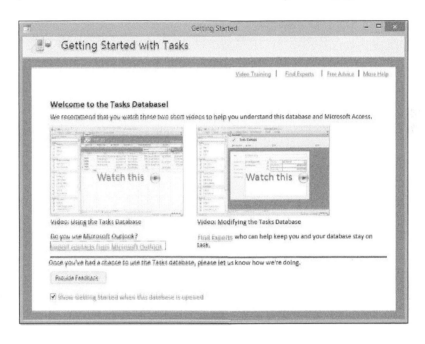

**FIGURE 1.28** Getting Started Page for Desktop Task Management Template

STEP 2 »

Because you downloaded a template, some objects will have already been created. You can work with these objects just as you did in the first three sections of this chapter. For example, you can enter data directly into any existing table in the database by opening the table, clicking in the first empty field, typing the data, tabbing to the next empty field, and then typing the data for the next field. You can also open any form that is part of the downloaded template and enter the data directly in the forms. Some templates will include queries and reports. Edit any object to meet your requirements.

STEP 3 »

Once the database is opened, review the objects listed in the Navigation Pane. Change the Navigation Pane category from Object Type to *Tables and Related Views* to become familiar with the relationships between the tables and other database objects. Note the tables and the objects that are based on them.

After noting the objects in the database, open the Relationships window to see the connections between them. Once you are familiar with the database design, you can enter your data.

Figure 1.29 displays the open Task Management database with the Navigation Pane set to display *Tables and Related Views*. The Tasks table displays with its related queries, forms, and reports. The Relationships window shows the relationship between the Contacts table and the Tasks table.

Relationships window

Navigation Pane displaying tables and related views

Tasks table

Queries, forms, and reports based on Task table

Join line indicates relationship

**FIGURE 1.29** Relationships Window for the Task Management Database

*Quick* Concepts

1. Name the three methods for creating a new database. ***p. 37***

2. What is a custom Web app, and what is required to build a custom Web app? ***p. 37***

3. What are two benefits of using a template to create a database? ***p. 38***

# Hands-On Exercises

## 4 Access Database Creation

After working with the Northwind Traders database on the job, you decide to use Access to create a personal contact database. Rather than start from scratch, you use an Access Contact Manager desktop template to jumpstart your database creation. A Web app is not necessary because you do not want to share your contacts with others.

**Skills covered:** Create a Desktop Database Using a Template • Add Records to a Downloaded Desktop Database Template • Explore the Database Objects in a Downloaded Desktop Database Template

## STEP 1 ≫ CREATE A DESKTOP DATABASE USING A TEMPLATE

You locate an Access desktop template that you can use to create your personal contact database. This template not only allows you to store names, addresses, telephone numbers, and other information, but also lets you categorize your contacts, send e-mail messages, and create maps of addresses. You download and save the template. Refer to Figure 1.30 as you complete Step 1.

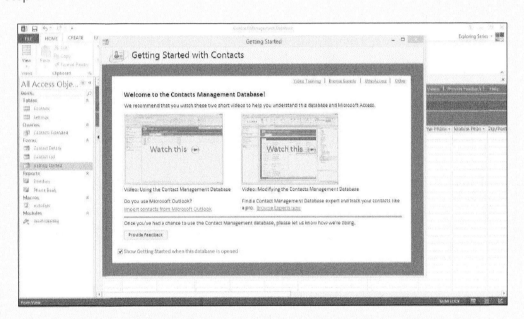

**FIGURE 1.30** Desktop Contacts Intro Screen

a. Open Access. Scroll down until you see the *Desktop contacts* template and click the template tile.

   The Create Intro Screen page for the Desktop contacts database opens.

b. Click the **Browse icon** to navigate to the folder where you are saving your files, enter **a01h4Contacts_LastFirst** as the file name, and then click **OK**.

c. Click **Create** to download the template.

d. Click **Enable Content** on the Security Warning message bar.

   The *Getting Started with Contacts* page displays, providing you with videos you can watch to learn how to use and modify the database as well as other helpful links.

---

> **TROUBLESHOOTING:** If the Getting Started page does not display, click Getting Started in the Forms category on the Navigation Pane.

---

> **TROUBLESHOOTING:** The Getting Started page opens every time you open the Contacts Management database. To close this page until you want to view it again, clear the *Show Getting Started when this database is opened* check box at the bottom-left corner of the dialog box before closing the Getting Started page.

 **e.** Close the Getting Started page.

  The database displays with the Contact List table open.

## STEP 2 ❯❯ ADD RECORDS TO A DOWNLOADED DESKTOP DATABASE TEMPLATE

Because the database opens in the Contact List form, you decide to begin by entering a contact—your dentist—in the form. Refer to Figure 1.31 as you complete Step 2.

**FIGURE 1.31** Contact Details Form

 **a.** Click in the empty first field of the first row. Enter the following information, pressing **Tab** between each entry. Do not press Tab after entering the ZIP/Postal Code.

| Field Name | Value to Type |
|---|---|
| First Name | Tanya |
| Last Name | Machuca |
| Company | Hobblecreek Mountain Dentistry |
| Job Title | D.D.S. |
| Category | Business (select from list) |
| E-mail Address | HMDentistry@email.com |
| Business Phone | 801-555-8102 |
| Home Phone | (leave blank) |
| Mobile Phone | 801-555-8921 |
| ZIP/Postal Code | 84664 |

 **b.** Click **Save and Close**.

 **c.** Double-click **Contact List** in the Forms group on the Navigation Pane.

**d.** Click **Open** in the first field of Dr. Machuca's record.

Open is a hyperlink to a different form in the database. The Contact Details form opens, displaying Dr. Machuca's information. More fields are available for you to use to store information.

**e.** Enter the following additional information to the record:

| Field Name | Value to Type |
|---|---|
| Street | 56 West 200 North |
| City | Mapleton |
| State/Province | UT |
| Country/Region | USA |
| Notes | Available Tuesday - Friday 7 a.m. to 4 p.m. |

**f.** Click the **Click to Map hyperlink** to view a map to Dr. Machuca's office. Close the map.

Bing displays a map to the address in the record. You can get directions, locate nearby businesses, and use many other options.

**g.** Click **Save and Close** in the top center of the form to close the Contact Details form.

The record is saved.

**h.** Click **New Contact** beneath the Contact List title bar.

The Contact Details form opens to a blank record.

**i.** Enter the following information for a new record, pressing **Tab** to move between fields. Some fields will be blank.

| Field Name | Value to Type |
|---|---|
| First Name | Rowan |
| Last Name | Westmoreland |
| Company | Phoenix Aesthetics |
| Job Title | Aesthetician |
| Mobile Phone | 801-555-2221 |
| Street | 425 North Main Street |
| City | Springville |
| State/Province | UT |
| ZIP/Postal Code | 84663 |
| Category | Personal |
| E-mail Address | Rowan55W5@email.com |
| Notes | Recommended by Michelle |

**j.** Click **Save and Close.**

## STEP 3 >> EXPLORE THE DATABASE OBJECTS IN A DOWNLOADED DESKTOP DATABASE TEMPLATE

You explore the objects created by the template so that you understand the organization of the database. Refer to Figure 1.32 as you complete Step 3.

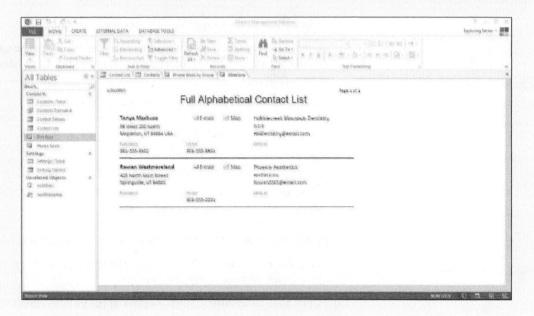

**FIGURE 1.32** Directory Form

a. Double-click the **Contacts table** in the Navigation Pane to open it.

The information you entered using the Contact List form and the Contact Details form displays in the Contacts table.

b. Click the **Reports group** in the Navigation Pane to expand the list of reports, if necessary.

The list of reports contained in the database file opens.

c. Double-click **Phone Book** in the Navigation Pane to open it.

The Phone Book report opens displaying the contact name and phone information organized by category.

d. Double-click the **Directory report** in the Navigation Pane to open it.

The Directory report opens, displaying a full alphabetical contact list. The Directory report was designed to display more fields than the Phone Book, but it is not organized by category.

e. Click **All Access Objects** on the Navigation Pane and select **Tables and Related Views**.

You can now see the objects that are based on the Contacts table.

f. Right-click the **Directory report tab** and click **Close All**.

g. Exit Access and submit your work based on your instructor's directions.

# Chapter Objectives Review

After reading this chapter, you have accomplished the following objectives:

## 1. Understand database fundamentals.

- A database is a collection of data organized as meaningful information that can be accessed, managed, stored, queried, sorted, and reported.
- Organize information in a database and recognize Access objects: An Access database is a structured collection of six types of objects—tables, forms, queries, reports, macros, and modules.
- The foundation of a database is its tables, the objects in which data is stored. Each table in the database is composed of records, and each record is in turn comprised of fields.
- The primary key in a table is the field (or combination of fields) that makes every record in a table unique.
- Examine the Access interface: Objects are organized and listed in the Navigation Pane. Access also uses a Tabbed Documents interface in which each object that is open has its own tab.
- Explore Access views: The Datasheet view enables the user to view, add, edit, and delete records, whereas the Design view is used to create and modify a table's design by specifying the fields it will contain, the fields' data types, and their associated properties.
- Open an Access file and work with Content Security: When a database is opened from a location that has not been designated as a trusted location or that does not have a digital signature from a publisher you can trust, Access displays a message bar with a security warning. Click the Enable Content button if you trust the database's source.

## 2. Use an existing database.

- Understand the difference between working in storage and memory: Access works primarily from storage. Records can be added, modified, or deleted in the database, and as the information is entered it is automatically saved.
- Add, edit, and delete records: A pencil icon displays in the row selector box to indicate when you are in editing mode. Moving to another record or clicking Save on the Quick Access Toolbar saves the changes.
- To add a new record, click *New (blank) record* on the navigation bar. To delete a record, click the row selector and click Delete in the Records group on the Home tab.
- Save As, Compact and Repair, and Back Up Access files: *Compact and Repair* reduces the size of the database, and Back Up creates a duplicate copy of the database.

## 3. Sort table data on one or multiple fields.

- Sorting changes the order of information, and information may be sorted by one or more fields.

## 4. Create, modify, and remove filters.

- A filter is a set of criteria that is applied to a table to display a subset of records in that table.
- *Filter by Selection* displays only the records that match the selected criteria.
- *Filter by Form* displays records based on multiple criteria and enables the user to apply logical operators and use comparison operators.

## 5. Know when to use Access or Excel to manage data.

- Use Access to manage data when you require multiple related tables to store your data; have a large amount of data; need to connect to and retrieve data from external databases; need to group, sort, and total data based on various parameters; and/or have an application that requires multiple users to connect to one data source.
- Use Excel to manage data when you need one worksheet to handle all of your data; have mostly numeric data; require subtotals and totals in your worksheet; want to primarily run a series of "what if" scenarios on your data; and/or need to create complex charts and/or graphs.

## 6. Understand relational power.

- Use the Relationships window: A relationship is a connection between two tables using a common field. The benefit of a relationship is to efficiently combine data from related tables for the purpose of creating queries, forms, and reports.
- Enforce referential integrity: Enforcing referential integrity when setting a table relationship ensures that data cannot be entered into a related table unless it first exists in the primary table.

## 7. Create a database.

- Create a Web application using a template: Creating a custom Web app enables you to create a database that you can build and use and share with others through the Web.
- Creating a blank desktop database: Creating a blank desktop database lets you create a database specific to your needs.
- Create a desktop database using a template: A template is a predefined database that includes professionally designed tables, forms, reports, and other objects that you can use to jumpstart the creation of your database.

# Key Terms Matching

Match the key terms with their definitions. Write the key term letter by the appropriate numbered definition.

a. Back Up Database
b. Compact and Repair
c. Custom Web app
d. Datasheet view
e. Design view
f. Field
g. Filter by Form
h. Filter by Selection
i. Form
j. Navigation Pane
k. Object

l. Primary key
m. Query
n. Record
o. Relational database management system (RDBMS)
p. Relationship
q. Report
r. Sort
s. Table
t. Template

1. _____ View that enables you to add, edit, and delete the records of a table. **p. 6**

2. _____ An Access object that enables you to enter, modify, or delete table data. **p. 4**

3. _____ An Access utility that reduces the size of the database and can repair a corrupt database. **p. 11**

4. _____ A main component that is created and used to make a database function. **p. 3**

5. _____ A filtering method that displays records based on multiple criteria **p. 22**

6. _____ A system that uses the relational model to manage groups of data (tables) and rules (relationships) between tables. **p. 30**

7. _____ A database that can be built, used, and shared with others through the use of a host server. **p. 37**

8. _____ An object that contains professional-looking formatted information from underlying tables or queries. **p. 4**

9. _____ An object used to store data, and the foundation of every database. **p. 3**

10. _____ An Access utility that creates a duplicate copy of the database. **p. 11**

11. _____ A predefined database that includes professionally designed tables, forms, reports, and other objects. **p. 37**

12. _____ A filtering method that displays only records that match selected criteria. **p. 21**

13. _____ A connection between two tables using a common field. **p. 29**

14. _____ A method of listing records in a specific sequence. **p. 20**

15. _____ View that enables you to create tables, add and delete fields, and modify field properties. **p. 8**

16. _____ An Access interface element that organizes and lists the database objects in a database. **p. 3**

17. _____ A question you ask that can help you find and retrieve table data meeting conditions you specify. **p. 4**

18. _____ The smallest data element in a table, such as first name, last name, address, or phone number. **p. 3**

19. _____ Complete set of all the fields (data elements) about one person, place, event, or concept. **p. 3**

20. _____ The field (or combination of fields) that uniquely identifies each record in a table. **p. 8**

# Multiple Choice

1. Which sequence represents the hierarchy of terms, from smallest to largest?

   (a) Database, table, record, field
   (b) Field, record, table, database
   (c) Record, field, table, database
   (d) Field, record, database, table

2. You edit several records in an Access table. When should you execute the Save command?

   (a) Immediately after you edit a record
   (b) When you close the table
   (c) Once at the end of the session
   (d) Records are saved automatically; the save command is not required.

3. Which of the following is *not* true of an Access database?

   (a) Short Text, Number, AutoNumber, and Currency are valid data types.
   (b) Every record in a table has the same fields as every other record.
   (c) Every table in a database contains the same number of records as every other table.
   (d) Each table should contain a primary key; however, a primary key is not required.

4. Which of the following is *true* regarding the record selector box?

   (a) An orange border surrounds the record selector box and the active record.
   (b) A pencil symbol indicates that the current record already has been saved.
   (c) An asterisk indicates the first record in the table.
   (d) An empty square indicates that the current record is selected.

5. Which of the following will be accepted as valid during data entry?

   (a) Adding a record with a duplicate primary key
   (b) Entering text into a numeric field
   (c) Entering numbers into a text field
   (d) Omitting an entry in a required field

6. You have finished an Access assignment and wish to turn it in to your instructor for evaluation. As you prepare to transfer the file, you discover that it has more than doubled in size. You should:

   (a) Delete extra tables or reports or fields to make the file smaller.

   (b) Zip the database file prior to sending it to your instructor.
   (c) Compact and repair the database before sending it to your instructor.
   (d) Turn it in; the size does not matter.

7. Which of the following conditions is available through *Filter by Selection*?

   (a) Equals condition
   (b) Delete condition
   (c) AND condition
   (d) OR condition

8. An Employees table is open in Datasheet view. You want to sort the names alphabetically by last name and then by first name (e.g., Smith, Andrew). To do this, you must:

   (a) First sort ascending on first name and then on last name.
   (b) First sort descending on first name and then on last name.
   (c) First sort ascending on last name and then on first name.
   (d) First sort descending on last name and then on first name.

9. Which of the following is *not* true when creating relationships between tables?

   (a) Join lines create a relationship between two tables.
   (b) The common fields used to create a relationship must both be primary keys.
   (c) The data types of common fields must be the same.
   (d) Enforcing referential integrity ensures that data cannot be entered into a related table unless it first exists in the primary table.

10. All of the following statements are *true* about creating a database *except*:

    (a) Creating a custom Web app requires that you use a host server.
    (b) When creating a blank desktop database, Access opens to a blank table in Datasheet view.
    (c) Using a template to create a database saves time because it includes predefined objects.
    (d) The objects provided in a template cannot be modified.

# Practice Exercises

## 1 Hotel Rewards

 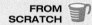

The Lakes Hotel and Conference Center caters to upscale business travelers and provides stylish hotel suites, sophisticated meeting and reception facilities, and state-of-the-art media equipment. The hotel is launching a rewards club to help the marketing department track the purchasing patterns of its most loyal customers. All of the hotel transactions will be stored in an Access database. Your task is to create a member table and enter sample customers. You will practice filtering on the table data. This exercise follows the same set of skills as used in Hands-On Exercises 1 and 2 in the chapter. Refer to Figure 1.33 as you complete this exercise.

| ID | LastName | FirstName | Address | City | Stat | Zip | Phone | DateOfMembership |
|---|---|---|---|---|---|---|---|---|
| 1 | Guerrassio | Janine | 1013 TRADERS TRAIL | GRAHAM | NC | 27253 | | 1/26/2015 |
| 2 | Gutierrez | Antonio | 100 PENNYPACKER CT | ELIZABETH CITY | NC | 27909 | 555-387-6894 | 1/29/2016 |
| 3 | Sigman | Hanni | 1922 WRIGHTSVILLE AVE | CARY | NC | 27513 | 555-794-8851 | 7/30/2016 |
| 4 | O'Brien | Lovie | 3413 KISTLER COURT | WILMINGTON | NC | 28409 | 555-557-8835 | 5/13/2015 |
| 5 | Ratanaphruks | Kritika | 4444 LLOYD CT | RALEIGH | NC | 27609 | | 3/18/2014 |
| 6 | Roski | Janice | 3904 HUNT CHASE CT | RALEIGH | NC | 27615 | | 7/3/2016 |
| 7 | Tutowiecki | Jerry | 775 BEAR RIDGE TRAIL | RALEIGH | NC | 27607 | 555-760-8879 | 5/21/2016 |
| 8 | Yingling | Bev | PO BOX 7045 | SALISBURY | NC | 53146 | | 5/17/2014 |
| 9 | Gray | Bob | 100 BIRDIE COURT | RALEIGH | NC | 27615 | 555-787-7688 | 9/1/2015 |
| 10 | Hauser | Bob | 10008 WHITESTONE RD | RALEIGH | NC | 27615 | 555-788-8596 | 8/1/2015 |
| * | (New) | | | | | | | |

**FIGURE 1.33** Enter Data into the Members Table

a. Open Access and click **Blank desktop database**.

b. Type **a01p1Rewards_LastFirst** in the **File Name box**. Click the **Browse icon**. Navigate to the location where you are saving your files in the File New Database dialog box, click **OK** to close the dialog box, and then click **Create** to create the new database.

c. Click **View** in the Views group on the TABLE TOOLS FIELDS tab to switch to Design view. Type **Members** in the **Save As dialog box** and click **OK**.

d. Type **LastName** under the ID field and press **Tab**. Accept **Short Text** as the Data Type. Type **FirstName** in the third row and press **Tab**. Accept **Short Text** as the Data Type.

e. Type the next five fields into the Field Name column: **Address**, **City**, **State**, **Zip**, and **Phone**. Accept **Short Text** as the Data Type for each of these fields.

f. Type **DateOfMembership** as the last Field Name and select **Date/Time** as the Data Type.

g. Click **View** in the Views group to switch to Datasheet view. Click **Yes** to save the table. Type the data as shown in Figure 1.33. Increase the column widths to fit the data as necessary. Press **Tab** to move to the next field.

h. Find a record that displays *Raleigh* as the value in the City field. Click **Raleigh** to select that data value.

i. Click **Selection** in the Sort & Filter group on the HOME tab. Select **Equals "Raleigh"**.

j. Find a record that displays *27612* as the value in the Zip field. Click **27612** to select that data value.

k. Click **Selection** in the Sort & Filter group on the HOME tab. Select **Equals "27612"**.

l. Click any value in the FirstName field. Click **Ascending** in the Sort & Filter group on the HOME tab. Click any value in the LastName field. Click **Ascending** in the Sort & Filter group on the HOME tab.

m. Click the **FILE tab**, click **Print**, and then click **Print Preview** to preview the sorted and filtered table.

n. Click **Close Print Preview** in the Close Preview group.

o. Close the table and save the changes.

p. Click the **FILE tab** and click **Compact and Repair Database** under *Advanced*.

q. Click the **FILE tab**, click **Save As**, and then double-click **Back Up Database**.

r. Click **Save** to accept the default backup file name with today's date.

s. Click the **FILE tab** and click **Exit** (to exit Access). Submit the database based on your instructor's directions.

The Custom Coffee Company provides coffee, tea, and snacks to offices in Miami. Custom Coffee also provides and maintains the equipment for brewing the beverages. The firm has a reputation for providing outstanding customer service. To improve customer service even further, the owner recently purchased an Access database to keep track of customers, orders, and products. This database will replace the Excel spreadsheets currently maintained by the office manager. The Excel spreadsheets are out of date, and they do not allow for data validation while data is being entered. The company hired you to verify and enter all the Excel data into the Access database. This exercise follows the same set of skills as used in Hands-On Exercises 1–3 in the chapter. Refer to Figure 1.34 as you complete this exercise.

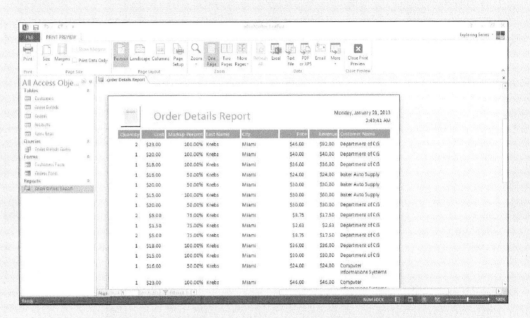

**FIGURE 1.34** Order Details Report Filtered for *YourName* and *Miami*

a. Open the *a01p2Coffee* file and save the database as **a01p2Coffee_LastFirst**.

b. Click the **DATABASE TOOLS tab** and click **Relationships** in the Relationships group. Review the table relationships. Take note of the join line between the Customers and Orders tables.

c. Click **Close** in the Relationships group.

d. Double-click the **Sales Reps table** in the Navigation Pane to open it. Replace *YourName* with your name in both the LastName and FirstName fields. For example, as the Access author, I used the name Cynthia Krebs in place of FirstName LastName. Close the table by clicking the **Close (X) button** on the right side of the Sales Reps window.

e. Double-click the **Customers Form** to open it. Click **New (blank) record** in the navigation bar at the bottom of the window. Add a new record by typing the following information; press **Tab** after each field.

| | |
|---|---|
| Customer Name: | *your name* Company |
| Contact: | *your name* |
| Email: | yourname@email.com |
| Address1: | 123 Main St |
| Address2: | (leave blank) |
| City: | Miami |
| State: | FL |
| Zip Code: | 33133 |
| Phone: | (305) 555-1234 |

```
Fax:                  (leave blank)
Service Start Date:   01/17/2016
Credit Rating:        A
Sales Rep ID:         2
```

Note the pencil in the top-left margin of the form window. This symbol indicates the new record has not been saved. Press **Tab**. The pencil symbol disappears, and the new customer is automatically saved to the table.

f. Close the Customers Form.

g. Double-click the **Orders Form** to open it. Click **New (blank) record** in the navigation bar at the bottom of the window. Add a new record by typing the following information:

```
Customer ID:    15 (Access will convert it to C0015)
Payment Type:   Cash (select using the arrow)
Comments:       Ship this order in 2 days
Product ID:     4 (Access will convert it to P0004)
Quantity:       2
```

h. Add a second product using the following information:

```
Product ID:    6 (Access will convert it to P0006)
Quantity:      1
```

i. Close the form.

j. Double-click the **Order Details Report** to open it in Report view. Click your name in the Last Name field, click **Selection** in the Sort & Filter group, and then click **Equals "Your Name"**.

k. Right-click **Miami** in the City field and select **Equals "Miami"** from the shortcut menu.

l. Click the **FILE tab**, click **Print**, and then click **Print Preview**.

m. Click **Close Print Preview** in the Close Preview group. Close the report.

n. Click the **FILE tab** and click **Compact & Repair Database**.

o. Click the **FILE tab**, click **Save As**, and then double-click **Back Up Database**. Use the default backup file name.

p. Close Access. Submit based on your instructor's directions.

## 3 Camping Trip

**FROM SCRATCH**

You and your friends have decided to spend your annual reunion camping at the Wawona Campground in Yosemite National Park. Wawona Campground is an extremely popular campground. Campground reservations are available in blocks of one month at a time, up to five months in advance, on the 15th of each month at 7 AM Pacific time. Nearly all reservations are filled the first day they become available, usually within seconds or minutes after 7 AM. Realizing that making reservations is a high-priority, critical task, and that there are many other tasks that must be completed before you can have a successful trip, your group decides to use the Access Task Management Database to begin getting organized for their trip on September 15, 2015. Other tasks can be entered at a later time. This exercise follows the same set of skills as used in Hands-On Exercises 3 and 4 in the chapter. Refer to Figures 1.35–1.38 as you complete this exercise.

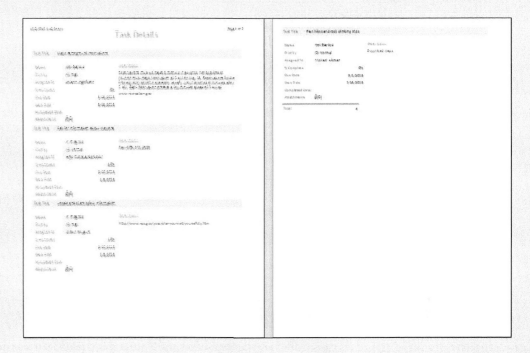

**FIGURE 1.35** Task Details Report

a. Open Access and click the **Desktop task management template** in the Access Backstage view.

b. Type **a01p3Camping_LastFirst** in the **File name box**. Click the **Browse icon**. Navigate to the location where you are saving your files in the File New Database dialog box, click **OK** to close the dialog box, and then click **Create** to create the new database.

c. Click the **Watch this arrow** for the *Using the Tasks Database* template video on the left side of the Getting Started page. If the Getting Started page does not open, open the Getting Started form in the Forms group in the Navigation Pane. Click **Watch this>>** and watch the video. Close the video when you have finished watching it. Click **Close** again to return to the *Getting Started with Tasks* page.

d. Remove the check in the *Show Getting Started when this database is opened* check box so that the page does not automatically display in the future. If you want to view Getting Started again, you can click **Getting Started** in the Forms category on the Navigation Pane. Click the **Close (X) button**.

e. Click **Relationships** in the Relationships group on the DATABASE TOOLS tab and note the relationship between the Contacts table and the Tasks table. Close the Relationships window.

f. Double-click **Contact List** in the Forms category on the Navigation Pane. Type the information for each field in the Contact list form using the information displayed in Figure 1.36, pressing **Tab** between each field.

**FIGURE 1.36** Contact List

g. Close the Contact List form. The Task List form displays because it was the form open when you downloaded the database.

h. Click the **Shutter Bar Open/Close button** to close the Navigation Pane, which enables you to see more table fields.

i. Enter the information for each field in the Task List form using the information displayed in Figure 1.37. In the Priority field, Status field, and Assigned To field, click the arrow and select the list of options. When typing the Start Date and Due Date, type the date and add **7 AM** after the date. Although the date does not show in the table, it is required.

**FIGURE 1.37** Task List Form

j. Close the Tasks table and click the **Shutter Bar Open/Close button** to open the Navigation Pane.

k. Double-click **Task Details** in the Forms category in the Navigation Pane.

l. Refer to Figure 1.38 to enter the information in the **Description box** and close the Task Details form.

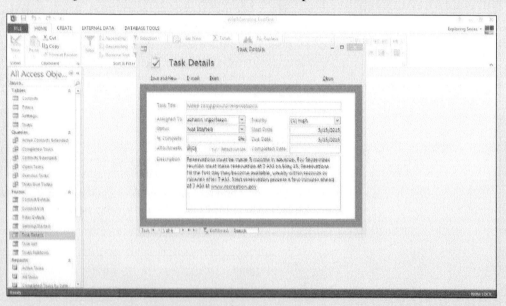

**FIGURE 1.38** Description in Task Details Form

m. Refer to Figure 1.35 and continue entering the descriptions for each of the records.

n. Double-click **Task Details** in the Reports category in the Navigation Pane to view the report displaying the details about the tasks you have created. Scroll down to see all tasks.

o. Click the **FILE tab**, click **Print**, and then click **Print Preview**.

p. Click **Two Pages** in the Zoom group on the Print Preview tab. Note the report format groups the information by Task Title.

q. Click **Close Print Preview** in the Close Preview group. Close the report.

r. Click the **FILE tab** and click **Compact & Repair Database**.

s. Click the **FILE tab**, click **Save As**, and then double-click **Back Up Database**. Use the default backup file name.

t. Close Access. Submit based on your instructor's directions.

## 1 Home Sales

**FROM SCRATCH**

You are the senior partner in a large, independent real estate firm that specializes in home sales. Most of your time is spent supervising the agents who work for your firm. The firm needs to create a database to hold all of the information on the properties it has listed. You will use the database to help find properties that match the goals of your customers. You will create the database, create two tables, add data to both tables, and create a relationship. Refer to Figure 1.39 as you complete this exercise.

**FIGURE 1.39** Properties Table

a. Open Access and click **Blank desktop database**. Type **a01m1Homes_LastFirst** in the **File Name box**. Click **Browse** and navigate to the location where you are saving your files. Click **OK** to close the dialog box and click **Create** to create the new database.

b. Switch to Design view. Type **Properties** in the **Save As dialog box** and click **OK**.

c. Type **DateListed** under the ID field and press **Tab**. Select **Date/Time** as the Data Type.

d. Type the remainder of the fields and Data Types as shown:

| Field Name | Data Type |
|---|---|
| DateSold | Date/Time |
| ListPrice | Currency |
| SalesPrice | Currency |
| SqFeet | Number |
| Beds | Number |
| Baths | Number |
| Address | Short Text |
| SubDivision | Number |
| AgentID | Number |
| Style | Short Text |
| Construction | Short Text |
| Garage | Short Text |
| YearBuilt | Number |

e. Switch to Datasheet view. Type the first 10 records as shown in Figure 1.39.

f. Open the *a01m1Properties.xlsx* workbook file in Excel. Click **row 2**, press and hold the **left mouse button**, and then drag through **row 70** so that all the data rows are selected. Click **Copy** in the Clipboard group on the HOME tab. Click **Yes** to save the data to the Clipboard when prompted. Close the Excel file.

g. Return to Access and click on the **asterisk (*)** on the first new row of the Properties table. Click **Paste** in the Clipboard group to paste all 69 rows into the Properties table. Save and close the table.

**DISCOVER**

h. Click **Table** in the Tables group on the CREATE tab. Click **View** in the Views group on the TABLE TOOLS FIELDS tab to switch to Design view. Save the table as **Agents**. Change the primary key from ID to **AgentID**. Add the following fields and switch to Datasheet view. Save changes to the table design when prompted.

| Field Name | Data Type |
|---|---|
| FirstName | Short Text |
| LastName | Short Text |
| Title | Short Text |

i. Enter the following data in the Agents table and close the table.

| AgentID | FirstName | LastName | Title |
|---|---|---|---|
| 1 | Kia | Hart | Broker |
| 2 | Keith | Martin | Agent |
| 3 | Kim | Yang | Agent |
| 4 | Steven | Dougherty | Agent in Training |
| 5 | Angela | Scott | Agent in Training |
| 6 | Juan | Resario | President |

j. Click the **DATABASE TOOLS tab** and click **Relationships** in the Relationships group. Add both tables to the Relationships window and close the Show Table dialog box.

k. Drag the bottom border of the Properties table downward until all fields display. Drag the **AgentID field** from the Agents table and drop it onto the **AgentID field** in the Properties table. Click the **Enforce Referential Integrity check box** in the Edit Relationships dialog box to activate it. Click **Create** and close the Relationships window. Click **Yes** to save your changes.

l. Open the **Properties** table. Click **Advanced** in the Sort & Filter group and click **Filter By Form**. Set the criteria to identify properties with a list price less than $300,000 and with two bedrooms. (You will use the expression <300000 for the criteria of the list price.) Display the results and sort by ascending list price. Save and close the table.

m. Compact, repair, and back up the database.

n. Exit Access. Submit the database based on your instructor's directions.

## 2 National Conference

The Association of Higher Education will host its National Conference on your campus next year. To facilitate the conference, the information technology department has replaced last year's Excel spreadsheets with an Access database containing information on the rooms, speakers, and sessions. Your assignment is to create a room itinerary that will list all of the sessions, dates, and times for each room. The list will be posted on the door of each room for the duration of the conference. Refer to Figure 1.40 as you complete this exercise.

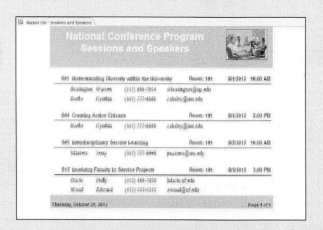

**FIGURE 1.40** Sessions and Speakers Report—Room 101

a. Open the *a01m2NatConf* file and save the database as **a01m2NatConf_LastFirst**.

b. Open the Relationships window.

c. Review the objects in the database to see if any of the existing objects will provide the room itinerary information displayed in Figure 1.40.

**d.** Open the SessionSpeaker table. Scroll to the first blank record at the bottom of the table and enter a new record using SpeakerID **99** and SessionID **09**. (Note: Speaker 99 does not exist.) How does Access respond? Close the dialog box, recognizing that you are not saving this record. Close the SessionSpeaker table. In the Relationships window, right-click the join line between the Speakers table and SessionSpeaker table and click **Delete**. Click **Yes** to permanently delete the selected relationship from the database. Close the Relationships window. Open the SessionSpeaker table and enter the same record again. How does Access respond this time? Close the SessionSpeaker table.

**e.** Open the Speakers table. Find and replace *YourName* with your name. Close the Speakers table.

**f.** Open the Speaker–Session Query and apply a filter to identify the sessions where you or Holly Davis are the speakers. Use *Filter by Form* and the Or tab. (Nine records should display.)

**g.** Sort the filtered results in ascending order by the RoomID field and save and close the query.

**h.** Open the Master List–Sessions and Speakers report. Right-click the **Master List–Sessions and Speakers tab** and select **Report View**.

**i.** Apply a filter that limits the report to sessions in Room 101 only.

**j.** Click the **FILE tab**, click **Print**, and then click **Print Preview**. Compare the report to Figure 1.40 and make any corrections necessary. Close Print Preview and close the report.

**k.** Compact and repair the database.

**l.** Back up the database. Use the default backup file name.

**m.** Exit Access. Submit based on your instructor's directions.

## 3 Used Cell Phones for Sale

You and a few of your classmates decide to start a new business selling used cell phones, MP3 players, and accessories. You will use an Access database to track your inventory. To begin, one person in your group will locate the Access database for this exercise, complete steps b through f, and then post the database to a SkyDrive folder. The next person in your group will retrieve the revised database and also complete steps b through f (and so on until everyone has completed steps b through f). After everyone has completed steps b through f, you will retrieve the database again and complete step g. At the completion of this exercise, each person will submit his or her own Word document containing the answers to the questions below.

**a.** Open the *a01m3Phones* database and save it as **a01m3PhonesGroupX_LastFirst**. (Replace *X* with the number assigned to your group by your instructor.)

**b.** Open the Inventory table and review the records in the table. Take note of the data in the TypeOfDevice column. Close the table and open the DeviceOptions table. Review the data and close the table.

**c.** Open the Relationships window. What is the benefit of the relationship between the Inventory table and the DeviceOptions table? Create a Word document with both the question and your answer. After you complete this exercise, you will submit this Word document to your instructor using the file name **a01m3PhonesAnswers_LastFirst**. Close the Relationships window.

**d.** Open the Inventory Form and add the information about your cell phone to the table (or search the Internet for any model if you do not have a cell phone) in the first new blank record. Enter your name in the SellerName field. With your information showing in the form, take a screenshot of the form using the Snipping Tool. Paste the image into the Word document you created in step c. Close the form.

**e.** Open the Inventory Report by Manufacturer in Report view. Filter the records for only items that have not been sold. Take a screenshot using the Snipping Tool and paste the image into the Word document. Close the report, close the database, and then exit Access.

**f.** Create a folder on your SkyDrive account named **Exploring Access** and share the folder with other members in your group and the instructor. Upload the database to this new folder and notify another person in your group. The next person will complete steps b through f, and then the next person, until all group members have added their information.

**g.** After all the new phone records have been added, each person in the group should download the **a01m3PhonesGroupX** database again and use filters to answer the following questions. Add the questions and your answers to the Word document you created.

    **1.** How many phones are still for sale? _____

    **2.** How many phones are made by Apple or Samsung? _____

    **3.** How many phones were sold in the first half of 2013? _____ List the ID numbers _____

    **4.** Sort the phones from lowest to highest asking price. Which phone is the least expensive? _____ Most expensive? _____

    **5.** How many items are not phones? _____

**h.** Use e-mail or text messaging to communicate with the other members in your group if you have any questions.

**i.** Submit the Word document based on your instructor's directions.

# Beyond the Classroom

### Northwind Revenue Report

RESEARCH CASE

Open the *a01b2NWind* file and save the database as **a01b2NWind_LastFirst**. Open the Employees table and replace *YourName* with your first and last names. Before you can filter the Revenue report, you need to update the criterion in the underlying query to match the dates in the database. Right-click the **Revenue query** in the Navigation Pane and click **Design view** in the shortcut menu. Scroll to the right until you see *OrderDate*. Right-click in the **Criteria row** under *OrderDate* and click **Zoom**. Change the criterion to **Between#1/1/2015#And#3/31/2015#** and click **OK**. Click **Run** in the Results group on the Query Tools Design tab and save the query. Open the Revenue report. Use the tools that you have learned in this chapter to filter the report for only your sales of Confections. Close the report. Compact, repair, and back up your database and exit Access.

### Lugo Computer Sales

DISASTER RECOVERY

You are having trouble with an Access 2013 database. One of the employees accidentally changed the CustomerID of Lugo Computer Sales. This change caused a problem in one of the relationships. Open the *a01b3Recover* file and save the database as **a01b3Recover_LastFirst**. Open the Customers and Orders tables and examine the data. Change the Lugo Computer Sales CustomerID in the Customers table back to the original number of 6. Reset the relationship between the Customers table and the Orders table and enforce referential integrity. Compact, repair, and back up your database and exit Access. Submit the database based on your instructor's directions.

### Financial Literacy

SOFT SKILLS CASE

The Cambridge Resources Group stated that surveyed executives ranked the "toll on productivity caused by financial stress" as one of the "most critical unaddressed issues in the workplace today." Dr. E. Thomas Garman*, the president of Personal Finance Employee Education Foundation, stated that "60% of employees live paycheck to paycheck" and that research shows that "those with more financial distress report poor health; financially distressed workers (40–50%) report that their financial problems cause their health woes; and that positive changes in financial behaviors are related to improved health."

Tracking your income and your expenses enables you to see where your money is going. With this information you can create a budget that will help you reach your goals. To aid you with this process, Microsoft created a downloadable Personal Account Ledger template. This database includes a form that enables you to record transactions; reports to display transactions, expenses by category, and income by category; and a tax report. Open *a01b4Ledger*, a database based on the Microsoft Personal Account Ledger, and save it as **a01b4Ledger_LastFirst**. Use the Account Transaction List to enter your income and expenses for the previous month. Then view the Income by Category report and the Expenses by Category report. Compact, repair, and back up your database and exit Access. Submit the database based on your instructor's directions.

* Employee Financial Wellness slideshare presentation, http://www.slideshare.net/irwink/Employee-Financial-Wellness, by Dr. E. Thomas Garman, President, Personal Finance Employee Education Foundation.

# Capstone Exercise

Your boss expressed concern about the accuracy of the inventory reports in the bookstore. He needs you to open the inventory database, make modifications to some records, and determine if the changes you make carry through to the other objects in the database. You will make changes to a form and verify those changes in a table, a query, and a report. When you have verified that the changes update automatically, you will compact and repair the database and make a backup of it.

## Database File Setup

You will open an original database file and save the database with a new name, replace an existing author's name with your name, create a table, create table relationships, sort, and apply a filter by selection.

a. Open the *a01c1Books* file and save the database as **a01c1Books_LastFirst**.

b. Create a new table in Design view. Save the table as **Publishers**. Change the primary key from ID to **PubID** with a Data Type of **Short Text**. Add the following fields and switch to Datasheet view. Save changes to the table design when prompted.

| Field Name | Data Type |
|---|---|
| PubName | Short Text |
| PubAddress | Short Text |
| PubCity | Short Text |
| PubState | Short Text |
| PubZIP | Short Text |

c. Enter the following data in the Publishers table and close the table.

| PubID | PubName | PubAddress | PubCity | PubState | PubZIP |
|---|---|---|---|---|---|
| BB | Bantam Books | 1540 Broadway | New York | NY | 10036 |
| FS | Farrar, Straus and Giroux | 12 Union Square West | New York | NY | 10003 |
| KN | Knopf | 299 Park Avenue | New York | NY | 10171 |
| LB | Little, Brown and Company | 1271 Avenue of the Americas | New York | NY | 10020 |
| PH | Pearson/ Prentice Hall | 1 Lake Street | Upper Saddle | NJ | 07458 |
| SS | Simon & Schuster | 100 Front Street | Riverside | NY | 08075 |

d. Open the Maintain Authors form.

e. Navigate to Record 7 and replace *YourName* with your name.

f. Add a new Title: **Technology in Action**. The ISBN is **0-13-148905-4**, the PubID is **PH**, the PublDate is **2015**, the Price is $89.95 (just type **89.95**, no $), and StockAmt is **95** units. Move to any other record to save the new record. Close the form.

g. Open the Maintain Authors form again and navigate to Record 7. The changes are there because Access works from storage, not memory. Close the form again.

## Sort a Query and Apply a Filter by Selection

You need to reorder a detail query so that the results are sorted alphabetically by the publisher name.

a. Open the Publishers, Books, and Authors Query.

b. Click in any record in the PubName column and sort the field in ascending order.

c. Check to make sure that four books list you as the author.

d. Click your name in the Author's Last Name field and filter the records to show only your books.

e. Close the query and save the changes.

## View a Report

You need to examine the Publishers, Books, and Authors Report to determine if the changes you made in the Maintain Authors form appear in the report.

a. Open the Publishers, Books, and Authors Report.

b. Check to make sure that the report shows four books listing you as the author.

c. View the layout of the report in Print Preview.

d. Close the report.

## Filter a Table

You need to examine the Books table to determine if the changes you made in the Maintain Authors form carried through to the related table. You also will filter the table to display books published after 2010 with fewer than 100 copies in inventory.

a. Open the Books table.

b. Use *Filter by Form* to create a filter that will identify all books published after 2010 with fewer than 100 items in stock.

c. Apply the filter and preview the filtered table.

d. Close the table and save the changes.

## Compact and Repair a Database and Back Up a Database

Now that you are satisfied that any changes made to a form or query carry through to the table, you are ready to compact, repair, and back up your file.

a. Compact and repair your database.

b. Create a backup copy of your database, accept the default file name, and save it.

c. Exit Access. Submit based on your instructor's directions.

# Tables and Queries in Relational Databases

**Access**

## Designing Databases and Extracting Data

Yuri Arcurs/Shutterstock

## OBJECTIVES — AFTER YOU READ THIS CHAPTER, YOU WILL BE ABLE TO:

1. Design a table p. 60
2. Create and modify tables p. 64
3. Share data p. 75
4. Establish table relationships p. 78
5. Create a single-table query p. 89
6. Specify query criteria for different data types p. 91
7. Understand query sort order p. 95
8. Run, copy, and modify a query p. 95
9. Use the Query Wizard p. 96
10. Create a multitable query p. 102
11. Modify a multitable query p. 103

## CASE STUDY | Bank Audit

During a year-end review, a bank auditor uncovers mishandled funds at Commonwealth Federal Bank in Wilmington, Delaware. In order to analyze the data in more detail, the auditor asks you to create an Access database so he can enter the compromised accounts, the associated customers, and the involved employees. Once the new database is created and all the data are entered, you will help the auditor answer questions by creating and running queries.

As you begin, you realize that some of the data are contained in Excel spreadsheets. After discussing this with the auditor, you decide importing these data directly into the new database would be best. Importing from Excel into Access is commonplace and should work well. Importing will also help avoid errors that are associated with data entry. Once the Excel data have been imported, you will use queries to determine which data do not belong in the database. Unaffected records will be deleted.

This chapter introduces the Bank database case study to present the basic principles of table and query design. You will use tables and forms to input data, and you will create queries and reports to extract information from the database in a useful and organized way. The value of that information depends entirely on the quality of the underlying data—the tables.

# Table Design, Creation, and Modification

Good database design begins with the tables. Tables provide the framework for all of the activities you perform in a database. If the framework is poorly designed, the rest of the database will be poorly designed as well. Whether you are experienced in designing tables or just learning how, the process should not be done haphazardly. You should follow a systematic approach when creating tables for a database. This process will take practice; however, over time, you will begin to see the patterns and eventually see the similarities among all databases.

In this section, you will learn the principles of good table design. You will review essential guidelines used when creating tables. After developing and testing the table design on paper, you will implement that design in Access. The first step is to list all the tables you need for the database and list all the fields in each table. While you learned to create tables in the previous chapter, in this chapter, you will learn to refine them by changing the properties of various fields. You will also be introduced to the concept of data validation. You want to make sure the data entered into the database are valid for the field and valid for the organization. Allowing invalid data into the tables will only cause problems later.

## Designing a Table

Recall that a table is a collection of records, with each record made up of a number of fields. During the table design process, think of the specific fields you need in each table; list the fields under the correct table and assign each field a data type (such as short text, number, or date) as well as its size (length) or format. The order of the fields within the table and the specific field names are not significant because they can be changed later. What is important is that the tables contain all necessary fields so that the system can produce the required information.

For example, consider the design process necessary to create a database for a bank. Most likely you have a bank account and know that the bank maintains data about you. Your bank has your name, address, phone number, and Social Security number. It also knows what accounts you have (checking, savings, money market), if you have a credit card with that bank, and what its balance is. Additionally, your bank keeps information about its branches around the city or state. If you think about the data your bank maintains, you could make a list of the categories of data needed to store that information. These categories for the bank—customers, accounts, branches—become the tables in the bank's database. A bank's customer list is an example of a table: It contains a record for each bank customer.

After the tables have been identified, add the necessary fields using these six guidelines. (These guidelines are discussed in detail in the following paragraphs.)

- Include the necessary data.
- Design for now and for the future.
- Store data in their smallest parts.
- Add calculated fields to a table.
- Design to accommodate date arithmetic.
- Link tables using common fields.

Figure 2.1 shows a customer table and two other tables found in a sample bank database. It also lists fields that would be needed in each table record.

**FIGURE 2.1** Rough Draft of Tables and Fields in a Sample Database

## Include Necessary Data

A good way to determine what data are necessary in tables is to consider the output you need. It will probably be necessary for you to create professional-looking reports for others, so begin by creating a rough draft of the reports you will need. Then design tables that contain the fields necessary to create those reports. In other words, ask yourself what information will be expected from the system and determine the data required to produce that information. Consider, for example, the tables and fields in Figure 2.1. Is there required information that could not be generated from those tables?

- You can determine which branch a customer uses because the Accounts table includes the CustomerID and the BranchID.
- You can determine who manages a particular branch and which accounts are located there because the Branch table contains the Manager and Location fields.
- You can determine how long a customer has banked with the branch because the date he or she opened the account is stored in the Accounts table.
- You cannot generate the monthly bank statement. In order to generate a customer bank statement (showing all deposits and withdrawals for the month), you would need to add an additional table—an Account Activity table.
- You cannot e-mail a customer because the Customers table does not contain an E-mail field.

If you discover a missing field, such as the E-mail field, you can insert a row anywhere in the appropriate table and add the missing field. The databases found in a real bank are more complex, with more tables and more fields; however, the concepts illustrated here apply both to our sample bank database and to real bank databases.

## Design for Now and for the Future

As the data requirements of an organization evolve over time, the information systems that hold the data must change as well. When designing a database, try to anticipate the future needs of the system and build in the flexibility to satisfy those demands. For example, when you add a text field, make sure that the number of characters allocated is sufficient to accommodate future expansion. On the other hand, if you include all the possible fields that anyone might ever need, you could drive up the cost of the database. Each additional field can increase the cost of the database, because it will require additional employee time to enter and maintain the data. The additional fields will also require more storage space, which you will need to calculate, especially when working with larger databases. Good database design must balance the data collection needs of the company with the cost associated with collection and storage. Plans must also include the frequency and cost necessary to modify and update the database.

Suppose you are designing a database for a college. You would need to store each student's name, address, and phone number. You would also need to store multiple phone numbers for most students—a cell phone number, a work number, and an emergency number. As a database designer, you will need to design the tables to accommodate multiple entries for similar data.

## Store Data in Their Smallest Parts

The table design in Figure 2.1 divides a customer's name into two fields (FirstName and LastName) to reference each field individually. You might think it easier to use a single field consisting of both the first and last name, but that approach is too limiting. Consider a list of customers stored as a single field:

- Sue Grater
- Rick Grater
- Nancy Gallagher
- Harry Weigner
- Barb Shank
- Pete Shank

The first problem in this approach is the lack of flexibility: You could not easily create a salutation for a letter of the form *Dear Sue* or *Dear Ms. Gallagher* because the first and last names are not accessible individually.

A second difficulty is that the list of customers cannot be easily displayed in alphabetical order by last name because the last name begins in the middle of the field. The names could easily be alphabetized by first name because the first name is at the beginning of the field. However, the most common way to sort names is by the last name, which can be done more efficiently if the last name is stored as a separate field.

Think of how an address might be used. The city, state, and postal code should always be stored as separate fields. Any type of mass mailing requires you to sort on ZIP codes to take advantage of bulk mail. Other applications may require you to select records from a particular state or postal code, which can be done more efficiently if you store the data as separate fields. Often database users enter the postal code, and the database automatically retrieves the city and state information. You may need to direct a mailing only to a neighborhood or to a single street. The guideline is simple: Store data in their smallest parts.

## Add Calculated Fields to a Table

A *calculated field* produces a value from an expression or function that references one or more existing fields. Access enables you to store calculated fields in a table using the calculated data type. An example of a calculated field can be found in the bank database. Suppose the bank pays its customers 1.0% interest on the principal each month. A calculated field, such as Monthly Interest, could store the expression Principal × 0.01. The interest amount would then appear on the customer's monthly bank statement.

Storing calculated data in a table enables you to add the data easily to queries, forms, and reports without the trouble of an additional calculation. Storing calculated data in a table may increase the size of the database slightly, but the benefits may outweigh this drawback. In the chapters ahead, you will examine calculations and calculated fields in greater detail. You will learn when to add calculated fields to a table and when to avoid them.

## Design to Accommodate Date Arithmetic

Calculated fields are frequently created with numeric data, as the preceding Monthly Interest field example illustrates. You can also create calculated fields using date/time data. If you want to store the length of time a customer has been a customer, you would first create a field to hold the start date for each customer. Next, you would create a calculated field that contains an expression that subtracts the start date from today's date. The resulting calculation would store the number of days each customer has been a customer. Divide the results by 365 to convert days to years. If you want to calculate days to years and account for leap year, you could divide the results by 365.25.

This same concept applies to bank accounts; a bank is likely to store the OpenDate for each account in the Accounts table, as shown in Figure 2.1. Using this date, you can subtract the open date from today's date and calculate the number of days the account has been open. (Again, divide the results by 365 to convert to years.) If you open the Accounts table at least one day later, the results of the calculated field will be different.

A person's age is another example of a calculated field using date arithmetic—the date of birth is subtracted from today's date and the result is divided by 365. It might seem easier to store a person's age rather than the birth date to avoid the calculation. But that would be a mistake because age changes over time and would need to be updated each time age changes. Storing the date of birth is much better because the data remains *constant*. You can use *date arithmetic* to subtract one date from another to find out the number of days, months, or years that have lapsed between them. You can also add or subtract a constant from a date.

## Plan for Common Fields Between Tables

As you create the tables and fields for the database, keep in mind that the tables will be joined in relationships using common fields. Draw a line between common fields to indicate the joins, as shown in Figure 2.2. These join lines will be created in Access when you learn to create table relationships later in the chapter. For now, you should name the common fields the same and make sure they have the same data type. For example, CustomerID in the Customers table will join to the CustomerID field in the Accounts table. CustomerID must have the same data type (in this case number/long integer) in both tables; otherwise, the join line will not be allowed.

**FIGURE 2.2** Create Relationships Using Common Fields

Avoid *data redundancy*, which is the unnecessary storing of duplicate data in two or more tables. You should avoid duplicate information in multiple tables in a database, because errors may result. Suppose the customer address data were stored in both the Customers and Accounts tables. If a customer moved to a new address, it is possible that the address would be updated in only one of the two tables. The result would be inconsistent and unreliable data. Depending on which table served as the source for the output, either the new or the old address might be given to someone requesting the information. Storing the address in only one table is more reliable.

# Creating and Modifying Tables

Tables can be created in a new blank database or in an existing database. You can create a table by:

**STEP 1 ≫**

- Typing a field name in a row in Design view.
- Entering table data into a new row in Datasheet view.
- Importing data from another database or application such as Excel.

Regardless of how a table is first created, you can always modify it later to include a new field or change an existing field. Figure 2.3 shows a table created by entering fields in Design view.

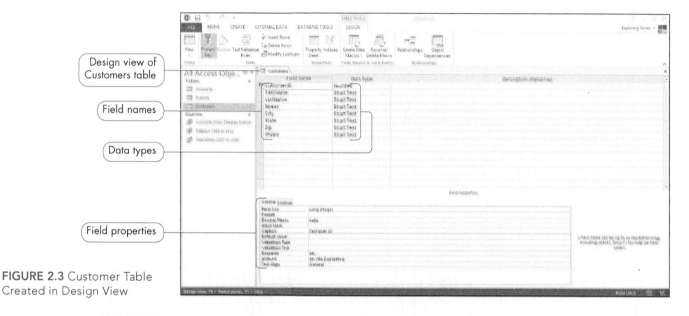

**FIGURE 2.3** Customer Table Created in Design View

**STEP 4 ≫**

When you add a new field in Design view, the field must be given a field name to identify the data it holds. The field name should be descriptive of the data and can be up to 64 characters in length, including letters, numbers, and spaces. Database developers use *CamelCase notation* for field names. Instead of spaces in multiword field names, use uppercase letters to distinguish the first letter of each new word, for example, ProductCost or LastName. It is best to avoid spaces in field names, because spaces can cause problems when creating the other objects—such as queries, forms, and reports—based on tables.

Fields may be renamed either in Design view or in Datasheet view. In Design view, double-click the field name you want to change, type the new field name, and then click Save on the Quick Access Toolbar. To rename a field in Datasheet view, double-click the field selector of the field that you want to rename, type the new field name, and then press Enter.

Fields can be also be deleted in Design view or Datasheet view. To delete a field in Datasheet view, select the field or fields you want to delete and press Delete. To delete fields in Design view, do the following:

1. Click the Record Selector of the field you want to delete to select it.
2. Click Delete Rows in the Tools group.

3. Click Yes in the message box that appears if you want to permanently delete the field(s). Click No if you do not want to delete the field(s).
4. Click Yes in the second message box that will appear if the selected field you are deleting is a primary key. Click No if you do not want to delete the primary key.

 **TIP** | **Freeze Fields in an Access Database**

To keep a field viewable while you are scrolling through a table, select the field or fields you want to freeze, right-click, and then click Freeze Fields. If you want the field(s) to remain frozen when you are finished working, save the changes when you close the table. To unfreeze all fields, right-click the field(s) and select Unfreeze All Fields.

## Determine Data Type

Every field also has a *data type* property that determines the type of data that can be entered and the operations that can be performed on that data. Access recognizes 12 data types. Table 2.1 lists these data types, their uses, and examples of the data type.

**TABLE 2.1  Data Types and Uses**

| Data Type | Description | Example |
|---|---|---|
| Short Text | Stores alphanumeric data, such as a customer's name or address. It can contain alphabetic characters, numbers, and/or special characters (e.g., an apostrophe in O'Malley). Social Security numbers, telephone numbers, and postal codes should be designated as text fields since they are not used in calculations and often contain special characters such as hyphens and parentheses. A short text field can hold up to 255 characters. Formerly Text data type. | 2184 Walnut Street |
| Long Text | Lengthy text or combinations of text and numbers, such as several sentences or paragraphs; used to hold descriptive data. Formerly Memo data type. | A description of product packaging |
| Number | Contains a value that can be used in a calculation, such as the number of credits a course is worth. The contents are restricted to numbers, a decimal point, and a plus or minus sign. | 12 |
| Date/Time | Holds dates or times and enables the values to be used in date or time arithmetic. | 10/31/2016<br>1:30:00 AM |
| Currency | Used for fields that contain monetary values. | $1,200 |
| AutoNumber | A special data type used to assign the next consecutive number each time you add a record. The value of an AutoNumber field is unique for each record in the file. | 1, 2, 3 |
| Yes/No | Assumes one of two values, such as Yes or No, True or False, or On or Off (also known as a Boolean). For example, is a student on the Dean's list: Yes or No. | Yes |
| OLE Object | Contains an object created by another application. OLE objects include spreadsheets, pictures, sounds, and graphics. | JPG image |
| Hyperlink | Stores a Web address (URL) or the path to a folder or file. Hyperlink fields can be clicked to retrieve a Web page or to launch a file stored locally. | http://www.keithmast.com |
| Attachment | Used to store multiple images, spreadsheet files, Word documents, and other types of supported files. | An Excel workbook |
| Calculated | The results of an expression that references one or more existing fields. | [IntRate] + 0.25 |
| Lookup Wizard | Creates a field that enables you to choose a value from another table or from a list of values by using a list box or a combo box. | Customers table with an AccountID field that looks up the Account ID from an Accounts table |

## Establish a Primary Key

**STEP 2 ▶▶** As you learned earlier, the primary key is the field (or combination of fields) that uniquely identifies each record in a table. Access does not require that each table have a primary key. However, good database design usually includes a primary key in each table. You should select unique and infrequently changing data for the primary key. For example, a complete address (street, city, state, and postal code) may be unique but would not make a good primary key because it is subject to change when someone moves.

You probably would not use a person's name as the primary key, because several people could have the same name. A customer's account number, on the other hand, is unique and is a frequent choice for the primary key, as in the Customers table in this chapter. The primary key can be easily identified in many tables—for example, a PartNumber in a parts table, the ISBN in the book database of a bookstore, or a StudentID that uniquely identifies a student. When no primary key occurs naturally, you can create a primary key field with the AutoNumber data type. The *AutoNumber* data type is a number that automatically increments each time a record is added.

In Figure 2.4, the book's ISBN is the natural primary key for the book table because no two book titles can have the same ISBN. This field uniquely identifies the records in the table. Figure 2.5 depicts the Speakers table, where no unique field can be identified from the data. Because of this, you can add the SpeakerID field with an AutoNumber data type. Access automatically numbers each speaker record sequentially with a unique ID as each record is added.

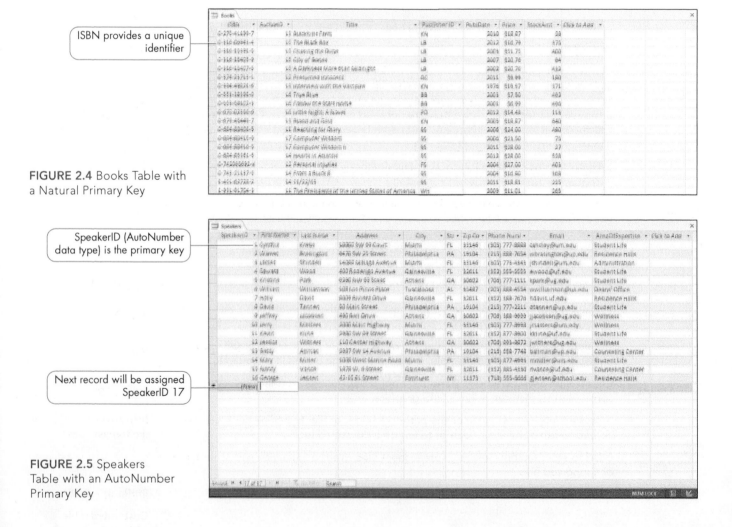

ISBN provides a unique identifier

**FIGURE 2.4** Books Table with a Natural Primary Key

SpeakerID (AutoNumber data type) is the primary key

Next record will be assigned SpeakerID 17

**FIGURE 2.5** Speakers Table with an AutoNumber Primary Key

## Explore a Foreign Key

A *foreign key* is a field in one table that is also the primary key of another table. The CustomerID is the primary key in the Customers table. It serves to uniquely identify each customer. It also appears as a foreign key in a related table. For example, the Accounts table contains the CustomerID field to establish which customer owns the account. A CustomerID can appear only once in the Customers table, but it may appear multiple times in the Accounts table (when viewed in Datasheet view) because one customer may own multiple accounts (checking, money market, home equity). Therefore, the CustomerID is the primary key in the Customers table and a foreign key in the Accounts table.

If you were asked to create an Access database for the speakers at a national conference, you would create a database with the tables Speakers and SessionSpeaker. You would add a primary key field to the Speakers table (SpeakerID) along with a speaker's FirstName and LastName fields; you would also add two fields to the SessionSpeaker table (SpeakerID and SessionID). The SpeakerID field in the Speakers table is a primary key and would not allow duplicates; the SpeakerID field in the SessionSpeaker table is a foreign key and would allow duplicates so that a speaker may speak more than once at the conference. The SpeakerID in the SessionSpeaker table enables you to join the two tables in a relationship. Figure 2.6 shows portions of the Speakers and SessionSpeaker tables.

SpeakerID is the primary key of the Speakers table (no duplicates)

SpeakerID is a foreign key in the Session Speaker table so speakers can be assigned multiple sessions

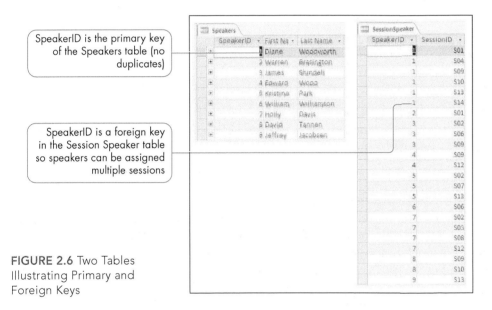

**FIGURE 2.6** Two Tables Illustrating Primary and Foreign Keys

## Work with Field Properties

**STEP 3 »**

While a field's data type determines the type of data that can be entered and the operations that can be performed on that data, it is its *field properties* that determine how the field looks and behaves.

Field Size is a commonly changed field property. A field with a *short text data type* can hold up to 255 characters; however, you can limit the characters by reducing the field size property. For example, you would limit the State field to only two characters because all state abbreviations are two letters. A field with a *number data type* can be set to Integer to display the field contents as integers from –32,768 to 32,768 or to Long Integer for larger values.

You can set a *caption property* to create a label more readable than a field. The caption displays at the top of a table or query column in Datasheet view and when the field is used in a report or form. For example, a field named ProductCostPerUnit could have the caption *Per Unit Product Cost*. Even if a caption is used, however, you must use the actual field name, ProductCostPerUnit, in any calculation.

## TIP | Best Fit Columns

If a field name is cut off in Datasheet view, you can adjust the column width by positioning the pointer on the vertical border on the right side of the column. When the pointer displays as a two-headed arrow, double-click the border. You can also click More in the Records group on the Home tab. Select Field Width and click Best Fit in the Column Width dialog box.

Set the validation rule property to restrict data entry in a field to ensure the correct type of data are entered or that the data do not violate other enforced properties. The *validation rule* checks the data entered when the user exits the field. If the data entered violate the validation rule, an error message displays and prevents the invalid data from being entered into the field. For example, if you have set the data type for a field as Number and then try to enter text in the field, you will receive an error message telling you that the value you entered does not match the Number data type in the column.

The field properties are set to default values according to the data type, but you can modify them if necessary. Common property types are defined in Table 2.2.

### TABLE 2.2 Common Access Table Property Types and Descriptions

| Property Type | Description |
| --- | --- |
| Field Size | Determines the maximum characters of a text field or the format of a number field. |
| Format | Changes the way a field is displayed or printed but does not affect the stored value. |
| Input Mask | Simplifies data entry by providing literal characters that are typed for every entry, such as hyphens in a Social Security Number or slashes in a date. It also imposes data validation by ensuring that data entered conform to the mask. |
| Caption | Enables an alternate name to be displayed other than the field name; alternate name appears in datasheets, forms, and reports. |
| Default Value | Enters automatically a predetermined value for a field each time a new record is added to the table. For example, if most customers live in Los Angeles, the default value for the City field could be set to Los Angeles to save data entry time and accuracy. |
| Validation Rule | Requires data entered to conform to a specified rule. |
| Validation Text | Specifies the error message that is displayed when the validation rule is violated. |
| Required | Indicates that a value for this field must be entered. |
| Allow Zero Length | Allows entry of zero length text strings ("") in a Hyperlink, or Short or Long Text fields. |
| Indexed | Increases the efficiency of a search on the designated field. |
| Expression | Used for calculated fields only. Enters the expression you want Access to evaluate and store. |
| Result Type | Used for calculated fields only. Enters the format for the calculated field results. |

## Enter Table Records in Datasheet View

STEP 5 ▶▶ While Design view is used to create and modify the table structure by enabling you to add and edit fields and set field properties, Datasheet view is used to add, edit, and delete records. As you have learned, the Datasheet view of an Access table resembles an Excel spreadsheet and displays data in a grid format—rows represent records and columns represent fields. Datasheet view indicates the current record using a gold border; you can select a record by clicking the record selector on the left side of each record. Use the new blank record (marked with an asterisk) at the end of the table to add a new record.

In Hands-On Exercise 1, you will create a new database and enter fields into a table. Then you will switch to the table's Design view to add additional fields and modify selected field properties of various fields within the table. Finally, you will enter data in the table in Datasheet view.

*Quick*
Concepts

1. What is meant by "Design for now and the future" when designing database fields? *p. 61*

2. What is the difference between a primary key and a foreign key? *p. 67*

3. What is a field property? Which field property creates a more readable label that displays in the top row in Datasheet view and in forms and reports? *p. 67*

## 1 Table Design, Creation, and Modification

Assisting the bank auditor at Commonwealth Federal Bank as he investigates the mishandled funds will be a great opportunity for you to showcase your Access skills. Be sure to check your work each step of the way, because your work will come under substantial scrutiny. Do a good job with this Access project and more opportunities might come your way.

**Skills covered:** Create a Table in Datasheet View • Delete a Field and Set a Table's Primary Key • Work with Field Properties • Create a New Field in Design View • Modify the Table in Datasheet View

### STEP 1 ≫ CREATE A TABLE IN DATASHEET VIEW

You create a new desktop database to store information about the mishandled funds database. You enter the data for the first record (BranchID, Manager, and Location). Refer to Figure 2.7 as you complete Step 1.

Step h: Type the data directly into the datasheet

Step i: Save the table as Branch

**FIGURE 2.7** Enter Data into the Branch Table in Datasheet View

a. Start Microsoft Office Access 2013 and click **Blank desktop database**.

b. Type **a02h1Bank_LastFirst** into the **File Name box**.

c. Click **Browse** to find the folder location designated by your instructor and click **OK**. Click **Create** to create the new database.

   Access will create the new database named *a02h1Bank_LastFirst* and a new table will automatically open in Datasheet view.

d. Click **Click to Add** and select **Short Text** as the Data type.

   *Click to Add* changes to *Field1. Field1* is selected to make it easier to change the field name.

e. Type **BranchID** and press **Tab**.

   A list of Data types for the third column opens so that you can select the data type for the third column.

f. Select **Short Text**, type **Manager**, and then press **Tab**.

g. Select **Short Text**, type **Location**, and then click in the first column next to the New Record asterisk.

h. Enter the data for the new table as shown in Figure 2.7, letting Access assign the ID field for each new record. Replace *YourLastName* with your own last name.

   Entering data in Datasheet view provides an easy way to create the table initially. You can now modify the table in Design view as described in the next several steps.

i. Click **Save** on the Quick Access Toolbar. Type **Branch** in the **Save As dialog box** and click **OK**.

# STEP 2 >> DELETE A FIELD AND SET A TABLE'S PRIMARY KEY

It is possible to modify tables even after data have been entered; however, pay attention to the messages from Access after you make a design change. In this step, you will be modifying the Branch table. You examine the design of the table and realize that the BranchID field is a unique identifier, making the ID field redundant. You delete the ID field and make the BranchID field the primary key. Refer to Figure 2.8 as you complete Step 2.

Step d: Click to establish primary key

Step a: Branch table in Design view

Step c: Selected field with orange border

**FIGURE 2.8** Branch Table in Design View

a. Click **View** in the Views group to switch to the Design view of the Branch table.

The Field Name for each of the four fields displays along with the Data Type.

b. Click the **ID field** to select it, if necessary. Click **Delete Rows** in the Tools group. Click **Yes** to both warning messages.

Access responds with a warning that you are about to permanently delete a field and a second warning that the field is the primary key. You delete the field because you will set the BranchID field as the primary key.

c. Click the **BranchID field,** if necessary.

The cell field name now has a orange border, as shown in Figure 2.8.

d. Click **Primary Key** in the Tools group on the DESIGN tab.

You set the BranchID as the primary key. The Indexed property in the *Field Properties* section at the bottom of the design window displays *Yes (No Duplicates).*

e. Click **Save** on the Quick Access Toolbar to save the table.

## TIP | Shortcut Menu

You can right-click a row selector to display a shortcut menu to copy a field, set the primary key, insert or delete rows, or to access field properties. Use the shortcut menu to make these specific changes to the design of a table.

## STEP 3 ≫ WORK WITH FIELD PROPERTIES

You need to modify the table design further to comply with the bank auditor's specifications. Be aware of messages from Access that indicate you may lose data. Refer to Figure 2.9 as you complete Step 3.

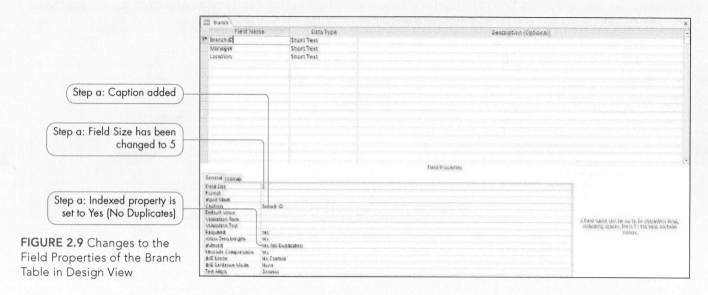

Step a: Caption added

Step a: Field Size has been changed to 5

Step a: Indexed property is set to Yes (No Duplicates)

**FIGURE 2.9** Changes to the Field Properties of the Branch Table in Design View

a. Click the **BranchID field name** in the top section of the design window; modify the BranchID field properties in the bottom of the design window.

   - Click in the **Field Size property** and change *255* to **5**.
   - Click in the **Caption property** and type **Branch ID**. Make sure *Branch* and *ID* have a space between them.
     A caption provides a more descriptive field name. It will appear as the column heading in Datasheet view.
   - Check the Indexed property; confirm it is *Yes (No Duplicates)*.

b. Click the **Manager field name** at the top of the window; modify the following field properties:

   - Click in the **Field Size property** and change *255* to **30**.
   - Click in the **Caption property** and type **Manager's Name**.

c. Click the **Location field name** and modify the following field properties:

   - Click in the **Field Size property** and change *255* to **30**.
   - Click in the **Caption property** and type **Branch Location**.

## STEP 4 ≫ CREATE A NEW FIELD IN DESIGN VIEW

You notify the auditor that a date field is missing in your new table. Modify the table to add the new field. The data can be entered at a later time. Refer to Figure 2.10 as you complete Step 4.

Step a: New field added

Step b: Date/Time data type added

Step f: Message indicating the field size was reduced

Step c: Description added

**FIGURE 2.10** Adding a New Field to the Branch Table

a. Click in the first blank row below the Location field name and type **StartDate**.

You added a new field to the table.

b. Press **Tab** to move to the Data Type column. Click the **Data Type arrow** and select **Date/Time**.

**TIP** **Keyboard Shortcut for Data Types**

You also can type the first letter of the data type, such as d for Date/Time, s for Short Text, or n for Number. To use the keyboard shortcut, click on the field name and press Tab to advance to the Data Type column. Next, type the first letter of the data type.

c. Press **Tab** to move to the Description column and type **This is the date the manager started working at this location.**

d. Click the **Format property**, click the arrow, and then select **Short Date** from the list of date formats.

e. Click in the **Caption property** and type **Manager's Start Date**.

f. Click **Save** on the Quick Access Toolbar.

A warning dialog box opens to indicate that "Some data may be lost" because the size of the BranchID, Manager, and Location field properties were shortened. It asks if you want to continue anyway. Always read the Access warning! In this case, you can click Yes to continue because you know that the existing data are no longer than the new field sizes.

g. Click **Yes** in the warning box.

## STEP 5 » MODIFY THE TABLE IN DATASHEET VIEW

As you work with the auditor, you will modify tables in the bank database from time to time. To modify the table, you will need to switch between Design view and Datasheet view. Refer to Figure 2.11 as you complete Step 5.

**FIGURE 2.11** Start Dates Added to the Branch Table

a.  Right-click the **Branch tab** and select **Datasheet View** from the shortcut menu. (To return to Design view, right-click the tab again and select Design view.)

The table displays in Datasheet view. The field captions display at the top of the columns, but they are cut off.

b.  Double-click the border between *Branch ID* and *Manager's Name*, the border between *Manager's Name* and *Branch Location*, the border between *Branch Location* and *Manager's Start Date*, and the border after *Manager's Start Date*.

The columns shrink or expand to display the best fit for the field name.

c.  Click inside the **Manager's Start Date** in the first record and click the **Calendar** next to the date field. Use the navigation arrows to find and select **December 3, 2014** from the calendar.

You can also enter the dates by typing them directly into the StartDate field.

d.  Type the start date directly in each field for the rest of the managers, as shown in Figure 2.11.

e.  Click the **Close (X) button** at the top-right corner of the datasheet, below the Ribbon.

> **TROUBLESHOOTING:** If you accidentally click the Close (X) button on top of the Ribbon, you will exit Access completely. To start again, launch Access and click the first file in the Recent list.

f.  Double-click the **Branch table** in the Navigation Pane to open the table. Check the start dates.

The start dates are still there even though you did not save your work in the previous step. Access saves the data to your storage location as soon as you move off the current record or close an object.

g.  Click the **FILE tab**, click **Print**, and then click **Print Preview**.

Occasionally, users will print an Access table. However, database developers usually create reports to print table data.

h.  Click **Close Print Preview** and close the Branch table.

i.  Keep the database open if you plan to continue with Hands-On Exercise 2. If not, close the database and exit Access.

# Multiple-Table Databases

In Figure 2.1, the sample bank database contains three tables—Customers, Accounts, and Branch. You created one table, the Branch table, in the previous section using the Datasheet view and modified the table fields in Design view. You will create the two remaining tables using a different method—importing data from Excel. In this section, you will learn how to import data from Excel, modify tables, create indexes, create relationships between tables, and enforce referential integrity.

## Sharing Data

Most companies store some type of data in Excel spreadsheets. Often, the data stored in those spreadsheets can be more efficiently managed in an Access database. Fortunately, Access provides you with a wizard that guides you through the process of importing data from Excel. The wizard can also guide you as you import data from other Access databases. You can import tables, queries, forms, reports, pages, macros, and modules from another database.

### Import an Excel Spreadsheet

STEP 1 ▶▶

STEP 2 ▶▶

Figures 2.12 through 2.17 show the steps of the Get External Data – Excel Spreadsheet feature. Launch the feature by clicking the External Data tab and clicking Excel in the Import & Link group. Figure 2.12 shows the first screen of the Get External Data – Excel Spreadsheet feature. In this step, you specify the source of the data. Locate the Excel file you want to import by clicking Browse. Then choose between three options for the incoming data: *Import the source data into a new table in the current database*; *Append a copy of the records to the table*, which adds the data to an existing table; or *Link to the data source by creating a linked table*, which creates a link to the Excel source. Importing or appending data stores a copy of the data in Access, whereas linking the data keeps the data in the original file and Access retrieves the data each time the database is opened.

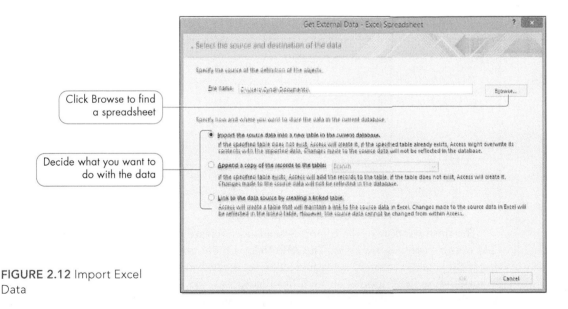

Click Browse to find a spreadsheet

Decide what you want to do with the data

**FIGURE 2.12** Import Excel Data

After you locate and select an Excel workbook, accept the default option (*Import the source data into a new table in the current database*) and click OK. The Import Spreadsheet Wizard dialog box launches and displays a list of the worksheets in the specified workbook. Select the worksheet you want to import and click Next. Figure 2.13 shows the Accounts worksheet selected. The bottom of the Import Spreadsheet Wizard dialog box displays a preview of the data stored in the specified worksheet.

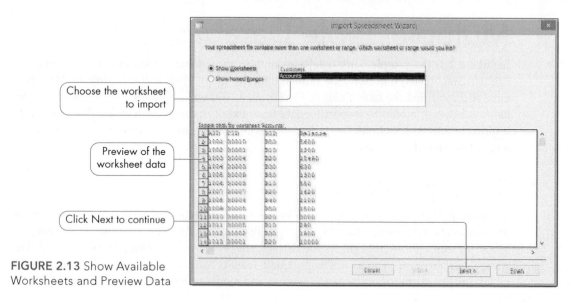

**FIGURE 2.13** Show Available Worksheets and Preview Data

Although a well-designed spreadsheet may include descriptive column headings that can be used as field names, not all spreadsheets are ready to import. You may have to revise the spreadsheet before importing it. The second window of the Import Spreadsheet Wizard dialog box contains a check box that enables you to convert the first row of column headings to field names in Access (see Figure 2.14). If a column heading row exists in the spreadsheet, check the box. If no column headings exist, leave the check box unchecked, and the data will import using Field1, Field2, Field3, and so forth as the field names.

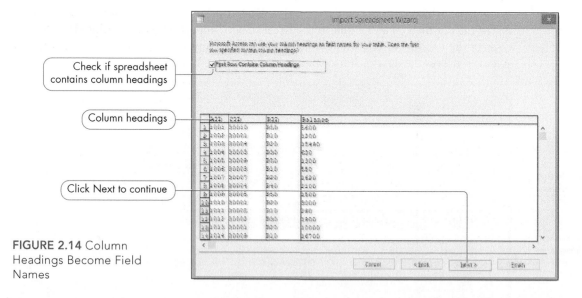

**FIGURE 2.14** Column Headings Become Field Names

The third window of the Import Spreadsheet Wizard dialog box enables you to specify field options (see Figure 2.15). The AID field is highlighted in this figure. Because it will become this table's primary key, you need to set the Indexed Property to *Yes (No Duplicates)*. To modify the field options of the other fields, click the Field Name column heading and make the changes. Not all Access table properties are supported by the wizard. You may need to open the table in Design view after importing it to make any additional field property changes.

When you set the primary key in Access, the *indexed property* is automatically set to *Yes (No Duplicates)*. The indexed property setting enables quick sorting in primary key order and quick retrieval based on the primary key. For non–primary key fields, it may be beneficial to set the Indexed property to *Yes (Duplicates OK)*. Again, Access uses indexing to sort and retrieve data quickly based on the indexed field. As a general rule, indexed fields are usually foreign keys and are numeric.

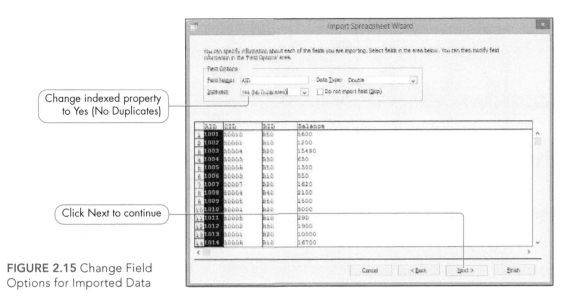

**FIGURE 2.15** Change Field Options for Imported Data

The fourth window of the Import Spreadsheet Wizard dialog box enables you to choose a primary key before the import takes place (see Figure 2.16). If the option *Let Access add primary key* is selected, Access will generate an AutoNumber field and designate it as the primary key. Otherwise, you can designate a field to be the primary key or choose to have no primary key. In the import depicted in the Figure 2.16, the Excel data have a unique identifier (AID) that will become the table's primary key.

**FIGURE 2.16** Set the Primary Key

Use the final window of the Import Spreadsheet Wizard to name the Access table. If the worksheet in the Excel workbook was named, Access uses the worksheet name as the table name (see Figure 2.17).

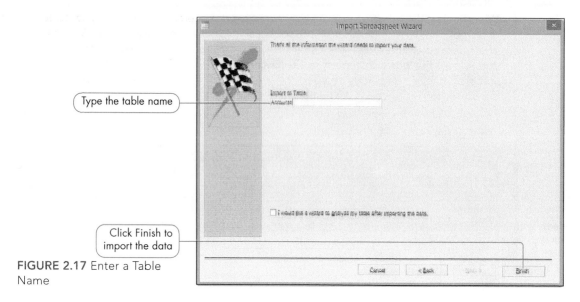

Type the table name

Click Finish to import the data

**FIGURE 2.17** Enter a Table Name

Finally, the Wizard will ask if you wish to save the import steps. If the same worksheet is imported from Excel to Access on a recurring basis, you could save the parameters and use them again. To save the import steps, such as the indexing option and any new field names, click Save Import Steps in the Save Import Steps group. Saving the import steps will help you import the data the next time it is needed.

### Modify an Imported Table's Design and Add Data

**STEP 3»** Importing data saves typing and prevents errors that may occur while entering data, but modifications will usually be required. After you have imported a table, open the table and examine the design to see if changes need to be made. You may need to modify the table by renaming fields so that they are more meaningful. To rename a field in Datasheet view, right-click the arrow next to the field name and click Rename Field. Type the new field name. To rename a field in Design view, select the field name and type the new name. In the bank example, you would change the name of the AID field to AccountID. Switch to Design view to modify the data type and field size.

**STEP 4»** You may need to add new fields or delete unnecessary fields. To add a new field in Datasheet view, right-click the field name to the right of where you want the new field to be added. Click Insert Field. To delete a field in Datasheet view, right-click the name of the field you want to delete and click Delete Field. To create a new field in Design view, click in the row below where you want the new field to be added and click Insert Rows in the Tools group on the Design tab. To delete a row in Design view, click in the row you want to delete and click Delete Rows in the Tools group on the Design tab. After making the modifications, you can add any data needed to the table.

## Establishing Table Relationships

As previously discussed, the benefit of a relationship is to efficiently combine data from related tables for the purpose of creating queries, forms, and reports. Because this is such an important concept in designing and creating relational databases, this chapter reviews creating relationships and enforcing referential integrity. To ensure you are creating redundancy, you should store like data items together in the same table. In the example we are using, the customer data are stored in the Customers table. The Branch table stores data about the bank's branches, management, and locations. The Accounts table stores data about account ownership and balances.

**STEP 5》**

Once you have created the tables by storing like data items together, you will be able to recognize that some tables have common fields with others. Our Accounts table shares a common field with the Customers table—the CustomerID. It also shares a common field with the Branch table—BranchID. These common fields can be used to establish relationships between two tables.

Once you determine the common fields, you drag the field name from one table to the field name on the table you want to be joined.

Figure 2.18 shows the Bank database with relationships created by joining common fields.

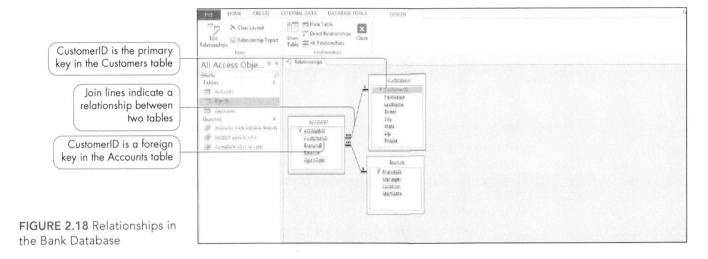

**FIGURE 2.18** Relationships in the Bank Database

The primary key of a table plays a significant role when setting relationships. You cannot join two tables unless a primary key has been set in the primary table. In our Bank database, the CustomerID has been set as the primary key in the Customers table. Therefore, a relationship can be set between the Customers table and the Accounts table. Similarly, the Branch table can be joined to the Accounts table because BranchID has been set as the primary key in the Branch table.

The other side of the relationship join line is most often a foreign key of the related table. A foreign key is a field in one table that is also the primary key of another table. In the previous example, CustomerID in the Accounts table is a foreign key; BranchID in the Accounts table is a foreign key. Relationships between tables will almost always be set using primary and foreign keys.

## Establish Referential Integrity

When you create a relationship in Access, the Edit Relationships dialog box displays. The first check box, Enforce Referential Integrity, should be checked in most cases. Remember, *referential integrity* enforces rules in a database that are used to preserve relationships between tables when records are changed.

**STEP 6》**

When referential integrity is enforced, you cannot enter a foreign key value in a related table unless the primary key value exists in the primary table. In the case of the Bank database, a customer's account information (which includes CustomerID) cannot be entered into the Accounts table unless the customer information is first entered into the Customers table. If you attempt to enter an account prior to entering the customer information, an error will appear, as shown in Figure 2.19. When referential integrity is enforced, you cannot delete a record in one table if it has related records.

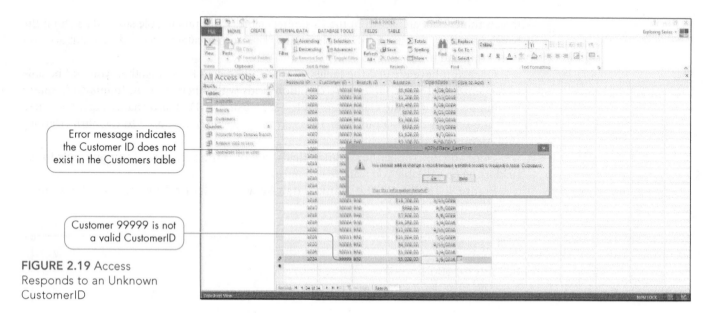

Error message indicates the Customer ID does not exist in the Customers table

Customer 99999 is not a valid CustomerID

**FIGURE 2.19** Access Responds to an Unknown CustomerID

## Set Cascade Options

When you create a relationship in Access and click the Enforce Referential Integrity check-box, Access gives you two additional options: Cascade Update Related Fields and Cascade Delete Related Records. Check the ***Cascade Update Related Fields*** option so that when the primary key is modified in a primary table, Access will automatically update all foreign key values in a related table (see Figure 2.20). If a CustomerID is updated for some reason, all the CustomerID references in the Accounts table will automatically be updated.

Check the ***Cascade Delete Related Records*** option so that when the primary key is deleted in a primary table, Access will automatically delete all records in related tables that reference the primary key (see Figure 2.20). If one branch of a bank closes and its record is deleted from the Branch table, any account that still remains with this branch would be deleted. Access will give a warning first and enable you to avoid the action. This may be a desired business rule, but it should be set with caution.

One-To-Many relationship

Click to Enforce Referential Integrity

Click Cascade Update in case the primary key changes

Click Cascade Delete with caution

**FIGURE 2.20** Cascade Options

## Establish a One-to-Many Relationship

Figure 2.20 also shows that the relationship that will be created will be a one-to-many relationship. Access provides three different relationships for joining your data: one-to-one, one-to-many, and many-to-many. The most common type by far is the one-to-many relationship. A ***one-to-many relationship*** is established when the primary key value in the primary table can match many of the foreign key values in the related table.

For example, a bank customer will be entered into the Customers table once and only once. The primary key value, which is also the customer's CustomerID number, might be 1585. That same customer could set up a checking, savings, and money market account.

With each account, the CustomerID (1585) is required and therefore will occur three times in the Accounts table. The value appears once in the Customers table and three times in the Accounts table. Therefore, the relationship between Customers and Accounts would be described as one to many.

Table 2.3 lists and describes all three types of relationships you can create between Access tables.

## TABLE 2.3  Relationship Types

| Relationship Type | Description |
|---|---|
| One-to-Many | The primary key table must have only one occurrence of each value. For example, each customer must have a unique identification number in the Customers table, or each employee must have a unique EmployeeID in the Employee table. The foreign key field in the second table may have repeating values. For example, one customer may have many different account numbers, or one employee can perform many services. |
| One-to-One | Two different tables use the same primary key. Exactly one record exists in the second table for each record in the first table. Sometimes security reasons require a table be split into two related tables. For example, anyone in the company can look in the Employee table and find the employee's office number, department assignment, or telephone extension. However, only a few people need to have access to the employee's network login password, salary, Social Security number, performance review, or marital status. Tables containing this information would use the same unique identifier to identify each employee. |
| Many-to-Many | This is an artificially constructed relationship giving many matching records in each direction between tables. It requires construction of a third table called a junction table. For example, a database might have a table for employees and one for projects. Several employees might be assigned to one project, but one employee might also be assigned to many different projects. When Access connects to databases using Oracle or other software, you find this relationship type. |

Figure 2.21 shows the Relationships window for the Bank database and all the relationships created using referential integrity. The join line between the CustomerID field in the Customers table and the CustomerID field in the Accounts table indicates that a one-to-many relationship has been set. You can rearrange the tables by dragging the tables by the title bar. You can switch the positions of the Branch and Accounts tables in the Relationships window without changing the relationship itself.

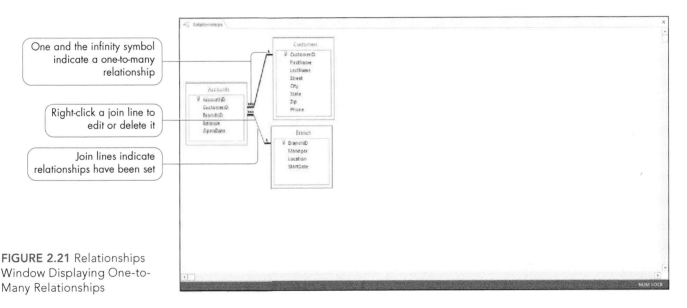

One and the infinity symbol indicate a one-to-many relationship

Right-click a join line to edit or delete it

Join lines indicate relationships have been set

**FIGURE 2.21** Relationships Window Displaying One-to-Many Relationships

**TIP** **Navigating Between the Relationships Window and a Table's Design**

When you right-click on a table's title bar in the Relationships window, the shortcut menu offers you a chance to open the table in Design view. This is a convenient feature because if you want to link one table to another table, the joined fields must have the same data type. This shortcut enables you to check the fields and revise them if necessary if a table contains a field with the wrong data type.

In the following Hands-On Exercise, you will create two additional tables in the Bank database by importing data from an Excel spreadsheet and from an Access database. You will establish and modify field properties. Then you will connect the newly imported data to the Branch table by establishing relationships between the tables.

 *Quick* Concepts

1. Describe a scenario that may require you to import Excel data into Access. **p. 75**

2. What is the purpose of setting a relationship between two tables? **p. 78**

3. Why would you enforce referential integrity when setting a relationship? **p. 79**

4. Give an example of two database tables that would contain a one-to-many relationship. Describe the relationship. **pp. 80–81**

# Hands-On Exercises

Watch the Video
for this Hands-
On Exercise!

MyITLab®
HOE2 Training

## 2 Multiple-Table Databases

You created a new Bank database, and you created a new Branch table. Now you are ready to import additional tables—one from an Excel spreadsheet and one from an Access database. Assume that the data are formatted correctly and are structured properly so that you can begin the import process.

**Skills covered:** Import Excel Data • Import Data from an Access Database • Modify an Imported Table's Design and Add Data • Add Data to an Imported Table • Establish Table Relationships • Test Referential Integrity

### STEP 1 ≫ IMPORT EXCEL DATA

You and the auditor have discovered several of Commonwealth's files that contain customer data. These files need to be analyzed, so you decide to import the data into Access. In this exercise, you import an Excel spreadsheet into the Bank database. Refer to Figure 2.22 as you complete Step 1.

**FIGURE 2.22** Imported Customers Table

a. Open *a02h1Bank_LastFirst* if you closed it at the end of Hands-On Exercise 1. Click the **FILE tab**, click **Save As**, and then click **Save As** in the *Save Database As* section. Type **a02h2Bank_LastFirst**, changing *h1 to h2*. Click **Save**.

b. If necessary, click **Enable Content** below the Ribbon to indicate you trust the contents of the database

> **TROUBLESHOOTING:** If you make any major mistakes in this exercise, you can close the file, open *a02h1Bank_LastFirst* again, and then start this exercise over.

c. Click the **EXTERNAL DATA tab** and click **Excel** in the Import & Link group to launch the Get External Data – Excel Spreadsheet feature. Select the **Import the source data into a new table in the current database option**, if necessary.

d. Click **Browse** and go to the student data folder. Select the *a02h2Customers* workbook. Click **Open** and click **OK** to open the Import Spreadsheet Wizard.

e. Ensure that the *First Row Contains Column Headings* check box is checked to tell Access that column headings exist in the Excel file.

   The field names CID, FirstName, LastName, Street, City, State, ZIP, and Phone will import from Excel along with the data stored in the rows in the worksheet. The field names will be modified later in Access.

f. Click **Next**.

g. Ensure that *CID* is displayed in the Field Name box in Field Options. Click the **Indexed arrow** and select **Yes (No Duplicates)**. Click **Next**.

The CID (CustomerID) will become the primary key in this table. It needs to be a unique identifier, so we must change the properties to no duplicates.

h. Click the **Choose my own primary key option**. Make sure that the CID field is selected. Click **Next**.

The final screen of the Import Spreadsheet Wizard asks you to name your table. The name of the Excel worksheet was Customers, and Access defaults to the worksheet name. It is an acceptable name.

i. Click **Finish** to accept the Customers table name.

A dialog box opens asking if you wish to save the steps of this import to use again. If this were sales data that was collected in Excel and updated to the database on a weekly basis, saving the import steps would save time. You do not need to save this example.

j. Click the **Close (X) button**.

The new table displays in the Navigation Pane and resides in the Bank database.

k. Open the imported Customers table in Datasheet view and double-click the border between each of the field names to adjust the columns to Best fit. Compare your table to Figure 2.22.

l. Close the table.

## STEP 2 ≫ IMPORT DATA FROM AN ACCESS DATABASE

The Customers spreadsheet that you imported contains customer information. The auditor asks you to import an Access database table that contains account information related to the mishandled funds. You use the Import Wizard to import the database table. Refer to Figure 2.23 as you complete Step 2.

**FIGURE 2.23** Imported Accounts Table

a. Click the **EXTERNAL DATA tab** and click **Access** in the Import & Link group to launch the Get External Data – Access Database feature. Select the **Import tables, queries, forms, reports, macros, and modules into the current database option**, if necessary.

b. Click **Browse** and go to the student data folder. Select the *a02h2Accounts* database. Click **Open** and click **OK** to open the Import Objects dialog box.

The Accounts table is active; you will import this table.

c. Ensure that the Accounts table is selected and click **OK**.

**d.** Click **Close** on the Save Import Steps dialog box.

The Navigation Pane contains three tables: Accounts, Branch, and Customers.

**e.** Open the imported Accounts table in Datasheet view and compare it to Figure 2.23.

## STEP 3 ≫ MODIFY AN IMPORTED TABLE'S DESIGN AND ADD DATA

When importing tables from either Excel or Access, the fields may have different data types and property settings than required to create table relationships. You need to modify the tables so that each field has the correct data type and field size. Refer to Figure 2.24 as you complete Step 3.

**FIGURE 2.24** Modified Accounts Table Design

**a.** Right-click the **Accounts table** in the Navigation Pane.

**b.** Click **Design View** to open the table in Design view.

The Accounts table displays with the primary key AID selected.

**c.** Change the AID field name to **AccountID**.

**d.** Change the Field Size property to **Long Integer** in the Field Properties at the bottom of the Design window.

Long Integer ensures that there will be enough numbers as the number of customers grows over time and may exceed 32,768 (the upper limit for Integer values).

**e.** Type **Account ID** in the **Caption property box** for the AccountID field. The caption contains a space between *Account* and *ID*.

**f.** Change the CID field name to **CustomerID**.

**g.** Change the Field Size property to **Long Integer** in the Field Properties at the bottom of the Design window.

You can select the Field Size option using the arrow, or you can type the first letter of the option you want. For example, type l for Long Integer or s for Single. Make sure the current option is completely selected before you type the letter.

**h.** Type **Customer ID** in the **Caption property box** for the CustomerID field. The caption contains a space between *Customer* and *ID*.

**i.** Click the **BID field**. Change the BID field name to **BranchID**.

**j.** Type **5** in the **Field Size property box** in the Field Properties.

**k.** Type **Branch ID** in the **Caption property box** for the Branch ID field.

**l.** Change the Data Type of the Balance field to **Currency**.

The Currency data type is used for fields that contain monetary values.

**m.** Change the Data Type of the OpenDate field to **Date/Time** and add **Short Date** in the Format field property. Type **Open Date** in the **Caption property box**.

The OpenDate field stores the date that each account was opened.

**n.** Click **View** in the Views group to switch to Datasheet view. Read the messages and click **Yes** twice.

In this case, it is OK to click Yes because the shortened fields will not cut off any data. Leave the table open.

**o.** Right-click the **Customers table** in the Navigation Pane and select **Design View** from the shortcut menu.

**p.** Change the CID field name to **CustomerID**. Change the Field Size property of the CustomerID field to **Long Integer** and add a caption, **Customer ID**. Take note of the intentional space between *Customer* and *ID*.

The Accounts table and the Customers table will be joined using the CustomerID field. Both fields must have the same data type.

**q.** Change the Field Size property to **20** for the FirstName, LastName, Street, and City fields. Change the Field Size for State to **2**.

**r.** Change the data type for ZIP and Phone to **Short Text**. Change the Field size property to **15** for both fields. Remove the @ symbol from the Format property where it exists for all fields in the Customers table.

**s.** Click the **Phone field name** and click **Input Mask** in Field Properties. Click **ellipsis (...)** on the right side to launch the Input Mask Wizard. Click **Yes** to save the table and click **Yes** to the *Some data may be lost* warning. Click **Finish** to apply the default phone number Input Mask.

The phone number input mask enables users to enter 6105551212, and Access will display it as (610)555-1212.

**t.** Click **Save** to save the design changes to the Customers table. Read the warning box and click **Yes**.

## STEP 4 ≫ ADD DATA TO AN IMPORTED TABLE

Now that you have created the Access tables, you add records. You may also need to update and delete records if you and the auditor decide the information is no longer needed. Refer to Figure 2.25 as you complete Step 4.

Step b: Enter yourself as a new customer

**FIGURE 2.25** Customers Table Displaying Your Information

**a.** Click **View** in the Views group to display the Customers table in Datasheet view.

The asterisk at the bottom of the table data in the row selector area is the indicator of a place to enter a new record.

**b.** Click the **Customer ID field** in the record after *30010*. Type **30011**. Fill in the rest of the data using your information as the customer. You may use a fictitious address and phone number.

Note the phone number format. The input mask you set formats the phone number.

**c.** Close the Customers table. The Accounts table tab is open.

> **TROUBLESHOOTING:** If the Accounts table is not open, double-click Accounts in the Navigation Pane.

**d.** Locate the new record indicator—the * in the row selector—and click in the **Account ID column**. Type **1024**. Type **30011** as the Customer ID and **B50** as the Branch ID. Type **14005** for the Balance field value. Type **8/7/2015** for the OpenDate.

e. Add the following records to the Accounts table:

| Account ID | Customer ID | Branch ID | Balance | Open Date |
|---|---|---|---|---|
| 1025 | 30006 | B40 | $11,010 | 3/13/2013 |
| 1026 | 30007 | B20 | $7,400 | 5/1/2014 |

f. Close the Accounts table; keep the database open.

# STEP 5 ▶ ESTABLISH TABLE RELATIONSHIPS

The tables for the bank investigation have been designed. Now you will need to establish connections between the tables. Look at the primary and foreign keys as a guide. Refer to Figure 2.26 as you complete Step 5.

FIGURE 2.26 Relationships Between Tables

a. Click the **DATABASE TOOLS tab** and click **Relationships** in the Relationships group.

The Relationships window opens and the Show Table dialog box appears.

> **TROUBLESHOOTING:** If the Show Table dialog box does not open, click Show Table in the Relationships group on the Relationships Tools Design tab.

b. Double-click each of the three tables displayed in the Show Table dialog box to add them to the Relationships window. (Alternatively, click a table and click **Add**.) Click **Close** in the Show Table dialog box.

> **TROUBLESHOOTING:** If you have a duplicate table, click the title bar of the duplicated table and press Delete.

c. Resize the Customers table box so all of the fields are visible. Arrange the tables as shown in Figure 2.26.

d. Drag the **BranchID field** in the Branch table onto the BranchID field in the Accounts table. The Edit Relationships dialog box opens. Click the **Enforce Referential Integrity** and **Cascade Update Related Fields check boxes**. Click **Create**.

A black line displays, joining the two tables. It has a 1 at the end near the Branch table and an infinity symbol on the end next to the Accounts table. You have established a one-to-many relationship between the Branch and Accounts tables.

e. Drag the **CustomerID field** in the Customers table onto the CustomerID field in the Accounts table. The Edit Relationships dialog box opens. Click the **Enforce Referential Integrity** and **Cascade Update Related Fields check boxes**. Click **Create**.

You have established a one-to-many relationship between the Customers and Accounts tables. A customer will have only a single CustomerID number. The same customer may have many different accounts: Savings, Checking, CDs, and so forth.

> **TROUBLESHOOTING:** If you get an error message when you click Create, verify that the data types of the joined fields are the same. To check the data types from the Relationships window, right-click the title bar of a table and select Table Design from the shortcut menu. Modify the data type and field size of the join fields if necessary.

   **f.** Click **Save** on the Quick Access Toolbar to save the changes to the relationships. Close the Relationships window.

## STEP 6 ≫ TEST REFERENTIAL INTEGRITY

The design of the Bank database must be 100% correct; otherwise, data entry may be compromised. Even though you are confident that the table relationships are correct, you decide to test them by entering some invalid data. If the relationships are not working, the invalid data will be rejected by Access. Refer to Figure 2.27 as you complete Step 6.

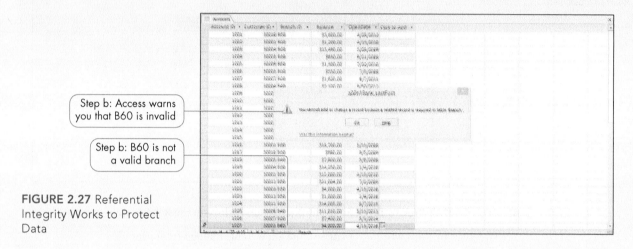

Step b: Access warns you that B60 is invalid

Step b: B60 is not a valid branch

**FIGURE 2.27** Referential Integrity Works to Protect Data

   **a.** Double-click the **Accounts table** to open it in Datasheet view.

   **b.** Add a new record, pressing **Tab** after each field: Account ID: **1027**, Customer ID: **30003**, Branch: **B60**, Balance: **4000**, OpenDate: **4/13/2016**.

     You attempted to enter a nonexistent BranchID and were not allowed to make that error. A warning message is telling you that a related record in the Branch table is required because the Accounts table and the Branch table are connected by a relationship with Enforce Referential Integrity checked.

   **c.** Click **OK**. Double-click the **Branch table** in the Navigation Pane and examine the data in the BranchID field. Notice the Branch table has no B60 record. Close the Branch table.

   **d.** Replace *B60* with **B50** in the new Accounts record and press **Tab** three times. As soon as the focus moves to the next record, the pencil symbol disappears and your data are saved.

     You successfully identified a BranchID that Access recognizes. Because referential integrity between the Accounts and Branch tables has been enforced, Access looks at each data entry item in a foreign key and matches it to a corresponding value in the table where it is the primary key. In step b, you attempted to enter a nonexistent BranchID and were not allowed to make that error. In step d, you entered a valid BranchID. Access examined the index for the BranchID in the Branch table and found a corresponding value for B50.

   **e.** Close the Accounts table. Reopen the Accounts table; you will find that the record you just entered for 1027 has been saved. Close the table.

     You have established a one-to-many relationship between the Customers and Accounts tables. A customer will have only a single CustomerID number. The same customer may have many different accounts: Savings, Checking, CDs, and so forth.

   **f.** Close all open tables, if necessary.

   **g.** Keep the database open if you plan to continue with Hands-On Exercise 3. If not, close the database and exit Access.

# Single-Table Queries

If you wanted to see which customers currently have an account with a balance over $5,000, you could find the answer by creating an Access query. A *query* enables you to ask questions about the data stored in a database and then provides the answers to the questions by providing subsets or summaries of data. Because data are stored in tables in a database, you always begin a query by asking, "Which table holds the data I want?" For the question about account balances over $5,000, you would reference the Accounts table. If you want to invite customers in a certain ZIP code to the Grand Opening of a new branch, you could create a query based on the Customers table.

You use the *Query Design view* to create queries. The Query Design view is divided into two parts: The top portion displays the tables, and the bottom portion (known as the query design grid) displays the fields and the criteria. You select only the fields you want arranged in the order that you want the resulting data displayed. The design grid also enables you to sort the records based on one or more fields. You can also create calculated fields to display data based on expressions that use the fields in the underlying table. For example, you could calculate the monthly interest earned on each bank account.

In this section, you will use the Query Design view and the Query Wizard to create queries that display only data that you select. Multitable queries will be covered in the next section.

## Creating a Single-Table Query

You can create a single-table query in two ways—by using the Simple Query Wizard or the Query Design tool in the Queries group on the Create tab. The Query Design tool is the most flexible way to create a query. You can add criteria to a query while in the Query Design view. After you design a query, you can display the results of the query by switching to Datasheet view. A query's datasheet looks and acts like a table's datasheet, except that it is usually a subset of the records found in the entire table. The subset shows only the records that match the criteria that were added in the query design. The subset may contain different sorting of the records than the sorting in the underlying table. Datasheet view allows you to enter a new record, modify an existing record, or delete a record. Any changes made in Datasheet view are reflected in the underlying table that the query is based upon.

**STEP 3** ⟩⟩    Be aware that query results display the actual records that are stored in the underlying table(s). Being able to correct an error immediately while it is displayed in query results is an advantage. You save time by not having to close the query, open the table, find the error, fix it, and then run the query again. However, you should use caution when editing records in query results since you will be changing the table data.

### Create a Single-Table Select Query

The Query Design tool is used to create *select queries*, a type of query that displays only the records that match criteria entered in Query Design view. To create a select query using the Query Design tool, do the following:

**STEP 2** ⟩⟩
1. Click the CREATE tab.
2. Click Query Design in the Queries group.
3. Select the table you need in your query from the Show Table dialog box.
4. Click Add to add the table to the top section of the query design and close the Show Table dialog box.
5. Drag the fields needed from the table to the query design grid (or alternatively, double-click the field names); then add criteria and sorting options.
6. Click Run in the Results group to show the results in Datasheet view.

## Use Query Design View

The Query Design view consists of two parts. The top portion contains tables with their respective field names. If a query contains more than one table, the join lines between tables will be displayed as they were created in the Relationships window.

The bottom portion (known as the query design grid) contains columns and rows. Each field in the query has its own column and contains multiple rows. The rows permit you to control the query results.

- The *Field row* displays the field name.
- The *Table row* displays the data source.
- The *Sort row* enables you to sort in ascending or descending order.
- The *Show row* controls whether the field will be displayed in the query results.
- The *Criteria row* is used to set the rules that determine which records will be selected, such as customers with account balances greater than $5,000.

Figure 2.28 displays the query design grid with the Show Table dialog box open. The Accounts table has been added from the Show Table dialog box. Figure 2.29 shows the Design view of a sample query with four fields, with a criterion set for one field and sorting set on another. The results of the query are shown in Datasheet view, as shown in Figure 2.30.

 **Examine the Records**

An experienced Access user always examines the records returned in the query results. Verify that the records in the query results match the criteria that you specified in Design view. As you add additional criteria, the number of records returned will usually decrease.

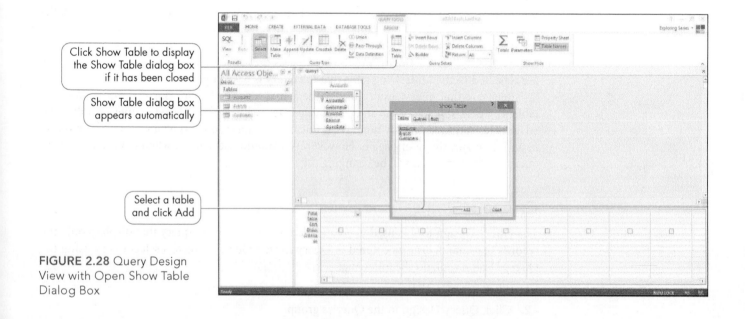

**FIGURE 2.28** Query Design View with Open Show Table Dialog Box

Click Show Table to display the Show Table dialog box if it has been closed

Show Table dialog box appears automatically

Select a table and click Add

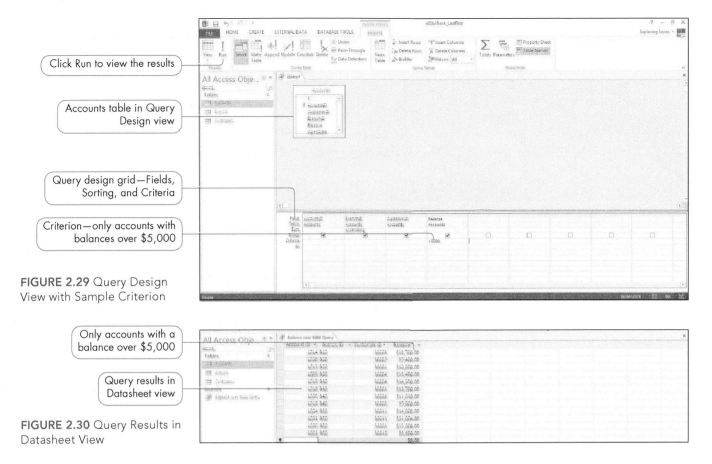

Click Run to view the results

Accounts table in Query Design view

Query design grid—Fields, Sorting, and Criteria

Criterion—only accounts with balances over $5,000

**FIGURE 2.29** Query Design View with Sample Criterion

Only accounts with a balance over $5,000

Query results in Datasheet view

**FIGURE 2.30** Query Results in Datasheet View

When you developed the tables, you toggled between the Design view and Datasheet view. Similarly, you will toggle between Design view and Datasheet view when you create queries. Use Design view to specify the criteria; you can use the results that display in Datasheet view to answer a question or to make a decision about the organization. Use Datasheet view to see the results of your query. Each time you need to fine-tune the query, switch back to Design view, make a change, and then test the results in Datasheet view. After you are satisfied with the query results, you may want to save the query so it can become a permanent part of the database and can be used later.

## Specifying Query Criteria for Different Data Types

When specifying the criteria for a query, you may need to include a *delimiter*—a special character that surrounds a criterion's value. The delimiter needed is determined by the field data type, and Access will automatically enter the delimiter for you for some data types. Text fields require quotation marks before and after the text. Access automatically adds the quotation marks around text, but to ensure that the correct delimiter is used, you may want to include the delimiters yourself.

Use plain digits (no delimiter) for the criteria of a numeric field, currency, or AutoNumber. You can enter numeric criteria with or without a decimal point and with or without a minus sign. Commas and dollar signs are not allowed.

When the criterion is in a date field, you enclose the criterion in pound signs, such as #10/14/2016#. Access accepts a date with or without the pound signs, but if you enter 1/1/2016 without the pound signs, Access will automatically add the pound signs when you move to another column in the design grid. The date value can be entered using any allowed format, such as February 2, 2016, 2/2/2016, or 2-Feb-16. You enter criteria for a Yes/No field as Yes or No. See Table 2.4 for query criteria and examples.

**TABLE 2.4  Query Criteria**

| Data Type | Criteria | Example |
|---|---|---|
| Text | "Harry" | For a FirstName field, displays only text that matches Harry exactly. |
| Numeric | 5000 | For a Quantity field, displays only numbers that match 5000 exactly. |
| Date | #2/2/2015# | For a ShippedDate field, shows orders shipped on February 2, 2015. |
| Yes/No | Yes | For a Discontinued field, returns records where the check box is selected. |

## Use Wildcards

Suppose you want to search for the last name of a customer, but you are not sure how to spell the name; however, you know that the name starts with the letters Sm. You can use a wildcard to search for the name. *Wildcards* are special characters that can represent one or more characters in a text value. A question mark is a wildcard that stands for a single character in the same position as the question mark, whereas an asterisk is a wildcard that stands for any number of characters in the same position as the asterisk. Use brackets to match any single character within the brackets, or use an exclamation mark inside brackets to match any character not in the brackets. Use the pound sign to match any single numeric character.

You can enter wildcard characters in the Criteria row of a query. Therefore, if you wanted to search for just names that start with the letters Sm, you can specify the criterion in the LastName field as Sm*. All last names that begin with Sm would display. For example, H?ll will return Hall, Hill, and Hull, whereas S*nd will return Sand, Stand, and StoryLand. Table 2.5 shows more query examples that use wildcards.

**TABLE 2.5  Query Criteria Using Wildcards**

| Character | Description | Example | Result |
|---|---|---|---|
| * | Matches for any number of characters in the same position as the asterisk | Sm* | Small, Smiley, Smith, Smithson |
| ? | Matches for a single character in the same position as the question mark | H?ll | Hall, Hill, Hull |
| [ ] | Matches any single character within the brackets | F[ae]ll | Fall and Fell, but not Fill or Full |
| [!] | Matches any character not in the brackets | F[!ae]ll | Fill and Full, but not Fall or Fell |

## Use Comparison Operators in Queries

A comparison operator, such as equal (=), not equal (<>), greater than (>), less than (<), greater than or equal to (>=), and less than or equal to (<=), can be used in the criteria of a query. Comparison operators enable you to limit the query results to only those records that meet the criteria. For example, if you only want to see accounts that have a balance greater than $5,000, you would type >5000 in the Criteria row. Table 2.6 shows more comparison operator examples as well as other sample expressions.

## TABLE 2.6 Comparison Operators in Queries

| Expression | Example |
|---|---|
| =10 | Equals 10 |
| <>10 | Not equal to 10 |
| >10 | Greater than 10 |
| >=10 | Greater than or equal to 10 |
| <10 | Less than 10 |
| <=10 | Less than or equal to 10 |

## Work with Null

Sometimes finding what is missing is an important part of making a decision. For example, if you need to know which orders have been completed but not shipped, you would create a query to find the orders with a missing ShipDate. Are there missing phone numbers or addresses for some of your customers? Create a query to find customers with a missing PhoneNumber. The term that Access uses for a blank field is *null*. Table 2.7 gives two illustrations of when to use the null criterion in a query.

## TABLE 2.7 Establishing Null Criteria Expressions

| Expression | Description | Example |
|---|---|---|
| Is Null | Use to find blank fields | For an Employee field in the Customers table when the customer has not been assigned a sales representative. |
| Is Not Null | Used to find fields with data | For a ShipDate field; a value inserted indicated the order was shipped to the customer. |

## Establish AND, OR, and NOT Criteria

Remember the earlier question, "Which customers currently have an account with a balance over $5,000?" This question was answered by creating a query with a single criterion, as shown in Figure 2.29. At times, questions are more specific and require queries with multiple criteria. For example, you may need to know "Which customers from the Eastern branch currently have an account with a balance over $5,000?" To answer this question, you need to specify criteria in multiple fields using the *AND logical operator*. When the criteria are in the same row of the query design grid, Access interprets the instructions using the AND operator. This means that the query results will display only records that match *all* criteria.

When you have multiple sets of criteria and you need to satisfy one set only, use the *OR logical operator*. The query results will display records that match any of the specified criteria. To use the OR operator, type your expression into the Criteria row, separating the criteria with the OR operator. Table 2.8 shows an example of an OR operator created using this method. You can also type the first expression into the Criteria row and then type the subsequent expression by using the Or row in the design grid. Figure 2.31b displays an example of an OR operator using this method.

The *NOT logical operator* returns all records except the specified criteria. For example, "Not Eastern" would return all accounts except those opened at the Eastern branch.

## TABLE 2.8 AND, OR, and NOT Queries

| Logical Operator | Example | Result |
|---|---|---|
| AND | "Eastern" AND "Campus" | For a Branch field, returns all records for the Eastern and Campus branches. |
| AND | >5000 AND <10000 | For a Balance field, returns all accounts with a balance greater than $5,000 and less than $10,000. |
| OR | 5000 OR 10000 | For a Balance field, returns all accounts with a balance of exactly $5,000 or $10,000. |
| NOT | Not "Campus" | For a Branch field, returns all records except those in the Campus branch. |

The first example in Figure 2.31 shows a query with an AND logical operator (criteria on the same row are implicitly joined by AND). It will return all of the B20 branch accounts with balances over $5,000. (Both conditions must be met for the record to be included.) The second example in Figure 2.31 shows a query with an OR logical operator. It will return all of the B20 branch accounts regardless of balance plus all accounts at any branch with a balance over $5,000. (One condition must be met for a record to be included.) The third example in Figure 2.31 shows a query that uses the NOT logical operator. It will return all of the accounts—excluding the B20 branch—with a balance over $5,000. The last example in Figure 2.31 shows a query that combines AND and OR logical operators. The top row will return B20 branch accounts with a balance over $5,000, and the second row will return B30 branch accounts with a balance over $15,000.

AND condition—criteria are in the same row

OR condition—criteria are in different rows

Use NOT to exclude specific records

Combination of AND and OR in the same query

**FIGURE 2.31** Query Design Views Showing the AND, OR, and NOT Conditions

### TIP | Finding Values in a Date Range

To find the values contained within a data range, use the > (greater than) and < (less than) operators. For example, to find the values of a date after January 1, 2015, and before December 31, 2015, use the criterion >1/1/2015 and <12/31/2015. You can also use the BETWEEN operator. For example BETWEEN 1/1/2015 and 12/31/2015.

# Understanding Query Sort Order

The *query sort order* determines the order of records in a query's Datasheet view. You can change the order of records by specifying the sort order in the Design view. When you want to sort using more than one field, the sort order is determined from left to right. The order of columns should be considered when first creating the query. For example, a query sorted by LastName and then by FirstName must have those two fields in the correct order in the design grid. You can change the order of the query fields in the design grid to change the sort order of the query results.

STEP 2>>

To change the order of fields, select the column you want to move by clicking the column selector. Release the mouse, then click again and drag the selected field to its new location. To insert additional columns in the design grid, select a column and click Insert Columns in the Query Setup group. The inserted column will insert to the left of the selected column. To delete a column, click the column selector to select the column and click the Delete Columns button on the Design tab or press Delete on the keyboard.

# Running, Copying, and Modifying a Query

Several ways exist to run a query. One method is to click Run in the Results group when you are in Design view. Another method is to locate the query in the Navigation Pane and double-click it. A similar method is to select the query and press Enter.

After you create a query, you may want to create a duplicate copy to use as the basis for creating a similar query. Duplicating a query saves time when you need the same tables and fields but with slightly different criteria.

## Run a Query

After you create a query and save it, you can run it directly from the Design view. You run a query by clicking the Run command (the red exclamation point) in the Results group on the Query Tools Design tab. You can also run a query from the Navigation Pane. Locate the query you want to run and double-click the query. The results will display as a tab in the main window.

## Copy a Query

Sometimes you have a one-of-a-kind question about your data. You would create a query to answer this question and then delete the query. However, sometimes you need a series of queries in which each query is similar to the first. For example, you need a list of accounts in each branch. In a case like this, you create a query for one branch and then save a copy of the query and give it a new name. Finally, you would change the criteria to match the second branch. To accomplish this, do the following:

1. Open the query you want to copy.
2. Click the FILE tab and click Save As.
3. Click Save Object As in the *File Types* section.
4. Ensure Save Object As is selected in the *Database File Types* section and click Save As.
5. Type the name you want to use for the new query in the Save As dialog box and click OK (see Figure 2.32).
6. Switch to Design view and modify the query criteria.

FIGURE 2.32 Using Save Object As to Copy a Query

You can also right-click the original query in the Navigation Pane and click Copy. Click in the Navigation Pane again and click Paste. Type a name for the new query in the Paste As dialog box.

# Using the Query Wizard

**STEP 1** You may also create a query using the Query Wizard. Like all of the Microsoft wizards, the **Simple Query Wizard** guides you through the query design process. The wizard is helpful for creating basic queries that do not require criteria. After the query is created using the Wizard, you can switch to Design view and add criteria manually. Even if you initiate the query with a wizard, you will need to learn how to modify it in Design view. Often, copying an existing query and making slight modifications to its design is much faster than starting at the beginning with the wizard. You also will need to know how to add additional tables and fields to an existing query when conditions change. To launch the Query Wizard, click the Create tab and click Query Wizard in the Queries group (see Figure 2.33).

FIGURE 2.33 Launching the Query Wizard

Select the Simple Query Wizard in the Query Wizard dialog box, as shown in Figure 2.34.

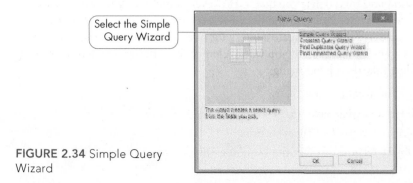

FIGURE 2.34 Simple Query Wizard

In the first step of the Simple Query Wizard dialog box, you specify the tables or queries and fields needed in your query. When you select a table from the Tables/Queries arrow (queries can also be based on other queries), a list of the table's fields displays in the Available Fields list box. See Figures 2.35 and 2.36.

**FIGURE 2.35** Specify Which Tables or Queries to Use

**FIGURE 2.36** Specify the Fields for the Query

Select the necessary fields and add them to the Selected Fields list box using the directional arrows shown in Figure 2.36.

In the next screen (shown in Figure 2.37), you choose between a detail and a summary query. The detail query shows every field of every record in the result. The summary query enables you to group data and view only summary records. For example, if you were interested in the total funds deposited at each of the bank branches, you would set the query to Summary, click Summary Options, and then click Sum on the Balance field. Access would then sum the balances of all accounts for each branch.

**FIGURE 2.37** Choose Detail or Summary Data

The final dialog box of the Simple Query Wizard asks for the name of the query. Assign a descriptive name to your queries so that you know what each does by looking at the query name. See Figure 2.38.

Type the Query name

**FIGURE 2.38** Name the Query

The next Hands-On Exercise enables you to create and run queries in order to find answers to questions you have about your data. You will use the Query Wizard to create a basic query and modify the query in Query Design view by adding an additional field and by adding query criteria.

**Quick Concepts** ✓

1. Define a query. Give an example. **p. 89**

2. Give an example of how to use the criteria row to find certain records in a table. **p. 90**

3. When would you need to use the "is null" and "is not null" criteria? **p. 93**

4. When would you want to copy a query? **p. 95**

# Hands-On Exercises

## 3 Single-Table Queries

The tables and table relationships have been created, and some data have been entered. Now, you need to begin the process of analyzing the bank data for the auditor. You will do so using queries. You decide to begin with the Accounts table.

**Skills covered:** Create a Query Using a Wizard • Specify Query Criteria and Query Sort Order • Change Query Data

---

### STEP 1 ≫ CREATE A QUERY USING A WIZARD

You decide to start with the Query Wizard, knowing you can always alter the design of the query later in Query Design view. You will show the results to the auditor using Datasheet view. Refer to Figure 2.39 as you complete Step 1.

**FIGURE 2.39** Query Results Before Criteria Are Applied

a. Open *a02h2Bank_LastFirst* if you closed it at the end of Hands-On Exercise 2. Save the database as **a02h3Bank_LastFirst**, changing *h2* to *h3*.

b. Click the **CREATE tab** and click **Query Wizard** in the Queries group to launch the New Query wizard.

The New Query Wizard dialog box opens. Simple Query Wizard is selected by default.

c. Click **OK**.

d. Verify that *Table: Accounts* is selected in the Tables/Query box.

e. Select **AccountID** from the **Available Fields list** and click >. Repeat the process with CustomerID, BranchID, and Balance.

The four fields should now display in the Selected Fields list box.

f. Click **Next**.

g. Confirm *Detail* is selected and click **Next**.

h. Name the query **Accounts from Campus Branch**. Click **Finish**.

This query name describes the data in the query results. Your query should have four fields: AccountID, CustomerID, BranchID, and Balance. The Navigation bar indicates 27 records meet the query criteria.

## STEP 2 ►► SPECIFY QUERY CRITERIA AND QUERY SORT ORDER

The auditor indicated that the problem seems to be confined to the Campus branch. You use this knowledge to revise the query to display only Campus accounts. Refer to Figure 2.40 as you complete Step 2.

Step c: Sort by Ascending AccountID

Step b: "B50" criterion added

**FIGURE 2.40** Enter Criteria and Add Sort Order

a. Click the **HOME tab** and click **View** in the Views group to view the Accounts from Campus Branch query in Design view.

You have created the Campus Branch Customers query to view only those accounts at the Campus branch. However, other branches' accounts also display. You need to limit the query results to only the records of interest.

b. Click in the **Criteria row** (fifth row) in the BranchID column and type **B50**.

B50 is the BranchID for the Campus branch. Access queries are not case sensitive; therefore, b50 and B50 will produce the same results. Access adds quotation marks around text criteria.

c. Click in the **Sort row** (third row) in the AccountID column and select **Ascending**.

d. Click **Run** in the Results group.

You should see nine records, all from Branch B50, in the query results.

## STEP 3 ►► CHANGE QUERY DATA

When the query results are on the screen, the auditor notices that some of the data are incorrect, and one of the accounts is missing. From your experience with Access, you explain to the auditor that the data can be changed directly in a query rather than switching back to the table. Refer to Figure 2.41 as you complete Step 3.

Step a: Balance of account 1020 was changed to $12,000

Step e: New record

**FIGURE 2.41** Changes Made in the Query Datasheet

a. Click on the **Balance field** in the record for account 1020. Change *$1,200* to **$12,000**. Press **Enter**. Save and close the query.

You are modifying the record directly in the query results.

b. Double-click the **Accounts table** in the Navigation Pane to open it.

Only one account shows a $12,000 balance. The Account ID is 1020 and the Customer ID is 30001. The change you made in the Accounts table from the Campus Branch query datasheet automatically changed the data stored in the underlying table.

c. Open the Customers table. Find the name of the customer whose CustomerID is 30001. Note that the account belongs to Allison Millward. Close the Customers table.

d. Add a new record to the Accounts table with the following data: **1028** (Account ID), **30005** (Customer ID), **B50** (Branch ID), and **8/4/2016** (Open Date). Press **Tab**.

---

**TROUBLESHOOTING:** If the Accounts table is not open, double-click Accounts in the Navigation Pane.

---

The new record is added to the Accounts table.

e. Double-click the **Accounts from Campus Branch query** in the Navigation Pane.

Customer 30005 now shows two accounts: one with a balance of $1,500 and one with a balance of $8,000.

f. Close the Accounts from Campus Branch query and close the Accounts table.

g. Keep the database open if you plan to continue with Hands-On Exercise 4. If not, close the database and exit Access.

# Multitable Queries

*Multitable queries* contain two or more tables. They enable you to take advantage of the relationships that have been set in your database. When you need to extract information from a database with a query, most times you will need to pull the data from multiple tables to provide the answers you need. One table may contain the core information that you need, while another table may contain the related data that makes the query relevant to the users.

For example, the sample bank database contains three tables: Customers, Accounts, and Branch. You connected the tables through relationships in order to store data efficiently and enforce consistent data entry. The Accounts table lists the balances of each account at the bank—the key financial information. However, the Accounts table does not list the contact information of the owner of the account. Therefore, the Customers table is needed to provide the additional information.

## Creating a Multitable Query

STEP 2 ❯❯  Creating a multitable query is similar to creating a single-table query; however, choosing the right tables and managing the table relationships will require some additional skills. First, you should only include related tables in a multitable query. *Related tables* are tables that are joined in a relationship using a common field. As a rule, related tables should already be established when you create a multitable query. Using Figure 2.42 as a guide, creating a query with the Accounts and Branch tables would be acceptable, as would using Accounts and Customers tables, or Accounts, Branch, and Customers tables. All three scenarios include related tables. Creating a query with the Branch and Customers tables would not be acceptable because these tables are *not* directly related. To create a multitable query, do the following:

1. Click the CREATE tab.
2. Click Query Design in the Queries group.
3. Select the table you need in your query from the Show Table dialog box.
4. Click Add to add the table to the top section of the query design.
5. Select the next table you want to add to the query and click Add. Continue selecting and adding tables to the top section of the query design until all the tables you need display.
6. Drag the fields needed from the tables to the query design grid (or alternatively, double-click the field names); then add criteria and sorting options.
7. Click Run in the Results group to show the results in Datasheet view.

### TIP | Print the Relationship Report to Help Create a Multitable Query

When creating a multitable query, you should only include related tables. As a guide, you can print the Relationship Report in the Tools group on the Relationship Tools Design tab when the Relationships window is open. This report will help you determine which tables are related in your database.

Refer to Figure 2.31 (the top image) showing the results of the query "Which customers from the Campus branch have an account with a balance over $5,000?" To make this report more understandable to others, we can modify the query by adding the Branch Location (in place of the BranchID) and the Customer LastName (in place of the CustomerID). To make these changes, we would need to add the Branch table (which contains the Location field) and the Customers table (which contains the LastName field) to the query design.

## Add Additional Tables to a Query

**STEP 1 »** To modify a saved query, open the query in Design view. If you wanted to change the Balance Over $5000 query as discussed earlier, first open the query in Design view. To add additional tables to a query, open the Navigation Pane (if necessary) and drag tables directly into the top portion of the query design grid. For example, the Branch and Customers tables were added to the query, as shown in Figure 2.42. The join lines between tables indicate that relationships were previously set in the Relationships window.

Join lines indicate new tables are related to the Accounts table

**FIGURE 2.42** Two Additional Tables Added to a Query

# Modifying a Multitable Query

**STEP 3 »** After creating a multitable query, you may find that you did not include all of the fields you needed, or you may find that you included fields that are unnecessary and complicate the results. You may find that other fields could be included that would make the results more understandable to others. To modify multitable queries, you use the same techniques you learned for single-table queries. Add tables using the Show Table dialog box; remove tables by clicking the unwanted table and pressing Delete. Add fields by double-clicking the field you want; remove fields by clicking the column selector and pressing Delete. Join lines between related tables should display automatically in a query if the relationships were previously established, as shown in Figure 2.42.

**TIP | Changes in Multitable Queries Do Not Affect Relationships**

When you add two or more tables to a query, join lines appear automatically. You can delete the join lines in a query with no impact on the relationships themselves. Deleting a join line only affects the relationships in the individual query. The next time you create a query with the same tables, the join lines will be restored. And, if you open the Relationships window, you will find the join lines intact.

## Add and Delete Fields in a Multitable Query

In Figure 2.43, three tables, as well as the join lines between the tables, display in the top pane of the Query Design view. All the fields from each of the tables are now available to be used in the query design grid. Figure 2.43 shows that Location (from the Branch table) replaced BranchID and LastName (from the Customers table) replaced CustomerID to make the results more useful. The BranchID was deleted from the query; therefore, the "B50" criterion was removed as well. "Campus" was added to the Location field's criteria row in order to extract the same results. Because criteria values are not case sensitive, typing "campus" is the same as typing "Campus," and both will return the same results. The results of the revised query are shown in Figure 2.44.

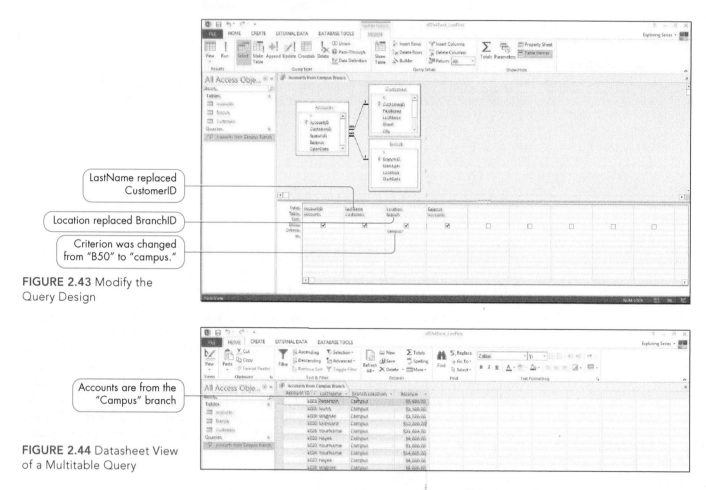

LastName replaced CustomerID

Location replaced BranchID

Criterion was changed from "B50" to "campus."

**FIGURE 2.43** Modify the Query Design

Accounts are from the "Campus" branch

**FIGURE 2.44** Datasheet View of a Multitable Query

## Add Join Lines in a Multitable Query

In Figure 2.45, two tables are added to the query design, but no join line connects them. The results of the query will be unpredictable and will display more records than expected. The Customers table contains 11 records, and the Branch table contains 5 records. Because Access does not know how to interpret the unrelated tables, the results will show 55 records—every possible combination of customer and branch (11 × 5). See Figure 2.46.

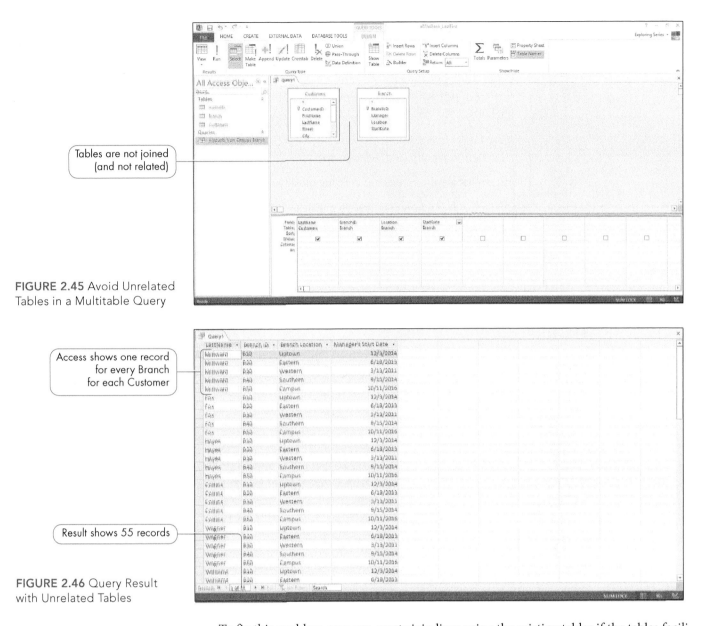

Tables are not joined (and not related)

**FIGURE 2.45** Avoid Unrelated Tables in a Multitable Query

Access shows one record for every Branch for each Customer

Result shows 55 records

**FIGURE 2.46** Query Result with Unrelated Tables

To fix this problem, you can create join lines using the existing tables if the tables facilitate this by having common fields. In a situation like this, in which there are no common fields, you must add an additional table that will provide a join between all three tables. In the Branch query, you can add the Accounts table, which will facilitate a join between the two existing tables, Customers and Branch. As soon as the third table is added to the query design, the join lines appear automatically, as shown in Figure 2.43.

Over time, your database will grow, and additional tables will be added. Occasionally, new tables are added to the database but not added to the Relationships window. When queries are created with the new tables, join lines will not be established. When this happens, add join lines to the new tables. Or you can create temporary join lines in the query design. These join lines will provide a temporary relationship between two tables and enable Access to interpret the query properly.

## Get Answers Using a Multitable Query

STEP 4 ▶▶  You can get key information from your database using a multitable query. For example, if you want to know how many orders each customer placed since the database was created, you would create a new query and add the Customers and Orders tables to the Query Design view. After you verify that the join lines are correct, you add the CustomerID field from the Customers table and the OrderID field from the Order table to the query design grid.

When you run the query, the results show duplicates in the CustomerID column because customers place multiple orders. Then return to the Query Design view and click Totals in the Show/Hide group. Both columns show the Group By option in the Total row. Change the total row of the OrderID field to Count and run the query again. This time the results show one row for each customer and the number of orders each customer placed since the database was created.

*Quick Concepts*

1. Define a multitable query. *p. 102*

2. What are the benefits of creating multitable queries? *p. 102*

3. What is the result of creating a query with two unrelated tables? *p. 104*

4. Describe the purpose adding a join line in a multitable query. *p. 105*

# Hands-On Exercises

Watch the Video
for this Hands-
On Exercise!

MyITLab®
HOE4 Training

## 4 Multitable Queries

Based on the auditor's request, you will need to evaluate the data further. This requires creating queries that are based on multiple tables rather than on a single table. You decide to open an existing query, add additional tables, and then save the query with a new name.

**Skills covered:** Add Additional Tables to a Query • Create a Multitable Query • Modify a Multitable Query • Get Answers Using a Multitable Query

---

### STEP 1 ≫ ADD ADDITIONAL TABLES TO A QUERY

The previous query was based on the Accounts table, but now you need to add information to the query that is in the Branch and Customers tables. You will need to add the Branch and Customers tables to the query. Refer to Figure 2.47 as you complete Step 1.

Steps c and l: Customers and Branch tables added

**FIGURE 2.47** Add Tables to Query Design View

a. Open *a02h3Bank_LastFirst* if you closed it at the end of Hands-On Exercise 3. Save the database as **a02h4Bank_LastFirst**, changing *h3* to *h4*.

b. Right-click the **Accounts from Campus Branch query** in the Navigation Pane and select **Design View** from the shortcut menu.

c. Drag the **Branch table** from the Navigation Pane to the top pane of the query design grid next to the Accounts table.

   A join line connects the Branch table to the Accounts table. The query inherits the join lines from the relationships created in the Relationships window.

d. Drag the **Location field** from the Branch table to the first empty column in the design grid.

   The Location field should be positioned to the right of the Balance column.

e. Click the **Show check box** under the BranchID field to clear the check box and hide this field in the results.

   The BranchID field is no longer needed because the Location field provides the same information. Because you unchecked the BranchID show check box, the BranchID field will not display the next time the query is opened.

f. Delete the B50 criterion in the BranchID field.

g. Type **Campus** as a criterion in the Location field and press **Enter**.

   Access adds quotation marks around *Campus* for you; quotes are required for text criteria. You are substituting the Location criterion *(Campus)* in place of the BranchID criterion (B50).

**h.** Remove Ascending from the AccountID sort row. Click in the **Sort row** of the Balance field. Click the arrow and select **Descending**.

**i.** Click **Run** in the Results group.

The BranchID field does not display in the Datasheet view because you hid the field in step e. Only Campus accounts should display in the datasheet (10 records). Next, you will add the Customer LastName and delete the CustomerID from the query.

**j.** Save the changes to the query design.

**k.** Click **View** in the Views group to return to the Design view.

The BranchID field has been removed from the grid.

**l.** Drag the **Customers table** from the Navigation Pane to the top section of the query design grid and reposition the tables so that the join lines are not blocked (see Figure 2.47).

The one-to-many relationship lines automatically connect the Customers table to the Accounts table (similar to step c on the previous page).

**m.** Drag the **LastName field** in the Customers table to the second column in the design grid.

The LastName field should be positioned to the right of the AccountID field.

**n.** Click the column selector in the CustomerID field to select it. Press **Delete**.

The CustomerID field is no longer needed in the results because we added the LastName field.

**o.** Click **Run** in the Results group.

The last names of the customers now display in the results.

**p.** Save and close the query.

## STEP 2 ➤ CREATE A MULTITABLE QUERY

After discussing the query results with the auditor, you realize that another query is needed to show those customers with account balances of $1,000 or less. You create the query and view the results in Datasheet view. Refer to Figure 2.48 as you complete Step 2.

Step d: Add the balance criterion

**FIGURE 2.48** Create a Multitable Query

**a.** Click the **CREATE tab** and click **Query Design** in the Queries group.

**b.** Double-click the **Branch table name** in the Show Table dialog box and double-click **Accounts** and **Customers** to add all three to the Query Design view. Click **Close** in the Show Table dialog box.

Three tables were added to the query.

c. Double-click the following fields to add them to the design grid: **LastName**, **FirstName**, **Balance**, and **Location**.

d. Type **<=1000** in the **Criteria row** of the Balance column.

e. Click **Run** in the Results group to see the query results.

Six records that have a balance of $1,000 or less display.

f. Click **Save** on the Quick Access Toolbar and type **Balance 1000 or Less** as the Query Name in the **Save As dialog box**. Click **OK**.

## STEP 3 ≫ MODIFY A MULTITABLE QUERY

The auditor requests additional changes to the Balance 1000 or Less query you just created. You will modify the criteria to display the accounts that were opened after January 1, 2011, with balances of $2,000 or less. Refer to Figure 2.49 as you complete Step 3.

**FIGURE 2.49** Query Using the AND Condition

a. Click **View** in the Views group to switch the *Balance 1000 or Less* query to Design view.

b. Type **<=2000** in place of *<=1000* in the **Criteria row** of the Balance field.

c. Double-click the **OpenDate field** in the Accounts table in the top section of the Query Design view to add it to the first blank column in the design grid.

d. Type **>=1/1/2011** in the **Criteria row** of the OpenDate field to extract only accounts that have been opened since January 2011.

After you type the expression and then move to a different column, Access will add the # symbols around the date automatically.

e. Click **Run** in the Results group to display the results of the query.

Five records display in the query results.

f. Click the **FILE tab**, click **Save As**, click **Save Object As**, and then click **Save As**. Type **OpenDate 2011 or Later** as the query name. Click **OK**.

g. Click **View** in the Views group to return to the Design view of the query.

h. Click in the **Sort row** of the OpenDate field and select **Ascending**.

i. Click **Run** in the Results group.

The records are sorted from the earliest open date after January 1, 2011, to the most recent open date.

j. Save and close the query.

# STEP 4 ≫ GET ANSWERS USING A MULTITABLE QUERY

The auditor wants to know the number of accounts each customer has opened. You create a query using a Totals row to obtain these data. Refer to Figure 2.50 as you complete Step 4.

Step f: Click Totals

Step g: Change to Count

**FIGURE 2.50** Number of Accounts Opened by a Customer

a. Click the **CREATE tab** and click **Query Design** in the Queries group.

b. Add the Accounts table and the Customers table to the top section of the Query Design view. Click **Close** in the Show Table dialog box.

c. Double-click the **CustomerID** in the Customers table in the top section of the Query Design view to add it to the first blank column in the design grid and double-click the **AccountID** in the Accounts table to add it to the second column.

d. Click **Run** in the Results group.

The results show there are 28 records. Every account a customer has opened is displayed. The auditor only wants the total number of accounts a customer has, so you need to modify the query.

e. Click **View** in the Views group to return to the Design view of the query.

f. Click **Totals** in the Show/Hide group.

Both columns show the Group By option in the Total row.

g. Click **Group By** in the Total row of the AccountID field and select **Count**.

h. Click **Run** in the Results group.

The results show one row for each customer and the number of accounts each customer has opened since the database was created.

i. Click **Save** on the Quick Access Toolbar and type **Number of Customer Accounts** as the query name. Close the query.

j. Submit based on your instructor's directions and close Access.

# Chapter Objectives Review

After reading this chapter, you have accomplished the following objectives:

## 1. Design a table.

- Include necessary data: Consider the output requirements when creating table structure. Determine the data required to produce the expected information.
- Design for now and for the future: When designing a database, try to anticipate the future needs of the system and build in the flexibility to satisfy those demands.
- Store data in its smallest parts: Store data in its smallest parts to make it more flexible. Storing a full name in a Name field is more limiting than storing a first name in a separate FirstName field and a last name in a separate LastName field.
- Add calculated fields to a table: A calculated field produces a value from an expression or function that references one or more existing fields. Storing calculated data in a table enables you to add the data easily to queries, forms, and reports without the trouble of an additional calculation.
- Design to accommodate date arithmetic: Calculated fields are frequently created with numeric data. You can use date arithmetic to subtract one date from another to find out the number of days, months, or years that have lapsed between them. You can also add or subtract a constant from a date.
- Plan for common fields between tables: Tables are joined in relationships using common fields. Name the common fields with the same name and make sure they have the same data type.

## 2. Create and modify tables.

- Create tables: Create tables in Datasheet view or Design view. You can also import data from another database or an application such as Excel.
- Determine data type: Data type properties determine the type of data that can be entered and the operations that can be performed on that data. Access recognizes 12 data types.
- Establish a primary key: The primary key is the field that uniquely identifies each record in a table.
- Explore a foreign key: A foreign key is a field in one table that is also the primary key of another table.
- Work with field properties: Field properties determine how the field looks and behaves. Examples of field properties are the field size property and the caption property.
- Enter table records in Datasheet view: Datasheet view is used to add, edit, and delete records. Design view is used to create and modify the table structure by enabling you to add and edit fields and set field properties.

## 3. Share data.

- Import data: You can import data from other applications such as an Excel spreadsheet or import data from another database by using the Import Wizard.
- Modify an imported table's design and add data: After importing a table, examine the design and make necessary modifications. Modifications may include changing a field name, adding new fields, or deleting unnecessary fields.

## 4. Establish table relationships.

- Set relationships in the Relationships window: Use Show Table to add tables to the Relationships window. Drag a field name from one table to the corresponding field name in another table to join the tables.
- Establish referential integrity: Referential integrity enforces rules in a database that are used to preserve relationships between tables when records are changed.
- Set cascade options: The Cascade Update Related Fields option ensures that when the primary key is modified in a primary table, Access will automatically update all foreign key values in a related table. The Cascade Delete Related Records option ensures that when the primary key is deleted in a primary table, Access will automatically delete all records in related tables that reference the primary key.
- Establish a one-to-many relationship: A one-to-many relationship is established when the primary key value in the primary table can match many of the foreign key values in the related table. One-to-one and many-to-many are also relationship possibilities, but one-to-many relationships are the most common.

## 5. Create a single-table query.

- Create a single-table select query: A single-table select query uses fields from one table to display only those records that match certain criteria.
- Use Query Design view: Use Query Design view to create and modify a query. The top portion of the view contains tables with their respective field names and displays the join lines between tables. The bottom portion, known as the query design grid, contains columns and rows that you use to control the query results.

## 6. Specify query criteria for different data types.

- Different data types require different syntax: Date fields are enclosed in pound signs (#) and text fields in quotations (""). Numeric and currency fields require no delimiters.
- Use wildcards: Wildcards are special characters that can represent one or more characters in a text value. A question mark is a wildcard that stands for a single character in the same position as the question mark, while an asterisk is a wildcard that stands for any number of characters in the same position as the asterisk.
- Use comparison operators in queries: Comparison operators such as equal (=), not equal (<>), greater than (>), less than (<), greater than or equal to (>=), and less than or equal to (<=) signs can be used in the criteria of a query to limit the query results to only those records that meet the criteria.

- Work with null: Access uses the term *null* for a blank field. Null criteria can be used to find missing information.
- Establish AND, OR, and NOT criteria: The AND, OR, and NOT logical operators are used when queries require multiple criteria. The AND logical operator returns only records that meet all criteria. The OR logical operator returns records meeting any of the specified criteria. The NOT logical operator returns all records except the specified criteria.

### 7. Understand query sort order.
- Query sort order: The query sort order determines the order of records in a query's Datasheet view. You can change the order of records by specifying the sort order in Design view.
- Determining sort order: The sort order is determined from the order of the fields from left to right. Move the field columns to position them in left to right sort order.

### 8. Run, copy, and modify a Query.
- Run a query: To obtain the results for a query, you must run the query. To run the query, click Run in the Results group when you are in Design view. Another method is to locate the query in the Navigation Pane and double-click it. A similar method is to select the query and press Enter.
- Copy a query: To save time, after specifying tables, fields, and conditions for one query, copy the query, rename it, and then modify the fields and criteria in the second query.

### 9. Use the Query Wizard.
- Create a query using the Query Wizard: The Query Wizard is an alternative method for creating queries. It enables you to select tables and fields from lists. The last step of the wizard prompts you to save the query.

### 10. Create a multitable query.
- Creating a multitable query: Multitable queries contain two or more tables enabling you to take advantage of the relationships that have been set in your database.
- Add additional tables to a query: Open the Navigation Pane and drag the tables from the Navigation Pane directly into the top section of the Query Design view.

### 11. Modify a multitable query.
- Add and delete fields in a multitable query: Multitable queries may need to be modified. Add fields by double-clicking the field name in the table you want; remove fields by clicking the column selector and pressing Delete.
- Add join lines in a multitable query: If the tables have a common field, create join lines by dragging the field name of one common field onto the field name of the other table. Or you can add an additional table that will provide a join between all three tables.
- Get answers using a multitable query: Use the total row options of a field such as Count to get answers.

# Key Terms Matching

Match the key terms with their definitions. Write the key term letter by the appropriate numbered definition.

a. AND logical operator
b. AutoNumber
c. CamelCase notation
d. Caption property
e. Cascade Update Related Fields
f. Criteria row
g. Data redundancy
h. Data type
i. Field property
j. Foreign key

k. Multitable query
l. Number data type
m. Null
n. One-to-many relationship
o. OR logical operator
p. Query
q. Referential Integrity
r. Simple Query Wizard
s. Sort row
t. Wildcard

1. _____ A special character that can represent one or more characters in the criterion of a query. **p. 92**

2. _____ A characteristic of a field that determines how a field looks and behaves. **p. 67**

3. _____ Returns only records that meet all criteria. **p. 93**

4. _____ A row in the Query Design view that determines which records will be selected. **p. 90**

5. _____ Determines the type of data that can be entered and the operations that can be performed on that data. **p. 65**

6. _____ Used to create a more readable label that displays in the top row in Datasheet view and in forms and reports. **p. 67**

7. _____ Enables you to ask questions about the data stored in a database. **p. 89**

8. _____ The term *Access* uses to describe a blank field. **p. 93**

9. _____ A data type that is a number that automatically increments each time a record is added. **p. 66**

10. _____ The unnecessary storing of duplicate data in two or more tables. **p. 64**

11. _____ A data type that can store only numerical data. **p. 67**

12. _____ A relationship established when the primary key value in the primary table can match many of the foreign key values in the related table. **p. 80**

13. _____ A field in one table that is also the primary key of another table. **p. 67**

14. _____ An option that directs Access to automatically update all foreign key values in a related table when the primary key value is modified in a primary table. **p. 80**

15. _____ Rules in a database that are used to preserve relationships between tables when records are changed. **p. 79**

16. _____ Uses no spaces in multiword field names, but uses uppercase letters to distinguish the first letter of each new word. **p. 64**

17. _____ A row in the Query Design view that enables you to reorder data in ascending or descending order. **p. 90**

18. _____ Contains two or more tables, enabling you to take advantage of the relationships that have been set in your database. **p. 102**

19. _____ Returns records meeting any of the specified criteria. **p. 93**

20. _____ Provides dialog boxes to guide you through the query design process. **p. 89**

# Multiple Choice

1. All of the following are suggested guidelines for table design *except*:
   - (a) Include all necessary data.
   - (b) Store data in its smallest parts.
   - (c) Avoid date arithmetic.
   - (d) Link tables using common fields.

2. Which of the following determines the type of data that can be entered and the operations that can be performed on that data?
   - (a) Field properties
   - (b) Data type
   - (c) Caption property
   - (d) Normalization

3. When entering, deleting, or editing table data:
   - (a) The table must be in Design view.
   - (b) The table must be in Datasheet view.
   - (c) The table may be in either Datasheet or Design view.
   - (d) Data may only be entered in a form.

4. When importing data into Access, which of the following statements is *true*?
   - (a) The Import Wizard only works for Excel files.
   - (b) The Import Wizard is found on the Create tab.
   - (c) You can assign a primary key while you are importing Excel data.
   - (d) The wizard will import the data in one step after you select the file.

5. The main reason to enforce referential integrity in Access is to:
   - (a) Limit the number of records in a table.
   - (b) Make it possible to delete records.
   - (c) Keep your database safe from unauthorized users.
   - (d) Keep invalid data from being entered into a table.

6. An illustration of a one-to-many relationship would be a:
   - (a) Person changes his/her primary address.
   - (b) Customer may have multiple orders.
   - (c) Bank branch location has an internal BranchID code.
   - (d) Balance field is totaled for all accounts for each person.

7. A query's specifications providing instructions about which records to include must be entered on the:
   - (a) Table row of the query design grid.
   - (b) Show row of the query design grid.
   - (c) Sort row of the query design grid.
   - (d) Criteria row of the query design grid.

8. When adding Value criteria to the Query Design view, the value you enter must be delimited by:
   - (a) Nothing ().
   - (b) Pound signs (#).
   - (c) Quotes (" ").
   - (d) At signs (@).

9. It is more efficient to make a copy of an existing query rather than create a new query when which of the following is *true*?
   - (a) The existing query contains only one table.
   - (b) The existing query and the new query use the same tables and fields.
   - (c) The existing query and the new query have the exact same criteria.
   - (d) The original query is no longer being used.

10. Which of the following is *true* for the Query Wizard?
    - (a) You can only select tables as a source.
    - (b) No criteria can be added.
    - (c) Fields from multiple tables are not allowed.
    - (d) You do not need a summary.

## 1 Our Corner Bookstore

**FROM SCRATCH**

Tom and Erin Mullaney own and operate a bookstore in Philadelphia, Pennsylvania. Erin asked you to help her create an Access database because of your experience in this class. You believe that you can help her by creating a database and importing the Excel spreadsheets they use to store the publishers and the books that they sell. You determine that a third table—for authors—is also required. Your task is to design and populate the three tables, set the table relationships, and enforce referential integrity. If you have problems, reread the detailed directions presented in the chapter. This exercise follows the same set of skills as used in Hands-On Exercises 1 and 2 in the chapter. Refer to Figure 2.51 as you complete this exercise.

**FIGURE 2.51** Books Relationships Window

a. Open Access and click **Blank desktop database**. Type **a02p1Books_LastFirst** in the **File Name box**. Click **Browse** to locate your student data files folder in the File New Database dialog box, click **OK** to close the dialog box, and then click **Create** to create the new database.

b. Type **11** in the **Click to Add column** and click **Click to Add**. The field name becomes *Field1*, and *Click to Add* now appears as the third column. Click in the third column, type **Benchloss**, and then press **Tab**. The process repeats for the fourth column; type **Michael R.** and press **Tab** twice.

c. The cursor returns to the first column where *(New)* is selected. Press **Tab**. Type the rest of the data using the following table. These data will become the records of the Author table.

| ID | Field1 | Field2 | Field3 |
|----|--------|--------|--------|
| 1 | 11 | Brenchloss | Michael R. |
| (New) | 12 | Turow | Scott |
| | 13 | Rice | Anne |
| | 14 | King | Stephen |
| | 15 | Connelly | Michael |
| | 16 | Rice | Luanne |
| | 17 | *your last name* | *your first name* |

d. Click **Save** on the Quick Access Toolbar. Type **Author** in the **Save As dialog box** and click **OK**.

e. Click **View** in the Views group to switch to the Design view of the Author table.

f. Select **Field1**—in the second row—in the top portion of the table design and type **AuthorID** to rename the field. In the *Field Properties* section in the lower portion of the table design, type **Author ID** in the **Caption property box** and verify that *Long Integer* displays for the Field Size property.

g. Select **Field2** and type **LastName** to rename the field. In the *Field Properties* section in the bottom portion of the Design view, type **Author's Last Name** in the **Caption property box** and type **20** as the field size.

h. Select **Field3** and type **FirstName** to rename the field. In the *Field Properties* section in the bottom portion of the table design, type **Author's First Name** as the caption and type **15** as the field size.

i. Click the **ID field row selector** (which shows the primary key) to select the row and click **Delete Rows** in the Tools group. Click **Yes** twice to confirm both messages.

j. Click the **AuthorID row selector** and click **Primary Key** in the Tools group to reset the primary key.

k. Click **Save** on the Quick Access Toolbar to save the design changes. Click **Yes** to the *Some data may be lost* message. Close the table.

**l.** Click the **EXTERNAL DATA tab** and click **Excel** in the Import & Link group to launch the Get External Data – Excel Spreadsheet feature. Verify the *Import the source data into a new table in the current database* option is selected, click **Browse**, and then go to the student data folder. Select the *a02p1Books* workbook, click **Open**, and then click **OK**. This workbook contains two worksheets. Follow these steps:

- Select the **Publishers worksheet** and click **Next**.
- Click the **First Row Contains Column Headings check box** and click **Next**.
- Select the **PubID field**, click the **Indexed arrow**, select **Yes (No Duplicates)**, and then click **Next**.
- Click the **Choose my own primary key arrow**, select **PubID**, if necessary, and then click **Next**.
- Accept the name *Publishers* for the table name, click **Finish**, and then click **Close** without saving the import steps.

**m.** Repeat the Import Wizard to import the Books worksheet from the *a02p1Books* workbook into the Access database. Follow these steps:

- Select the **Books worksheet** and click **Next**.
- Ensure the *First Row Contains Column Headings* check box is checked and click **Next**.
- Click on the **ISBN column**, set the Indexed property box to **Yes (No Duplicates)**, and then click **Next**.
- Click the **Choose my own primary key arrow**, select **ISBN** as the primary key field, and then click **Next**.
- Accept the name *Books* as the table name. Click **Finish** and click **Close** without saving the import steps.

**n.** Right-click the **Books table** in the Navigation Pane and select **Design View**. Make the following changes:

- Change the PubID field name to **PublisherID**.
- Change the Caption property to **Publisher ID**.
- Change the PublisherID Field Size property to **2**.
- Click the **ISBN field** and change the Field Size property to **13**.
- Change the AuthorCode field name to **AuthorID**.
- Change the AuthorID Field Size property to **Long Integer**.
- Click the **ISBN field row selector** (which shows the primary key) to select the row. Drag the row up to the first position.
- Click **Save** on the Quick Access Toolbar to save the design changes to the Books table. Click **Yes** to the *Some data may be lost* warning.
- Close the table.

**o.** Right-click the **Publishers table** in the Navigation Pane and select **Design View**. Make the following changes:

- Change the PubID field name to **PublisherID**.
- Change the PublisherID Field Size property to **2**.
- Change the Caption property to **Publisher's ID**.
- Change the Field Size property to **50** for the PubName and PubAddress fields.
- Change the Pub Address field name to **PubAddress** (remove the space).
- Change the PubCity Field Size property to **30**.
- Change the PubState Field Size property to **2**.
- Change the Pub ZIP field name to **PubZIP** (remove the space).
- Click **Save** on the Quick Access Toolbar to save the design changes to the Publishers table. Click **Yes** to the *Some data may be lost* warning. Close all open tables.

**p.** Click the **DATABASE TOOLS tab** and click **Relationships** in the Relationships group. Click **Show Table** if necessary. Follow these steps:

- Double-click each table name in the Show Table dialog box to add it to the Relationships window and close the Show Table dialog box.
- Drag the **AuthorID field** from the Author table onto the AuthorID field in the Books table.

- Click the **Enforce Referential Integrity** and **Cascade Update Related Fields check boxes** in the Edit Relationships dialog box. Click **Create** to create a one-to-many relationship between the Author and Books tables.
- Drag the **PublisherID field** from the Publishers table onto the PublisherID field in the Books table.
- Click the **Enforce Referential Integrity** and **Cascade Update Related Fields check boxes** in the Edit Relationships dialog box. Click **Create** to create a one-to-many relationship between the Publishers and Books tables.
- Click **Save** on the Quick Access Toolbar to save the changes to the Relationships window and click **Close**.

q. Click the **FILE tab** and click **Close** to exit Access.

r. Submit based on your instructor's directions.

## 2 Morgan Insurance Company

The Morgan Insurance Company offers a full range of insurance services in four locations: Miami, Boston, Chicago, and Philadelphia. They store all of the firm's employee data in an Excel spreadsheet. This file contains employee name and address, job performance, salary, and title. The firm is converting from Excel to Access. A database file containing two of the tables already exists; your job is to import the employee data from Excel for the third table. Once imported, you need to modify field properties and set new relationships. The owner of the company, Victor Reed, is concerned that some of the Atlanta and Boston salaries may be below the guidelines published by the national office. He asks that you investigate the salaries of the two offices and create a separate query for each city. If you have problems, reread the detailed directions presented in the chapter. This exercise follows the same set of skills as used in Hands-On Exercises 2–4 in the chapter. Refer to Figure 2.52 as you complete this exercise.

**FIGURE 2.52** Boston Salaries Query Design

a. Open *a02p2Insurance*. Click the **FILE tab**, click **Save As**, and then click **Save As** again to save the database as **a02p2Insurance_LastFirst**. Double-click the **Location table** and look at the contents to become familiar with the field names and the type of information stored in the table. Repeat with the Titles table.

b. Click the **EXTERNAL DATA tab**, click **Excel** in the Import & Link group, and then do the following:
- Click **Browse** and locate the *a02p2Employees* workbook in your student data files location. Select the file, click **Open**, and then click **OK**.
- Select the **Employees worksheet**, if necessary, and click **Next**.
- Click the **First Row Contains Column Headings check box** and click **Next**.
- Click the **Indexed arrow** for the EmployeeID field, select **Yes (No Duplicates)**, and then click **Next**.

- Click **Choose my own primary key arrow**, select the **EmployeeID** as the primary key, and then click **Next**.
- Accept the name *Employees* for the table name, click **Finish**, and then click **Close** without saving the import steps.

c. Double-click the **Employees table** in the Navigation Pane, click the **HOME tab**, and then click **View** in the Views group to switch to the Design view of the Employees table. Make the following changes:

- Click the **LastName field** and change the Field Size property to **20**.
- Change the Caption property to **Last Name**.
- Click the **FirstName field** and change the Field Size property to **20**.
- Change the Caption property to **First Name**.
- Click the **LocationID field** and change the Field Size property to **3**.
- Change the Caption property to **Location ID**.
- Click the **TitleID field** and change the Field Size property to **3**.
- Change the Caption property to **Title ID**.
- Change the Salary field data type to **Currency** and change *General Number* in the Format property in field properties to **Currency**.
- Save the design changes. Click **Yes** to the *Some data may be lost* warning.

d. Click **View** in the Views group to view the Employees table in Datasheet view and examine the data. Click any record in the Title ID and click **Ascending** in the Sort & Filter group on the HOME tab. Multiple employees are associated with the T01, T02, T03, and T04 titles.

e. Double-click the **Titles table** in the Navigation Pane to open it in Datasheet view. Notice the T04 title is not in the list.

f. Add a new record in the first blank record at the bottom of the Titles table. Use the following data:

- Type **T04** in the **TitleID field**.
- Type **Senior Account Rep** in the **Title field**.
- Type **A marketing position requiring a technical background and at least three years of experience** in the **Description field**.
- Type **Four-year degree** in the **Education Requirements field**.
- Type **45000** in the **Minimum Salary field**.
- Type **75000** in the **Maximum Salary field**.

g. Close all tables. Click **Yes** if you are asked to save changes to the Employees table.

h. Click the **DATABASE TOOLS tab** and click **Relationships** in the Relationships group. Click **Show Table** if necessary. Follow these steps:

- Double-click each table name in the Show Table dialog box to add them to the Relationships window and close the Show Table dialog box.
- Adjust the height of the tables so that all fields display.
- Drag the **LocationID field** in the Location table onto the LocationID field in the Employees table.
- Click the **Enforce Referential Integrity** and **Cascade Update Related Fields check boxes** in the Edit Relationships dialog box. Click **Create** to create a one-to-many relationship between the Location and Employees tables.
- Drag the **TitleID field** in the Titles table onto the TitleID field in the Employees table.
- Click the **Enforce Referential Integrity** and **Cascade Update Related Fields check boxes** in the Edit Relationships dialog box. Click **Create** to create a one-to-many relationship between the Titles and Employees tables.
- Click **Save** on the Quick Access Toolbar to save the changes to the Relationships window and close the Relationships window.

i. Click the **CREATE tab** and click the **Query Wizard** in the Queries group. Follow these steps:

- Select **Simple Query Wizard** and click **OK**.
- Select **Table: Employees** in the Tables/Queries box, if necessary.
- Double-click **LastName** in the **Available Fields list** to move it to the Selected Fields list.
- Double-click **FirstName** in the **Available Fields list** to move it to the Selected Fields list.

- Double-click **LocationID** in the **Available Fields list** to move it to the Selected Fields list.
- Click **Next**.
- Select the **Detail (shows every field of every record) option**, if necessary, and click **Next**.
- Type **Employees Location** as the query title and click **Finish**.

j. Click the **CREATE tab** and click the **Query Wizard** in the Queries group. Follow these steps:
- Select **Simple Query Wizard** and click **OK**.
- Select **Table: Location** in the Tables/Queries box.
- Double-click **Location** in the **Available Fields list** to move it to the Selected Fields list.
- Select **Table: Employees** in the Tables/Queries box.
- Double-click **LastName**, **FirstName**, and **Salary**.
- Select **Table: Titles** in the Tables/Queries box.
- Double-click **MinimumSalary** and **MaximumSalary**. Click **Next**.
- Select the **Detail (shows every field of every record) option**, if necessary, and click **Next**.
- Type **Atlanta Salaries** as the query title and click **Finish**.

k. Click the **HOME tab** and click **View** to switch to the Design view of the Atlanta Salaries Query. In the Criteria row of the Location field, type **Atlanta**. Click in the **Sort row** in the Salary field and select **Ascending**. Click **Run** in the Results group on the DESIGN tab. Visually inspect the data to see if any of the Atlanta employees have a salary less than the minimum or greater than the maximum when compared to the published salary range. These salaries will need to be updated later. Save and close the query.

l. Right-click on the **Atlanta Salaries query** in the Navigation Pane and select **Copy**. Right-click a blank area in the Navigation Pane and select **Paste**. In the Paste As dialog box, type **Boston Salaries** for the query name. Click **OK**.

m. Right-click on the **Boston Salaries query** in the Navigation Pane and select **Design View**. In the Criteria row of the Location field, replace *Atlanta* with **Boston**. Click **Run** in the Results group on the DESIGN tab. Visually inspect the data to see if any of the Boston employees have a salary less than the minimum or greater than the maximum when compared to the published salary range. Save and close the query.

n. Click the **FILE tab** and click **Close** to exit Access.

o. Submit based on your instructor's directions.

# Mid-Level Exercises

## 1 My Game Collection

ANALYSIS
CASE

Over the years, you have collected quite a few video games, so you cataloged them in an Access database. After opening the database, you create two tables—one to identify the game system that plays your game and the other to identify the category or genre of the game. Then, you will join each table in a relationship so that you can query the database. Refer to Figure 2.53 as you complete this exercise.

**FIGURE 2.53** Game List Query

a. Open *a02m1Games* and save the database as **a02m1Games_LastFirst**. Open the *Games* table and review the fields containing the game information.

b. Click the **CREATE tab** and click **Table Design** in the Tables group.

c. Type **SystemID** for the first Field Name and select **Number** as the Data Type.

d. Type **SystemName** for the second Field Name and accept **Short Text** as the Data Type.

e. Change to Design view. Delete the ID row. Make **SystemID** the primary key and change the Data Type to **AutoNumber**. Add the caption **System ID**.

f. Change the SystemName Field Size property to **15**. Add the caption **System Name**, making sure there is a space between System and Name. Save the table as **System**, saving the changes to the table design. Switch to Datasheet view.

g. Add the system names to the System table as shown below, letting Access use AutoNumber to create the SystemID field. Close the table.

| System ID | System Name |
|-----------|-------------|
| 1 | XBOX 360 |
| 2 | PS3 |
| 3 | Wii |
| 4 | NES |
| 5 | PC Game |
| 6 | Nintendo 3DS |

h. Click the **CREATE tab** and click **Table Design** in the Tables group. Delete the existing ID row. Type **CategoryID** for the first Field Name and select **AutoNumber** as the Data Type. Set the CategoryID as the **Primary Key**.

i. Type **CategoryDescription** for the second Field Name and accept **Short Text** as the Data Type. Change the Field Size property to **25**. Add the caption **Category Description**, making sure there is a space between Category and Description. Save the table as **Category**, saving the changes to the table design. Switch to Datasheet view.

**j.** Add the category descriptions to the Category table as shown below, letting Access use AutoNumber to create the CategoryID field. Close the table.

| CategoryID | Category Description |
|---|---|
| 1 | Action |
| 2 | Adventure |
| 3 | Arcade |
| 4 | Racing |
| 5 | Rhythm |
| 6 | Role-playing |
| 7 | Simulation |
| 8 | Sports |

**k.** Click the **DATABASE TOOLS tab** and click **Relationships** in the Relationships group. Add all three tables to the Relationships window and close the Show Table dialog box. Create a one-to-many relationship between CategoryID in the Category table and CategoryID in the Games table. Enforce referential integrity and cascade update related fields.

**l.** Create a one-to-many relationship between SystemID in the System table and SystemID in the Games table. Enforce referential integrity and cascade update related fields. Close the Relationships window, saving changes.

**m.** Use the Query Wizard to create a simple query using the Games table. Use the following fields in the query: GameName, Rating. Save the query using the title **Ratings Query**.

**n.** Switch to Query Design view. Sort the rating field in ascending order and run the query. Close the query, saving the changes to the design of the Ratings Query.

**o.** Create a multitable query in Design view using all three tables. Use the following fields: GameName, CategoryDescription, Rating, SystemName, and DateAcquired.

**p.** Sort the query in Ascending order by GameName and run the query. Save the query as **Game List Query** and close the query.

**q.** Copy the **Game List Query** and paste it in the Navigation Pane using the name **PS3 Games**. Modify the query in Design view by using **PS3** as the criteria for SystemName. Remove the sort by GameName and sort in ascending order by CategoryDescription. The query results should include 7 records.

**r.** Close the PS3 Games query, saving the changes to the design.

**s.** Assume you are going home for Thanksgiving and you want to take your Wii gaming system and games home with you—but you only want to take home games with a rating of Everyone. Create a query named **Thanksgiving Games** that shows the name of the game, its rating, the category description of the games, and the system name. The results of the query will tell you which games to pack.

**t.** Submit based on your instructor's directions.

## 2 The Prestige Hotel

The Prestige Hotel chain caters to upscale business travelers and provides state-of-the-art conference, meeting, and reception facilities. It prides itself on its international, four-star cuisine. Last year, it began a member reward club to help the marketing department track the purchasing patterns of its most loyal customers. All of the hotel transactions are stored in the database. Your task is to help the managers of the Prestige Hotel in Denver and Chicago identify their customers who stayed in a room last year and who had three persons in their party. Refer to Figure 2.54 as you complete this exercise.

**FIGURE 2.54** Denver Rooms 3 Guests Query

**a.** Open *a02m2Hotel* and save the file as **a02m2Hotel_LastFirst**. Review the data contained in the three tables. Specifically, look for the tables and fields containing the information you need: dates of stays in Denver suites, the members' names, and the numbers in the parties.

**b.** Import the location data from the Excel file *a02m2Location* into your database as a new table. The first row does contain column headings. Set the LocationID Indexed property to **Yes (No Duplicates)** and set the Data Type to **Long Integer**. Select the **LocationID field** as the primary key. Name the table **Location**. Do not save the import steps.

**c.** Open the Relationships window and create a relationship between the Location table and the Orders table using the LocationID field. Enforce referential integrity and select **Cascade Update Related Fields**. Create a relationship between the Orders and Members tables using the MemNumber field, ensuring that you enforce referential integrity and cascade update related fields. Create a relationship between the Orders and Service tables using the ServiceID field, ensuring that you enforce referential integrity and cascade update related fields. Save and close the Relationships window.

**d.** Open the Members table and find Bryan Gray's name. Replace his name with your own first and last names. Use Find to locate Nicole Lee's name and replace it with your name. Close the table.

**e.** Create a query using the following fields: ServiceDate (Orders table), City (Location table), NoInParty (Orders table), ServiceName (Service table), FirstName (Members table), and LastName (Members table). Set the criteria to limit the output to **Denver**. Use the Between command to only show services from **7/1/2012** to **6/30/2013**. Set the Number in Party criterion to **3**. Sort the results in ascending order by the Service Date. Compare your query to Figure 2.54.

**f.** Run the query and examine the number of records in the status bar at the bottom of the query. It should display *154*. If your number of records is different, examine the criteria.

**g.** Change the order of the query fields so that they display as FirstName, LastName, ServiceDate, City, NoInParty, and ServiceName.

**h.** Save the query as **Denver Rooms 3 Guests**. Close the query and copy and paste it, renaming the new query **Chicago Rooms 3 Guests**; one of your colleagues in Chicago asked for your help in analyzing the guest data.

**i.** Open the Chicago Rooms 3 Guests query in Design view and change the criterion for Denver to **Chicago**. Run and save the changes. You should have 179 results.

**j.** Combine the two previous queries into a third query named **Denver and Chicago Rooms 3 Guests**. Use the criteria from the two individual queries to create a combination AND–OR condition. The records in the combined query should equal the sum of the records in the two individual queries (333 records).

**k.** Submit based on your instructor's directions.

## 3 Used Cell Phones for Sale

COLLABORATION
CASE

ANALYSIS
CASE

You and a few of your classmates started a new business selling used cell phones, MP3 players, and accessories. You have been using an Access database to track your inventory. You decide to improve the data entry process by adding three additional tables. After the new tables are added and the relationships set, you will create several queries to analyze the data. In order to collaborate with the other members of your group, you will post an Access database and two Excel files to a SkyDrive folder. At the completion of this exercise, each person will submit his or her own Word document containing the answers to the questions below.

a. Open the *a02m3Phones* database and save the file as **a02m3Phones_GroupX**. Close the database. (This step will be completed by only one person in your group. Replace *X* with the number assigned to your group by your instructor.) Create a folder on your SkyDrive account named **Exploring Access** and share the folder with the other members in your group and the instructor. Upload the database to this new folder and notify the other members in your group.

b. Download the database from the Exploring Access SkyDrive folder created in step a and save it locally as **a02m3Phones_GroupX_LastFirst**. (Everyone in the group will complete this step.) Open the database, open the Inventory table, and than review the records in the table. Take note of the data in the TypeOfDevice column; this field is joined to the DeviceOptions table, and the *enforce referential integrity* option has been set. Only the options in the DeviceOptions table are allowed to be entered. What other fields in this table could be joined to a table in the same way? Type your answer into a Word document named **a02m3Phones_Answers_LastFirst**.

c. Import the data in the *a02m3Carriers* Excel spreadsheet into a new table named **Carriers**. Let Access add a primary key field (ID). Open the table and verify that the data imported correctly. Change the ID field to **CarrierID**. Save and close the Carriers table.

d. Open the Inventory table in Design view and add a new field under the Carrier field named **CarrierID**. Set the Data Type to **Number**. Save and close the table. Open the Relationships window and the Carriers table. Create a relationship between the Carriers table and the Inventory table using the CarrierID field. Enforce referential integrity. Take a screen shot of the Relationships window using the Snipping Tool and paste the image into the Word document you created in step b. Close the Relationships window.

e. Open the Inventory table and the Carriers table. Using the CarrierID field in the Carriers table, enter the correct CarrierID into each record in the Inventory table.

f. Repeat steps c, d, and e for the fields Manufacturer and Color. To do this, one member of the group must create an Excel spreadsheet named **a02m3Manufacturers**, which contains all the manufacturers found in the Inventory table. Another member of the group must create an Excel spreadsheet named **a02m3Colors**, which contains all the colors found in the Inventory table. Both of these Excel spreadsheets must be saved to the Exploring Access folder created in step a so all members can access the data.

g. Create relationships between the tables based on common fields. Take a screen shot of the Relationships window using the Snipping Tool and paste the image into the Word document. Close the Relationships window.

DISCOVER

h. After all the new tables have been added, each person in the group should create all of the following queries. Make sure the text fields from the supporting tables appear in the queries (not the ID fields). Save each query as noted below. Take a screen shot of the datasheet of each query using the Snipping Tool and paste the image into the Word document.

   1. Display all the phones that are still for sale (SellDate is Null). Save as **qry1 Phones For Sale**.
   2. Display all the phones that are not made by Apple. Save as **qry2 Not Apple Phones**.
   3. List the Manufacturer and Model and asking price of sold phones; also include phones that are less than $50. Sort by asking price; only include tables that are required. Save as **qry3 Phones Sold or less than $50**.
   4. Display the phones that were purchased before 4/1/2012. Exclude the sold phones. Sort by purchase date. Save as **qry4 Obsolete Phones**.

i. Use e-mail or text messaging to communicate with other members in your group if you have any questions.

j. Exit all applications. Submit both the Word document and the database based on your instructor's directions.

# Beyond the Classroom

### Database Administrator Position

You arrive at Secure Systems, Inc., for a database administrator position interview. After meeting the human resources coordinator, you are given a test to demonstrate your skills in Access. You are asked to create a database from scratch to keep track of all the candidates for the positions currently open at Secure Systems. Use the Internet to search for information about database management. One useful site is published by the federal government's Bureau of Labor Statistics. It compiles an Occupational Outlook Handbook describing various positions, the type of working environment, the education necessary, salary information, and the projected growth. The Web site is http://www.bls.gov/ooh. After researching the database administrator position requirement, create a database using these requirements:

a. Name the database **a02b2Admin_LastFirst**.

b. Create three tables including these fields: Candidates (CandidateID, FirstName, LastName, Phone, Email), JobOpenings (Job OpeningID, JobName, Required Skill, HourlyPayRate, DataPosted, Supervisor), and Interviews (InterviewSequenceID, CandidateID, JobOpeningID, InterviewedBy, DateOfInterview, Rank).

c. Set the table relationships.

d. Add 10 candidates—yourself and 9 other students in your class.

e. Add the Database Administrator job and four other sample jobs.

f. Add eight sample interviews—four for the Database Administrator position and four others. Rank each candidate on a scale of 1 to 5 (5 is highest).

g. Create a query that lists the LastName, FirstName, JobOpeningID, InterviewedBy, DateofInterview, and Rank fields. Display only Database Administrator interviews with a ranking of 4 or 5. Sort by last name and first name. Run the query.

h. Compact and repair the database. Close Access. Submit based on your instructor's directions.

---

### May Beverage Sales

A coworker called you into his office, explained that he was having difficulty with Microsoft Access 2013, and asked you to look at his work. Open *a02b3Traders* and save it as **a02b3Traders_LastFirst**. It contains two queries, *May 2015 Orders of Beverages and Confections* and *2015 Beverage Sales by Ship Country*. The May 2015 Orders of Beverages and Confections query is supposed to have only information from May 2015. You find other dates included in the results. Change the criteria to exclude the other dates. The 2015 Beverage Sales by Ship Country query returns no results. Check the criteria in all fields and modify so that the correct results are returned. After you find and correct the error(s), compact and repair the database. Close Access. Submit based on your instructor's directions.

---

## Conflict Database

After watching the Conflict: Sexual Harassment video, search the Web for the Equal Employment Opportunities Commission (EEOC) government site. Open the EEOC site and read the *About EEOC: Overview* information. Open a Word document and save it as **a02b4Harrassment_Answers_LastFirst**. Type a paragraph about the responsibilities of the EEOC.

Locate the *EEOC Laws, Regulations, Guidance & MOUs* page. The *Discrimination by Type* section includes a list of hyperlinks to discrimination type pages—pages that include laws, regulations and policy guidance, and also fact sheets, Q&As, best practices, and other information organized by basis of discrimination. Select a discrimination link and review the material on the page. Type two to three additional paragraphs in the Word document to summarize what you have read. Be sure to use good grammar, punctuation, and spelling in your document. Save the Word document and submit based on your instructor's directions.

# Capstone Exercise

The Morris Arboretum in Chestnut Hill, Pennsylvania, tracks donors in Excel. They also use Excel to store a list of plants in stock. As donors contribute funds to the Arboretum, they can elect to receive a plant gift from the Arboretum. These plants are both rare plants and hard-to-find old favorites, and they are part of the annual appeal and membership drive to benefit the Arboretum's programs. The organization has grown, and the files are too large and inefficient to handle in Excel. Your task will be to begin the conversion of the files from Excel to Access.

## Create a New Database

You need to examine the data in the Excel worksheets to determine which fields will become the primary keys in each table and which fields will become the foreign keys. Primary and foreign keys are used to form the relationships between tables.

a. Open the *a02c1Donors* Excel workbook.

b. Open the *a02c1Plants* Excel workbook.

c. Examine the data in each worksheet and identify the column that will become the primary key in an Access table. Identify the foreign keys in each table.

d. Create a new, blank database named **a02c1Arbor_LastFirst**.

## Create a New Table

Use the new blank table created automatically by Access to hold the donations as they are received from the donors.

a. Switch to Design view and save the table as **Donations**.

b. Add the remaining field names in Design view. Note: The data for this table will be added later in this exercise.

- Change *ID* to **DonationID** with the **AutoNumber Data Type**.

- Add **DonorID** (a foreign key) with the **Number Data Type** and a field size of **Long Integer**.

- Add **PlantID** (a foreign key) as **Number Data** and a field size of **Long Integer**.

- Enter two additional fields with an appropriate data type and field properties. Hint: You need the date of donation and the amount of donation.

c. Verify the primary key is *DonationID*.

d. Save the table. Close the table.

## Import Data from Excel

You need to use the Import Spreadsheet Data Wizard twice to import a worksheet from each Excel workbook into Access. You need to select the worksheets, specify the primary keys, set the indexing option, and name the newly imported tables (see Figures 2.12 through 2.17).

a. Click the **EXTERNAL DATA tab** and click **Excel** in the Import & Link group.

b. Locate and select the *a02c1Donors* workbook.

c. Set the DonorID field Indexed option to **Yes (No Duplicates)**.

d. Select **DonorID** as the primary key when prompted.

e. Accept the table name *Donors*.

f. Import the *a02c1Plants* file, set the **ID field** as the primary key, and then change the indexing option to **Yes (No Duplicates)**.

g. Accept the table name *Plants*.

h. Open each table in Datasheet view to examine the data.

i. Change the ID field name in the Plants table to **PlantID**.

## Create Relationships

You need to create the relationships between the tables using the Relationships window. Identify the primary key fields in each table and connect them with their foreign key counterparts in related tables. Enforce referential integrity and cascade and update related fields.

a. Open the Donors table in Design view and change the Field Size property for DonorID to **Long Integer** so it matches the Field Size property of DonorID in the Donations table.

b. Open the Plants table in Design view and change the Field Size property for PlantID to **Long Integer** so it matches the Field Size property for PlantID in the Donations table.

c. Close the open tables and open the Relationships window.

d. Add the three tables to the Relationships window using the Show Table dialog box. Close the Show Tables dialog box.

e. Drag the **DonorID field** in the Donors table onto the DonorID field in the Donations table. Enforce referential integrity and cascade and update related fields. Drag the **PlantID field** from the Plants table onto the PlantID field of the Donations table. Enforce referential integrity and check the **Cascade Update Related Fields option**.

f. Close the Relationships window and save your changes.

## Add Sample Data to the Donations Table

Add 10 records to the Donations table.

a. Add the following records to the Donations table.

| Donation ID | Donor ID | Plant ID | Date Of Donation | Amount Of Donation |
|---|---|---|---|---|
| 10 | 8228 | 611 | 3/1/2015 | $150 |
| 18 | 5448 | 190 | 3/1/2015 | $15 |
| 6 | 4091 | 457 | 3/12/2015 | $125 |
| 7 | 11976 | 205 | 3/14/2015 | $100 |
| 1 | 1000 | 25 | 3/17/2015 | $120 |
| 12 | 1444 | 38 | 3/19/2015 | $50 |
| 2 | 1444 | 38 | 4/3/2015 | $50 |
| 4 | 10520 | 49 | 4/12/2015 | $460 |
| 5 | 3072 | 102 | 4/19/2015 | $450 |
| 21 | 1204 | 25 | 4/22/2012 | $120 |

b. Sort the Donations table by the AmountOfDonation field in descending order.

## Use the Query Wizard

Use the Query Wizard to create a query of all donations greater than $100 in the Donations table. Use the following guidelines:

a. Include the DonorID and AmountOfDonation fields.

b. Name the query **Donations Over 100**.

c. Add criteria to include only donations of more than $100.

d. Sort by ascending AmountOfDonation.

e. Save and close the query.

## Create a Query in Design View

You need to create a query that identifies the people who made a donation after April 1, 2015. The query should list the date of the donation, donor's full name (LastName, FirstName), phone number, the amount of the donation, and name of the plant they want. Sort the query by date of donation, then by donor last name. This list will be given to the Arboretum staff so they can notify the donors that a plant is ready for pickup.

a. Click the **CREATE tab** and click **Query Design** in the Queries group.

b. Add the tables and fields necessary to produce the query as stated previously. Name the query **Plant Pickup List**.

c. Run and print the query from Datasheet view.

## Modify a Query in Design View

a. Copy the Plant Pickup List query on the Navigation Pane and paste it using **ENewsletter** as the query name.

b. Open the ENewsletter query in Design view and delete the DateofDonation column.

c. Add the ENewsletter field to the design and set it to sort in Ascending order. Position the ENewsletter field on the grid so that the query sorts first by ENewsletter and then by LastName.

d. Compact and repair the database. Close Access.

e. Submit based on your instructor's directions.

# Customize, Analyze, and Summarize Query Data

## Creating and Using Queries to Make Decisions

## OBJECTIVES    AFTER YOU READ THIS CHAPTER, YOU WILL BE ABLE TO:

1. Create a calculated field in a query p. 130
2. Format and save calculated results p. 133
3. Create expressions with the Expression Builder p. 141
4. Use built-in functions in Access p. 143
5. Add aggregate functions to datasheets p. 151
6. Create queries with aggregate functions p. 152

## CASE STUDY | Housing Slump Means Opportunity for College Students

Two students from Passaic County Community College (PCCC) decided they would take advantage of the declining housing market. After taking several business courses at PCCC and a weekend seminar in real estate investing, Donald Carter and Matthew Nevoso were ready to test their skills in the marketplace. Don and Matt had a simple strategy—buy distressed properties at a significant discount, then resell the properties for a profit one year later when the market rebounds.

As they drove through the surrounding neighborhoods, if they noticed a For Sale sign in a yard, they would call the listing agent and ask for the key information such as the asking price, the number of bedrooms, square feet, and days on the market. Because they were just starting out, they decided to target houses that were priced at $150,000 or below and only houses that had been on the market at least six months.

For the first two months, they gathered lots of information and began to get a feel for the houses and prices in the area. Some neighborhoods were definitely more distressed than others! But they still had not made any offers. The two PCCC investors realized they needed a more scientific approach to finding an investment property. Based on a tip from the real estate seminar, they decide to create a database using Access 2013, using data from free lists of homes for sale. They would then like to use Access to help them find houses that meet their criteria. Once the data is in Access, you can help Don and Matt easily identify the qualifying properties. This new database approach should help them become more successful and hopefully help them acquire their first investment property.

# Calculations and Expressions

One reason you might choose Excel over a program like Word is for the ability to perform calculations. At first glance, you may not see an obvious location for you to enter a calculation in Access. However, Access includes many of the same built-in calculations and functions that Excel does.

So, why do you need to create calculated fields? Similar to Excel, there are going to be times when you have to process data into information. For example, it could be as simple as needing to calculate a paycheck amount. If you have one field storing the number of hours worked and another field storing the hourly pay rate, you would be able to multiply them together to get the total amount the person is owed. Basic calculations such as these can be done using a query, so you do not have to rely on doing calculations by hand, which can lead to mistakes.

Unfortunately, calculations may not always be that easy. We did not consider some of the common deductions, such as Social Security, Medicare/FICA, federal and state income taxes, unemployment insurance, and possibly union dues. Some of these may be a flat rate, and others may be calculated based on your paycheck amount.

Expressions go beyond simple mathematical functions. Access includes extremely powerful logical functions as well. For example, your employees will claim a certain number of allowances. Based on the number of allowances an employee claims, the amount deducted from the paycheck will be different. This advanced topic will not be covered in this chapter.

When working with Access, there will be times when you need to create arithmetic calculations—using expressions and functions—in your database. In Access 2013, you can add calculations to tables, queries, forms, and reports. Often, rather than storing a calculated value, you would instead store the components of it and calculate the field when necessary. For example, if you have a list price and amount ordered, you would not need to also store the total amount due, because this is the list price multiplied by the amount ordered. Calculating fields rather than storing them will reduce the likelihood of errors and inconsistencies and also save space, as you are storing less information.

In this section, you will learn about the order of operations and how to create a calculated field in a query.

## Creating a Calculated Field in a Query

When creating a query, in addition to using fields from tables, you may also need to create a calculation based on the fields from one or more tables. For example, a table might contain the times when employees clock in and out of work. You could create a calculated field (as defined in an earlier chapter) to determine, or calculate, how many hours each employee worked by subtracting the ClockIn field from the ClockOut field. You create calculated fields in the Design view of a query. A formula used to calculate new fields from the values in existing fields is known as an *expression*. An expression can consist of a number of different elements to produce the desired output. The elements used in an expression may include the following:

- Identifiers (the names of fields, controls, or properties)
- Arithmetic operators (for example, *, /, +, or –)
- Functions (built-in functions like Date or Pmt)
- Values that do not change, known as *constants* (numbers such as 30 or 0.5)

You can use calculations to create a new value based on an existing field, verify data entered, set grouping levels in reports, or help set query criteria.

## Understand the Order of Operations

The *order of operations* determines the sequence by which operations are calculated in an expression. You may remember PEMDAS from a math class, or the mnemonic device "Please Excuse My Dear Aunt Sally." Evaluate expressions in parentheses first, then exponents, then multiplication and division, and, finally, addition and subtraction. Table 3.1 shows some examples of the order of operations. You must have a solid understanding of these rules in order to create calculated fields in Access. Access, like Excel, uses the following symbols:

- Parentheses ( )
- Exponentiation ^
- Multiplication *
- Division /
- Addition +
- Subtraction –

**TABLE 3.1  Examples of Order of Operations**

| Expression | Order to Perform Calculations | Output |
|---|---|---|
| =2+3*3 | Multiply first and then add. | 11 |
| =(2+3)*3 | Add the values inside the parentheses first and then multiply. | 15 |
| =2+2^3 | Evaluate the exponent first, $2^3$=2*2*2 (or 8). Then add. | 10 |
| =10/2+3 | Divide first and then add. | 8 |
| =10/(2+3) | Add first to simplify the parenthetical expression and then divide. | 2 |
| =10*2–3*2 | Multiply first and then subtract. | 14 |

## Build Expressions with Correct Syntax

Expressions are entered in the first row of the query design grid. You must follow the correct *syntax*, which dictates the structure and components required to perform the necessary calculations in an equation or evaluate expressions. You can create expressions to perform calculations using field names, constants, and functions. If you use a field name, such as Balance, in an expression, you must spell the field name correctly; otherwise, Access displays an error. Access ignores spaces in calculations.

For example, if you worked at a company that was planning on allowing customers to pay off their balance in 12 monthly payments, you would divide the balance by 12. However, let's say you wanted to add a 3.5% surcharge. In this case, you would multiply the balance by 0.035 (3.5%) and then divide that total by 12. An example of an expression with correct syntax is:

STEP 1 »

Balance*0.035/12

If you type the preceding function into a line in a query and save the query, you may be surprised to see Access add a few things to the line (see Figure 3.1):

Expr1: [Balance]*0.035/12

Access made a few changes to your entry. First, it removed extra spaces. Secondly, Access added brackets [ ] around the Balance field, which Access uses to indicate a field name. In addition, you see that Access added *Expr1:* to the start of the line. This is how Access assigns a column heading to this field. If you were to run the query, the column heading would be *Expr1.* As this is not a descriptive name, it would probably be better to include your own title. If you wanted to name this column MonthlySurcharge, you would start the expression with the name, followed by a colon, followed by the expression:

MonthlySurcharge: Balance*0.035/12

Field calculates
monthly surcharge

**FIGURE 3.1** Calculated Field
in a Query Design

## TIP | Avoid Spaces in Calculated Field Names

Although you can use spaces in calculated field names, it is a good habit not to use spaces. For example, use NewPrice: [Price]*1.1 rather than New Price: [Price]*1.1. If you avoid spaces in calculated field names, it will be easier to reference these fields in other queries, related forms, and related reports. If you want a column heading to have spaces in it, you should set the Caption property, which will be discussed later in this section.

Again, if you saved the query, Access would add brackets around the Balance field.

In calculated fields, the parts of the formula are usually a constant (for example, 0.035 and 12 in the preceding example), a field name (for example, Balance), or another calculated field. Figure 3.1 shows the MonthlySurcharge field, calculated by multiplying the Balance field by 0.035 (or 3.5%) and dividing by 12. This calculation shows what a customer would pay as a monthly surcharge if you offered him or her the monthly payments and added a 3.5% fee.

The arithmetic operators, the * symbol (multiply) and the / symbol (divide), first multiply [Balance] by 0.035 and then divide the result by 12. There is no real issue in this example with order of operations because the order of operations states that multiplication and division are at the same level of precedence. In other words, if you state 12*3/3, whether you do the multiplication or division first, the result will be exactly the same (12).

The query results, as shown in Figure 3.2, display a decimal number in the MonthlySurcharge column. Notice the results are not formatted well. This will be addressed later in this section.

MonthlySurcharge
shows many digits

**FIGURE 3.2** Results of a
Calculated Field in a Query

Another example of when to use a calculated field is calculating a price increase for a product or service. Suppose you need to calculate a 10% price increase on certain products you sell. You could name the calculated field NewPrice and use the expression (CurrentPrice) + (CurrentPrice × 0.10). The first segment represents the current price, and the second segment adds an additional 10%. (Recall that to get 10% of a number, you would multiply by 0.10.) The expression would be entered into the query design grid as follows:

NewPrice: [CurrentPrice] + [CurrentPrice]*0.10

Note that if you are adept at math, you may find other ways to calculate this increase.

## TIP | Use Zoom (Shift+F2) to View Long Expressions

To see the entire calculated field expression, click the field in Query Design view and press Shift+F2. A new window will appear to enable you to easily see and edit the entire contents of the cell. Access refers to this window as the Zoom dialog box, as shown in Figure 3.3.

Zoom can also be used in a number of other contexts. If you are ever having trouble viewing the entirety of a text box, try using Shift+F2 to expand it. Once you are done modifying a field, click the X in the top-right corner of the Zoom dialog box.

MonthlySurcharge field zoomed in

**FIGURE 3.3** Using Zoom to See an Entire Field

# Formatting and Saving Calculated Results

In the previous example, we saw inconsistent results in the formatting, with some results showing only two decimal places and others showing many decimal places. In Figure 3.2, the MonthlySurcharge field was extremely difficult to read. Part of the purpose of queries is to perform calculations, but an overlooked portion of that is the formatting. You can create a clever calculation, but if it is not labeled and formatted correctly, it may leave your users confused. Spending a few moments formatting your output will make your query more usable.

There is a way to give Access instructions as to how to format the field. You can use the **Property Sheet** to do so. The Property Sheet enables you to change settings such as number format, number of decimal places, and caption, among many others. You can select a predefined format (for example, currency), change the number of decimal places, and also change the caption, as you did in the earlier chapter on tables. To format the calculated results:

STEP 2 >>

1. Open the query in Design view.
2. Click in the calculated field cell (the cell you just created).
3. On the QUERY TOOLS DESIGN tab, click Property Sheet in the Show/Hide group.
4. To change the format, click the *Format property* arrow and select your desired format. For numeric fields, the Decimal Places property will allow you to choose exactly how many decimal places display.

5. To change the caption, click in the text box next to the caption and type your desired column heading. This will override the column name, much like the caption property does for a field name in a table, as shown in a previous chapter.

Formats vary based on the data type. A currency field will have options related to number format, whereas a date/time field will have options related to changing the display of the date and/or time. Figure 3.4 shows the Property Sheet options related to a numeric field.

**FIGURE 3.4** Property Sheet

## Recover from Common Errors

A number of common errors can occur while creating calculated fields. Access may not provide as much assistance as you may be used to in cases like this. The following are three common errors that occur when you begin creating formulas.

STEP 3 >>

- Forgetting the colon between the column title and the formula
  - A correct formula would look like this:

    Expr1: [Balance]*0.035/12

    If you forget the colon, the formula looks like this instead:

    Expr1 [Balance]*0.035/12

    and you will get an error about invalid syntax.
- Typing a field name incorrectly
  - If your field name is Balance and you mistype it, you will not get an error until you attempt to run the query. You may end up with a formula that looks like this:

    Expr1: [Baalnce]*0.035/12
  - When you run the query, you will be prompted by Access to give a value for Baalnce.
- Forgetting the order of operations
  - If you do not check your formulas, you may get bad values. For example, the following would not produce the expected output:

    Expr2: [NumberOfDays] + 7/365
  - If you need addition to be done before division, you must remember the parentheses:

    Expr2: ([NumberOfDays] + 7)/365

## Verify Calculated Results

STEP 4 > After your query runs, look at the field values in the Datasheet view and look at the calculated values. Ask yourself, "Does the data make sense?" Assume you are calculating a mortgage payment for a $300,000 house, with monthly payments for 20 years. If your formula is incorrect, you may end up calculating a monthly payment such as $30,000. If you look at your data, you should say to yourself, "Does it make sense for me to pay $30,000 a month for a mortgage?" or perhaps "Does it make sense that, on a $300,000 loan, my total repayment is $7,200,000 ($30,000 a month times 12 months a year times 20 years)?" In a real-world scenario, you will not be given step-by-step directions, and you will need to apply critical thinking skills to your work. Access will calculate exactly what you tell it to calculate, even if you make logical errors in the calculation. Although it will catch some errors, it will not catch or note logic errors.

Use a calculator to manually calculate some of the results in the calculated fields and compare the answers to the datasheet results. Another method to verify the results is to copy and paste all or part of the datasheet into Excel. Recreate the calculations in Excel and compare the answers to the query results in Access. The Access calculated field, the calculator, and the Excel calculations should all return identical results.

In the first Hands-On Exercise, you will create a query with a calculated field, format the results, learn how to recover from common errors, and verify your results.

*Quick*
Concepts

1. Briefly describe the order of operations. Give an example of how order of operations makes a difference in a calculation. **p. 131**

2. When might you need a calculated field in a query? Give an example. **p. 130**

3. Define syntax. How does Access respond to incorrect syntax? **p. 131**

4. Why is it important to verify calculated results? **p. 135**

# Hands-On Exercises

## 1 Calculations and Expressions

Using the data from the homes for sale lists that Don and Matt acquired, you are able to help them target properties that meet their criteria. As you examine the data, you discover other ways to analyze the properties. You create several queries and present your results to the two investors for their comments.

**Skills covered:** Create a Query with a Calculated Field • Format and Save Calculated Results • Recover from Common Errors • Verify the Calculated Results

## STEP 1 >> CREATE A QUERY WITH A CALCULATED FIELD

You begin your analysis by creating a query using the Properties and Agents tables. The Properties table contains all the properties the investors will evaluate; the Agents table contains a list of real estate agents who represent the properties' sellers. In this exercise, add the fields you need and only show properties that have not been sold. Refer to Figure 3.5 as you complete Step 1.

**FIGURE 3.5** Query Results for Properties NOT Sold

a. Open *a03h1Property*. Save the database as **a03h1Property_LastFirst**.

> **TROUBLESHOOTING:** Throughout the remainder of this chapter and textbook, click Enable Content whenever you are working with student files.

> **TROUBLESHOOTING:** If you make any major mistakes in this exercise, you can delete the *a03h1Property_LastFirst* file, repeat step a above, and then start this exercise over.

b. Open the Agents table and replace *Angela Scott* with your name. Close the table.

c. Click the **CREATE tab** and click **Query Design** in the Queries group to create a new query.

The Show Table dialog box opens so you can specify the table(s) and/or queries to include in the query design.

d. Select the **Agents table** and click **Add**. Select the **Properties table** and click **Add**. Close the Show Table dialog box.

e. Double-click the **FirstName** and **LastName fields** in the Agents table to add them to the design grid.

f. Double-click the **ListPrice**, **SqFeet**, and **Sold fields** in the Properties table to add them to the query design grid.

g. Click **Run** in the Results group to display the results in Datasheet view.

You should see 303 properties in the results.

h. Switch to Design view. Type **No** in the Criteria row of the Sold field.

i. Select **Ascending** from the Sort row of the ListPrice field.

j. Click **Run** to see the results.

You only want to see properties that were not sold. There should now be 213 properties in the datasheet.

k. Click **Save** on the Quick Access Toolbar and type **Price Per Sq Ft** as the Query Name in the Save As dialog box. Click **OK**.

l. Switch to Design view. Click in the top row of the first blank column of the query design grid and use **Shift+F2** to show the Zoom dialog box. Type **PricePerSqFt: ListPrice/SqFeet** and click **OK**.

Access inserts square brackets around the fields for you. The new field divides the values in the ListPrice field by the values in the SqFeet field. The : after *PricePerSqFt* is required.

m. Click **Run** in the Results group to view the results.

The new calculated field, PricePerSqFt, is displayed. Compare your results to those shown in Figure 3.5.

---

**TROUBLESHOOTING:** If you see pound signs (#####) in an Access column, use the vertical lines between column indicators to increase the width.

---

**TROUBLESHOOTING:** If, when you run the query, you are prompted for PricePerSqFt, cancel and return to Design view. Ensure you have entered the formula from step l to the field line of the query, not the criteria line.

---

n. Save the changes to the query and close the query.

# STEP 2 >> FORMAT AND SAVE CALCULATED RESULTS

Don and Matt would like the field formatted differently. You will change the format to Currency and add a caption to the calculated field. Refer to Figure 3.6 as you complete Step 2.

Steps d–e: PricePerSqFt field formatted as Currency with added caption

**FIGURE 3.6** Results of Calculated Field Creation

a. Make a copy of the Price Per Sq Ft query. Name the copy **Price Per Sq Ft Formatted**.

b. Open the Price Per Sq Ft Formatted query in Design view.

c. Click in the **PricePerSqFt calculated field cell**. Click **Property Sheet** in the Show/Hide group on the DESIGN tab.

   The Property Sheet displays on the right side of your screen.

d. Click the **Format box**. Click the **Format property arrow** and select **Currency**.

e. Click in the **Caption box** and type **Price Per Sq Ft**. Press **Enter**. Close the Property Sheet.

f. Click **Run** to view your changes.

   The calculated field values are formatted as Currency, and the column heading displays *Price Per Sq Ft* instead of *PricePerSqFt*.

g. Save the changes to the query.

# STEP 3 >> RECOVER FROM COMMON ERRORS

A few errors arise as you test the new calculated fields. You check the spelling of the field names in the calculated fields because that is a common mistake. Refer to Figure 3.7 as you complete Step 3.

Step g: Same results ($100.00) for every record

**FIGURE 3.7** Results of a Misspelled Field Name

a. Switch to Design view of the Price Per Sq Ft Formatted query. Scroll to the first blank column of the query design grid and click in the top row.

b. Use **Shift+F2** to display the Zoom dialog box. Type **WrongPricePerSqFt: xListPrice/ xSqFeet**. Click the **Close (X) button** in the top-right corner of the Zoom dialog box.

Be sure that you added the extra *x*'s to the field names. You are intentionally misspelling the field names to see how Access will respond. Access inserts square brackets around the field names for you.

c. Click **Property Sheet** in the Show/Hide group of the DESIGN tab. Click the **Format box**. From the menu, select **Currency**. Click in the **Caption box** and type **Wrong Price Per Sq Ft**. Close the Property Sheet.

d. Click **Run** in the Results group.

You should see the Enter Parameter Value dialog box. The dialog box indicates that Access does not recognize xListPrice in the tables defined for this query in the first record. When Access does not recognize a field name, it will ask you to supply a value.

e. Type **100000** in the first parameter box. Press **Enter** or click **OK**.

Another Enter Parameter Value dialog box displays, asking that you supply a value for xSqFeet. Again, this error occurs because the tables defined for this query do not contain an xSqFeet field.

f. Type **1000** in the second parameter box and press **Enter**.

The query has the necessary information to run and returns the results in Datasheet view.

g. Examine the results of the calculation for *Wrong Price Per Sq Ft*. You may have to scroll right to see the results.

All of the records show 100 because you entered the values 100000 and 1000, respectively, into the parameter boxes. The two values are treated as constants and give the same results for all the records.

h. Return to Design view. Press **Shift+F2** to zoom. Correct the errors in the WrongPricePerSqFt field by changing the formula to **WrongPricePerSqFt: [ListPrice]/ [SqFeet]**. Click the **Close (X) button** in the top-right corner of the Zoom dialog box to close it.

i. Run and save the query. Close the query.

The calculated values in the last two columns should be the same.

# STEP 4 >> VERIFY THE CALCULATED RESULTS

Because you are in charge of the Access database, you decide to verify your data prior to showing it to the investors. You use two methods to check your calculations: estimation and checking your results using Excel. Refer to Figure 3.8 as you complete Step 4.

Step e: Column G results should match first 10 results in column F

**FIGURE 3.8** Results Validated in Excel

a. Open the Price Per Sq Ft query in Datasheet view. Examine the PricePerSqFt field.

One of the ways to verify the accuracy of the calculated data is to ask yourself if the numbers make sense.

b. Locate the second record with *Bill Sabey* as the listing agent, an asking price of *$119,990*, and square footage of *1202*. Ask yourself if the calculated value of *$99.83* makes sense.

The sale price is $119,990, and the square footage is 1202. You can verify the calculated field easily by rounding the two numbers (to 120,000 and 1,200) and dividing the values in your head (120,000 divided by 1,200 = 100) to verify that the calculated value, $99.83 per square foot, makes sense.

> **TROUBLESHOOTING:** If the second record is not the one listed above, ensure you have sorted the query by the List Price in ascending order, as specified in Step 1i.

c. Open a new, blank workbook in Excel and switch to Access. Drag over the record selector for the first 10 records (the tenth record has a list price of $163,737). Click **Copy** in the Clipboard group on the HOME tab.

You will verify the calculation in the first 10 records by pasting the results in Excel.

d. Switch to Excel and, click **Paste** in the Clipboard group on the HOME tab.

The field names display in the first row, and the 10 records display in the next 10 rows. The fields are located in columns A–F. The calculated field results are pasted in column F as values rather than as a formula.

> **TROUBLESHOOTING:** If you see pound signs (#####) in an Excel column, use the vertical lines between column indicators to increase the width.

e. Type =C2/D2 in **cell G2** and press **Enter**. Copy the formula from **cell G2** and paste it into **cells G3 to G11**.

The formula divides the list price by the square feet. Compare the results in columns F and G. The numbers should be the same, except for a slight difference due to rounding.

> **TROUBLESHOOTING:** If the values differ, look at both the Excel and Access formulas. Determine which is correct, and then find and fix the error in the incorrect formula.

f. Save the Excel workbook as **a03Property_LastFirst**. Exit Excel.

g. Keep the database open if you plan to continue with the next Hands-On Exercise. If not, close the database and exit Access.

# The Expression Builder and Functions

In the last Hands-On Exercise, you calculated the price per square foot for real estate properties. That simple calculation helped you to evaluate all the properties on the investment list. You were able to type the expression manually.

When you encounter more complex expressions, you can use the *Expression Builder* tool to help you create more complicated expressions. When you create an expression in the field cell, you must increase the column width to see the entire expression. The Expression Builder's size enables you to easily see complex formulas and functions in their entirety. In addition, it provides easy access to objects, operators, functions, and explanations for functions.

In this section, you will learn how to create expressions using the Expression Builder. You also will learn how to use built-in functions.

## Creating Expressions with the Expression Builder

Launch the Expression Builder while in the query design grid to assist with creating a calculated field (or other expression). (See "Launch the Expression Builder" later in this section for directions.) The Expression Builder helps you create expressions by supplying you with the fields, operators, and functions you need to create them. When you use the Expression Builder to help you create expressions, you can eliminate spelling errors in field names. Another advantage is when you are inserting functions; functions require specific arguments in a specific order. When you insert a function using the Expression Builder, the builder gives you placeholders that tell you which values belong where.

You may not always need the Expression Builder. As you become familiar with programs like Access, some of the more common tasks may become second nature to you. Rather than clicking to find what you need, you may be able to do your day-to-day work without the aid of the Expression Builder. However, when working with a less familiar calculation, having this tool gives you extra support.

Though you will learn about the Expression Builder in queries in this chapter, this tool can be used in many other areas. You can also use the Expression Builder when working with forms and reports. For example, if you need to perform a calculation in a form or report, you can launch the Expression Builder to assist you with this task. The same skills you learn here can be applied there as well.

### TIP  Missing Field Names

If you have not yet saved your query, you may not see the names of the fields you are working with. This is especially true of any calculated fields you want to use as part of another expression. If you cannot see a field you need to use, exit the Expression Builder, save the query, and close and reopen the query. Once you reenter the Expression Builder, you should see the missing fields.

### Create an Expression

The left column of the Expression Builder dialog box contains Expression Elements (see Figure 3.9), which include the built-in functions, the tables and other objects from the current database, and common expressions. Select an item in this column.

The middle column displays the Expression Categories based on the item selected in the Expression Elements box (see Figure 3.9). For example, when the Built-In Functions item is selected in the Expression Elements box, the available built-in function categories, such as the Math category, are displayed in the Expression Categories box.

The right column displays the Expression Values, if any, for the categories that you selected in the Expression Categories box (see Figure 3.9). For example, if you click Built-In Functions in the Expression Elements box and click Date/Time in the Expression Categories box, the Expression Values box lists all of the built-in functions in the Date/Time category.

You can create an expression by manually typing text in the expression box or by double-clicking the elements from the bottom section in the Expression Builder dialog box. For example, to create a calculated field using the fields in the tables, type the calculated field name and type a colon. Next, click the desired table listed in the Expression Elements section and double-click the field you want. Click the Operators item in the Expression Elements section and choose an operator (such as + or *) from the Expression Categories section (or just type the operator). The Expression Builder is flexible and will enable you to find what you need while still enabling you to modify the expression manually.

Calculated fields are relatively simple to create, and most Access developers can create them without the Expression Builder. The main reason to use the builder for a calculated field is to eliminate spelling errors in field names. Using functions in Access almost always requires the Expression Builder because the syntax of functions can be difficult to remember. When you double-click the Functions command in the Expression Elements box and click Built-In Functions, the Expression Categories box lists all the available functions in Access. The Expression Values box lists the functions in each of the categories. When you find the function you need, double-click it and the function displays in the expression box. You can see the «placeholder text» where the arguments belong; replace each placeholder text with the argument values, either numbers or fields from a table.

## Launch the Expression Builder

STEP 1 >> To launch the Expression Builder:

1. Open a query in Design view (or create a new query).
2. Verify the QUERY TOOLS DESIGN tab is selected on the Ribbon.
3. Click the top cell of a blank column (also known as the Field cell, because it appears in the row labeled Field) where you would like your expression to appear.
4. Click Builder in the Query Setup group, and the Expression Builder launches (see Figure 3.9). (You can also launch the Expression Builder by right-clicking the cell where you want the expression and selecting Build from the shortcut menu.)

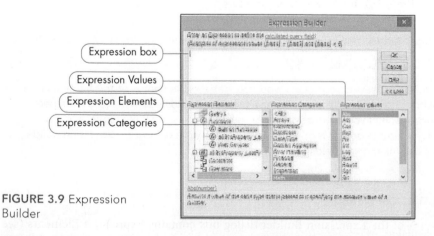

FIGURE 3.9 Expression Builder

5. The top section of the Expression Builder dialog box contains a rectangular area (known as the *expression box*) where you create an expression. You can type your expression in the expression box manually, or you can use the Expression Elements, Expression Categories, and Expression Values in the bottom portion of the Expression Builder. The bottom area allows you to browse for functions, tables, queries, and more. Refer to Figure 3.9.

6. Double-click an item in the *Expression Categories* or *Expression Values* section to add it automatically to the expression box, thus allowing you to use this interface to avoid typographical errors.

7. After you create the expression, click OK to close the Expression Builder window. The expression is then entered into the current cell in the query design grid. From the query design, click Run in the Results group to view the results (in Datasheet view). If the results are incorrect, you can return to Design view and use the Expression Builder again to correct the expression.

# Using Built-In Functions in Access

STEP 2 ❯❯ Similar to Excel, a number of functions are built into Access. A *function* is a predefined computation that performs a complex calculation. It produces a result based on inputs known as arguments. An *argument* is any data that is needed to produce the output for a function. The term *argument*, outside of computers, can mean a fact. For example, in court, you may have a judge ask a lawyer to present his argument. Similarly, Access will need arguments, or facts, to execute a function. Arguments can be a variable (such as a field name) or a constant (such as a number). Some functions require no arguments, but many require at least one. Some functions have optional arguments, which are not required but may be necessary for your task.

Many of the tasks that are built in are tasks that would otherwise be difficult to perform. If you had to figure out the payment of a loan or determine the year portion of a date without functions, it would not be an easy task.

Once you identify what you need a function to do, you can check the Built-In Functions in the Expression Builder to see if the function exists. If it does, add the function to the expression box and replace the «placeholder text» with the argument values. Functions work the same in Access and Excel and other programming languages (such as Visual Basic). There are nearly 150 built-in functions in Access, and many of them will not apply to the task you are performing. Be aware that if you want to perform complex operations, there may be a function that can do it for you. In cases like this, search engines or Microsoft Help are extremely useful. This chapter will demonstrate one function.

## Calculate Payments with the Pmt Function

Figure 3.10 shows the *Pmt function*, which calculates the periodic loan payment given the interest rate per period (for example, monthly), term of the loan (in months), and the original value of the loan (the principal). To use this function, you will need to supply at least three arguments as field names from underlying tables or as constants:

- The first argument is the interest rate per period. Interest rates are usually stated as annual rates, so you will need to convert the annual interest rate to the rate per period. For example, if a loan is paid monthly, you can calculate the rate by dividing the yearly rate by 12.

- The second argument is the number of periods. Because loan terms are usually stated in years, you will need to multiply the number of years by the number of payments per year. For example, a monthly payment would be calculated as the number of years multiplied by 12.

- The third argument is the present value—or principal—of the loan. It is the amount a customer is borrowing.

- The last two arguments—future value and type—are both optional, so they are usually 0 or blank. The future value shows the amount the borrower will owe after the final payment has been made. The type tells Access whether the payment is made at the beginning or the end of the period.

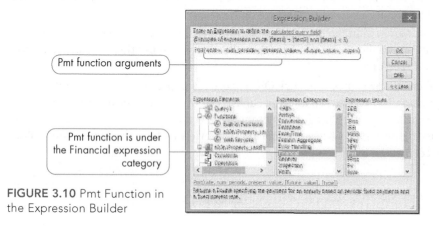

**FIGURE 3.10** Pmt Function in the Expression Builder

The following example shows how to use the Pmt function to calculate the monthly payment on a $12,500 loan, at a 5.0% interest rate, with a four-year loan term.

Function: Pmt(*rate, num_periods, present_value, future_value, type*)

Example: Pmt(0.06/12, 5*12, 12500)

The Pmt function will return a negative value (as a loan payment is considered a debit). If you would like to display this as a positive number, you will need to negate it.

Table 3.2 describes the arguments for the Pmt function in more detail.

## TABLE 3.2 Arguments of the Pmt Function

| Part | Description |
| --- | --- |
| ( ) | Items inside the parentheses are arguments for the function. The arguments are separated by commas. Some arguments are optional; some arguments have a default value. In the Pmt function, the first three arguments are required and the last two are optional. |
| rate | Required. Expression or value specifying interest rate per period, usually monthly. A mortgage with an annual percentage rate of **6.0%** with monthly payments would have a rate entered as **0.06/12**, since the rate of 6% would be entered as .06, and because there are 12 months in a year. A loan with a 4% interest rate paid quarterly would be expressed as .04/4 for the same reason. A common cause of issues with this function is that people forget to divide the annual percentage rate by the number of periods in a year. |
| num_periods | Required. Expression or integer value specifying total number of payment periods in the loan. For example, monthly payments on a five-year car loan give a total of 5 * 12 (or 60) payment periods. Quarterly payments on a six-year loan would give a total of 6 * 4 (or 24) payment periods. |
| present_value | Required. Expression or value specifying the present value of the money you borrow. If you borrow $12,500 for a car, the value would be 12500. |
| future_value | *Optional* (can be left blank). Expression or value specifying the future value after you've made the final payment. Most consumer loans have a future value of $0 after the final payment. However, if you want to save $50,000 over 18 years for your child's education, then 50000 is the future value. Zero is assumed if left blank. |
| type | *Optional* (can be left blank). Value (0 or 1) identifying when payments are due. Use 0 if payments are due at the end of the payment period (the default), or 1 if payments are due at the beginning of the period. Zero is assumed if left blank. |

In the second Hands-On Exercise, you will practice using the Expression Builder to add and modify a field, and use a built-in function.

*Quick Concepts*

1. List two benefits of creating expressions with the Expression Builder. **p. 141**

2. Give an example of a built-in function. **p. 143**

3. What is an argument in a function? Give an example. **p. 143**

4. Describe a scenario where you might use the Pmt function. **p. 143**

# Hands-On Exercises

## 2 The Expression Builder and Functions

When Don and Matt ask you to calculate the price per bedroom and the price per room for each property, you use the Expression Builder to make the task easier. You also add two additional fields that calculate the days on market and the estimated commission for each property.

**Skills covered:** Use the Expression Builder to Add and Modify a Field • Use Built-In Functions

## STEP 1 » USE THE EXPRESSION BUILDER TO ADD AND MODIFY A FIELD

You create a copy of the Price Per Sq Ft Formatted query from the previous Hands-On Exercise and paste it using a new name. You will add a few more calculated fields to the new query. You will create one calculation to determine the price per bedroom for each house. You will create a second field to calculate the price per room. For this calculation, you will assume that each property has a kitchen, a living room, a dining room, and the listed bedrooms and bathrooms. The calculations you will create are shown in Figure 3.11. Your expected output is shown in Figure 3.12.

Step b: ListPriceCalculations query created as copy of PricePerSqFtFormatted query

Steps e–i: PricePerBR calculation

Steps r–u: PricePerRoom calculation

**FIGURE 3.11** Design View of Query

a. Open *a03h1Property_LastFirst* if you closed it at the end of Hands-On Exercise 1 and save it as **a03h2Property_LastFirst**, changing *h1* to *h2*.

b. Create a copy of the Price Per Sq Ft Formatted query with the name **List Price Calculations**.

The new query is displayed in the Navigation Pane. The name of the query suggests it should contain calculations based on each property's list price.

c. Open the List Price Calculations query in Design view. Click the **WrongPricePerSqFt field**. Click **Delete Columns** in the Query Setup group on the QUERY TOOLS DESIGN tab.

> **TROUBLESHOOTING:** If instead of the column being deleted, a new row named *Delete* appears on the bottom half of the screen, close the query without saving, open in Design view once more, and ensure you are clicking Delete Columns in the Query Setup group. If you click Delete under Query Type, you will get very different results.

d. Click in the top cell in the PricePerSqFt column and click **Builder** in the Query Setup group.

The Expression Builder dialog box opens, displaying the current formula.

> **TROUBLESHOOTING:** If the Builder is gray and cannot be clicked, ensure you have clicked in the top cell of the column.

e. Change the PricePerSqFt field name to **PricePerBR**.

f. Double-click the **[SqFeet] field** in the expression and press **Delete**.

g. Click the **plus sign** (+) under Expression Elements, next to the *a03h2Property_LastFirst* database in the Expression Elements box, to expand the list. Click + next to *Tables* and click the table named **Properties**.

The fields from the Properties table are now listed in the middle column (Expression Categories).

h. Double-click the **Beds field** to add it to the expression box.

The expression now reads *PricePerBR: [ListPrice]/[Properties]![Beds]*.

i. Highlight the **[Properties]! prefix** in front of *Beds* and press **Delete**.

The expression now reads *PricePerBR: [ListPrice]/[Beds]*. As the Beds field name is unique within our query, the table name is not necessary. Removing this makes the query easier to read. If a field named Beds appeared in more than one table in our query, removing the table name would cause problems.

j. Click **OK** and click **Run** to view the query results.

Notice the column heading still reads Price Per Sq Ft. Also notice the column's contents are formatted as Currency. These settings were copied when we copied the query.

k. Switch to Design view and ensure the **PricePerBR field** is selected. Click **Property Sheet** in the Show/Hide group and change the **Caption** to **Price Per Bedroom**. Close the Property Sheet. Run the query and examine the changes.

The PricePerBR column now has an appropriate caption.

l. Switch to Design view. Select the entire **PricePerBR expression**, right-click the selected expression, and then select **Copy**. Right-click in the top cell of the next blank column and select **Paste**.

You will edit the copy so that it reflects the price per room. As stated already, you assume the kitchen, living room, dining room, and the bedrooms and bathrooms will make up the number of rooms. Your final formula would be the list price divided by the total number of rooms, which is the number of bedrooms (in the Beds field), plus the number of bathrooms (found in the Baths field), plus 3 (a constant representing the kitchen, living room, and dining room).

m. Click **Builder** in the Query Setup group.

n. Change the PricePerBR field name to **PricePerRoom**.

o. Add **parentheses** before the [Beds] portion of the formula. Type a **plus sign** (+) after *[Beds]*.

As you want the addition to be done first, the order of operations states we must enclose the addition in parentheses. The expression box should read *PricePerRoom: [ListPrice]/([Beds]+*

p. Click the **plus sign** (+) next to the *a03h2Property_LastFirst* database in the Expression Elements box to expand the list. Click the **plus sign** (+) next to *Tables* and click the **Properties table**.

The fields from the Properties table are now listed in the Expression Categories box.

q. Double-click the **Baths field** to add it to the expression box.

The expression now reads *PricePerRoom: [ListPrice]/([Beds]+[Properties]![Baths]*.

**r.** Type another plus sign after *[Baths]* and type **3)**.

The expression now reads *PricePerRoom: [ListPrice]/([Beds]+[Properties]![Baths]+3)*.

**s.** Delete the *[Properties]!* portion of the expression and click **OK** to close the Expression Builder.

The expression now reads *PricePerRoom: [ListPrice]/([Beds]+[Baths]+3)*.

**t.** Click **Property Sheet**. Type **Price Per Room** in the **Caption box**. Close the Property Sheet.

**u.** Run the query. Widen the PricePerRoom column if necessary in order to see all the values.

**FIGURE 3.12** Final Results of Query

**v.** Save and close the query.

---

**TIP** **Switching Between Object Views**

You can switch between object views quickly by clicking View, or you can click the View arrow and select the desired view from the list. Another way to switch between views is to right-click the object tab and select the view from the shortcut menu.

**TIP** **Expression Builder and Property Sheet**

You can launch the Expression Builder by either clicking Builder in the Query Setup group on the Design tab or by right-clicking in the top row of the query design grid and selecting Build. Similarly, you can display the Property Sheet by clicking Property Sheet in the Show/Hide group on the Design tab or by right-clicking the top row of the query design grid and selecting Properties from the shortcut menu.

## STEP 2 >> USE BUILT-IN FUNCTIONS

Don and Matt feel like they are close to making an offer on a house. They would like to restrict the query to houses that cost $150,000 or less. They would also like to calculate the estimated mortgage payment for each house. You create this calculation using the Pmt function. You will use the Pmt function to calculate an estimated house payment for each of the sold properties. You make the following assumptions: 100% of the sale price will be financed, a 30-year term, monthly payments, and a fixed 6.0% annual interest rate. Refer to Figures 3.13 and 3.14 as you complete Step 2.

**FIGURE 3.13** Pmt Function Calculating Mortgage Costs

a. Create a copy of the Price Per Sq Ft Formatted query named **Mortgage Payments**.

The new query is displayed in the Navigation Pane.

b. Right-click **Mortgage Payments** and select **Design View**.

c. Delete the WrongPricePerSqFt field.

The WrongPricePerSqFt field is not needed for this query.

> **TROUBLESHOOTING:** If you do not see the WrongPricePerSqFt field, ensure you copied the correct query.

d. Type <=**150000** in the Criteria row of the ListPrice column. Press **Enter**.

The query, when it is run, will show only the houses that cost $150,000 or less.

e. Click in the top cell of the first blank column. Click **Builder** in the Query Setup group to open the Expression Builder dialog box.

f. Double-click **Functions** in the Expression Elements box and click **Built-In Functions**.

g. Click **Financial** in the Expression Categories box.

h. Double-click **Pmt** in the Expression Values box.

The expression box displays:

*Pmt(«rate», «num_periods», «present_value», «future_value», «type»)*

i. Position the insertion point before the Pmt function. Type **Payment:** to the left of the Pmt function.

The expression box now displays:

*Payment:Pmt(«rate», «num_periods», «present_value», «future_value», «type»)*

> **TROUBLESHOOTING:** If you forget to add the calculated field name to the left of the expression, Access will add *Expr1* to the front of your expression for you. You can edit the Expr1 name later, after the Expression Builder is closed.

**j.** Click each argument to select it and substitute the appropriate information. Make sure there is a comma between each argument.

| Argument | Replacement Value |
|---|---|
| «rate» | 0.06/12 |
| «num_periods» | 360 |
| «present_value» | [ListPrice]*0.8 |
| «future_value» | 0 |
| «type» | 0 |

Note the loan is a 30-year loan with 12 payments per year, hence the 360 value for the number of payments. Also note, Don and Matt plan on financing 80% of the cost, putting 20% down. Therefore, you need to multiply the list price times 0.8 (80%).

**k.** Examine Figure 3.13 to make sure that you have entered the correct arguments. Click **OK**.

**l.** Click **OK**. Open the **Property Sheet** for *Payment* and change the format to **Currency**. Close the Property Sheet. **Run** the query.

Notice the payment amounts are negative numbers (displayed in parentheses). You will edit the formula to change the negative payment values to positive.

**m.** Right-click the **Mortgage Payments tab** and select **Design View**. Click **Builder**. Add a **minus sign** (–) to the left of *[ListPrice]* and click **OK**.

By adding the negative sign in front of the ListPrice field, you ensure the value is displayed as a positive number. The expression now reads *Payment: Pmt(0.06/12,360, –[ListPrice]*0.8,0,0)*.

The calculated field values should now appear as positive values formatted as currency, as shown in Figure 3.14.

> Steps l–n: Payment field displayed as a positive number, formatted as Currency

**FIGURE 3.14** Results of Mortgage Payments Query

**n.** Click **OK**. Run the query and examine the results.

The query displays a column containing the calculated monthly mortgage payment, formatted as currency.

**o.** Save and close the query. Keep the database open if you plan to continue with the next Hands-On Exercise. If not, close the database and exit Access.

# Aggregate Functions

**Aggregate functions** perform calculations on an entire column of data and return a single value. Aggregate functions—such as Sum, Avg, and Count—are used when you need to evaluate a group of record values rather than the individual records in a table or query.

Access refers to aggregate functions as Totals. Totals can be added to the Datasheet view of a query, or they can be added to a query's Design view. Based on the data type, different aggregate functions will be available. Numeric fields are eligible for all of the functions, whereas Short Text fields are not. A list of common aggregate functions is shown in Table 3.4.

A car dealer's monthly inventory report is a good example of a report that might contain aggregate information. The cars would be grouped by model, then by options package and color. At the end of the report, a summary page would list the count of cars in each model for quick reference by the sales reps. In the property database, aggregate information could be grouped by county or by subdivision. For example, the average home price per county could be presented in a query or a report. This would give prospective buyers a good idea of home prices in their target counties. Almost every company or organization that uses a database will require some type of aggregate data.

## TABLE 3.4 Common Aggregate Functions

| Function | Description | Use with Data Type(s) |
|---|---|---|
| AVG | Calculates the average value for a column. The function ignores null values. | Number, Currency, Date/Time |
| COUNT | Counts the number of items in a column. The function ignores null values. | All data types except a column of multivalued lists. |
| MAXIMUM | Returns the item with the highest value. For text data, the highest value is "Z." The function ignores null values. | Number, Currency, Date/Time, Short Text |
| MINIMUM | Returns the item with the lowest value. For text data, the lowest value is "a." The function ignores null values. | Number, Currency, Date/Time, Short Text |
| SUM | Adds the items in a column. Works only on numeric and currency data. | Number, Currency |

In this section, you will learn how to create and work with aggregate functions. Specifically, you will learn how to use the Total row and create a totals query.

## Adding Aggregate Functions to Datasheets

Aggregate functions are most commonly used in tables, queries, and reports. Occasionally, aggregate functions are also added to the *form footer* section of forms. Aggregate data helps users evaluate the values in a single record as compared to the aggregate of all the records. If you are considering buying a property in Bergen County, New Jersey, for $150,000, and the average price of a property in that county is $450,000, you know you are getting a good deal (or buying a bad property).

Access provides two methods of adding aggregate functions to a query—a **Total row**, which displays the results of the aggregate function as the last row in the Datasheet view of a table or query, and a totals query created in Query Design view.

The first method enables you to add a Total row to the Datasheet view. This method is quick and easy and has the advantage of showing the total information while still showing the individual records. Adding a Total row to a query or table can be accomplished by most users, even those who are not familiar with designing a query. Note the Total row values cannot be modified; you can change the aggregate function displayed there, but you cannot overwrite the numbers.

## Add a Total Row in a Query or Table

STEP 1 » Figure 3.15 shows the Total row added to the Datasheet view of a query. You can choose any of the aggregate functions that apply to numeric fields. Follow these steps to add a Total row to a query or table:

1. Ensure you are viewing the query in Datasheet view.
2. Click Totals in the Records group on the HOME tab. The Total row is added at the bottom of the datasheet, below the new record row of the query or table.
3. In the new Total row, you can select one of the aggregate functions by clicking in the cell and clicking the arrow. The list of aggregate functions includes Sum, Avg, Count, and others.

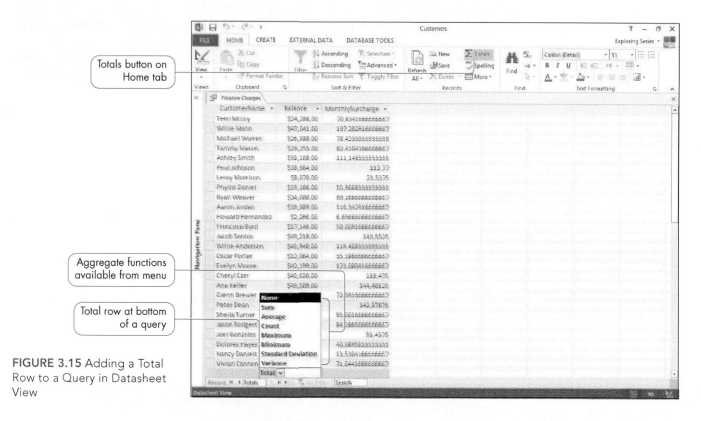

**FIGURE 3.15** Adding a Total Row to a Query in Datasheet View

Callouts:
- Totals button on Home tab
- Aggregate functions available from menu
- Total row at bottom of a query

# Creating Queries with Aggregate Functions

The second method to display aggregate functions requires you to alter the design of a query and add a Total row in the Query Design view. Once the totals data is assembled, you can use it to make decisions. For example, you can use the Count function to show the number of houses sold. You could also use the Avg function to show the average sale price for houses. This method has the advantage of enabling you to group your data by categories.

Many times, you will need to find some sort of averages for fields, and you may need to do more in-depth statistics than just an overall set as we did in the previous few pages. Instead of wanting to see the average sale price for houses, you may want to see the average sale price by city. Using the total row in the previous example, this is not feasible. Another limitation of the previous example is that I might want to see the average sale price, minimum sale price, and maximum sale price. Using the previous method, we would have to put the sale price field into our query three times, leading to repeated columns.

Instead of showing detail, we can quickly see the overall statistics for the entire table or query. For example, if you want to see the number of listings, average value, and the average size in square feet for all properties in your table, you can run a totals query to get that data and not see details. Instead of doing that, we can create a different type of query to summarize our data.

## Create a Basic Totals Query

A *totals query* contains an additional row in the query design grid and is used to display aggregate data when the query is run. Figure 3.16 shows a totals query in Design view, and Figure 3.17 shows the results.

To create a Totals query:

1. Create a query in Design view and add the fields for which you want to get statistics. For example, in the preceding example, we would add the Listing, List Price, and Square Feet fields.
2. Click Totals in the Show/Hide group on the QUERY TOOLS DESIGN tab to display the total row. A new row should display in your query between the Table and Sort options. You will notice it defaults to Group By.
3. For each field, select the menu next to Group By and select the aggregate function you want applied to that field. For example, we want to count the number of listings and average both the list price and square feet values.
4. If you would like to apply specific formats, display the Property Sheet (as we did earlier in this chapter) and adjust the settings for each field.
5. Run the query to see your results.

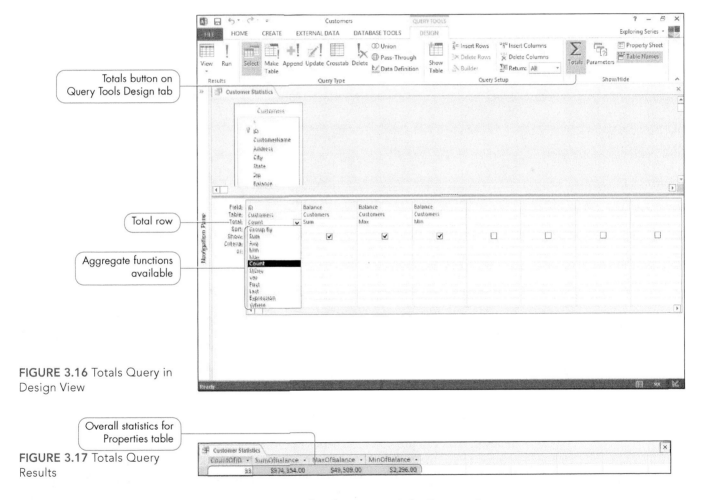

**Totals button on Query Tools Design tab**

**Total row**

**Aggregate functions available**

**FIGURE 3.16** Totals Query in Design View

**Overall statistics for Properties table**

**FIGURE 3.17** Totals Query Results

## Create a Totals Query with Grouping

*Grouping* a query allows you to summarize your data by the values of a field. For example, you want to see the results not for the entire table, but instead by state. You can add the State field as a grouping level, and Access will show you the statistics you request for each state.

To group an existing query, add the field you wish to group by to the query in Design view. You would then verify the Total row displays Group By (see Figure 3.18). So if you want to see the results by state, add the State field to the query and leave the Total with the default of Group By. You may want to move this column to the beginning, as it will make your query easier to read.

Figure 3.18 shows the Design view of a totals query with five columns, one of which is the grouping field. Figure 3.19 shows the results of this query.

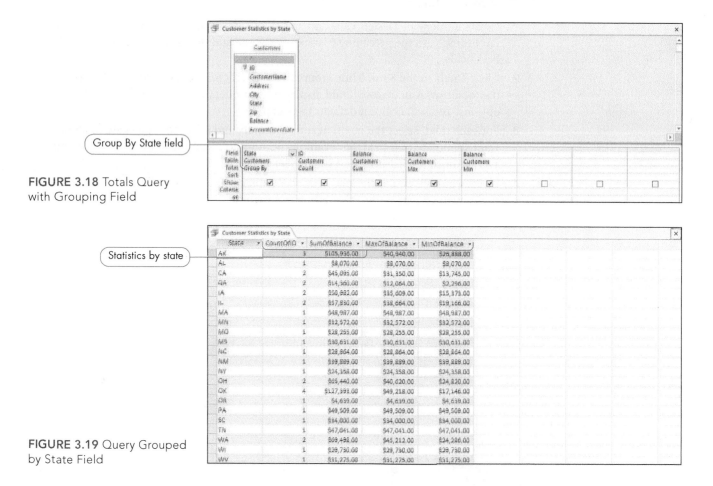

**Group By State field**

**FIGURE 3.18** Totals Query with Grouping Field

**Statistics by state**

**FIGURE 3.19** Query Grouped by State Field

---

## TIP Too Much Grouping

Beware that the more grouping levels you add, the less valuable the data is probably going to be; a typical totals query will group by only a few columns. As the purpose of grouping is to get some sort of aggregate data (such as a sum) for related data, grouping by more fields leads to less data being summarized.

## Create a Totals Query with a Condition

Totals queries can provide even better information if you add criteria. For example, if you wanted to see the number of houses, average price, and average square feet for only the unsold properties, grouped by state, you can add the Sold field to the query. You would set the criteria to No to indicate that the Sold field is no. You should select Where from the menu in the Total row for any field you add to which you wish to apply criteria. Figure 3.20 shows a query with a condition added, and Figure 3.21 shows the results. You can compare this to Figure 3.19 to see the change in results.

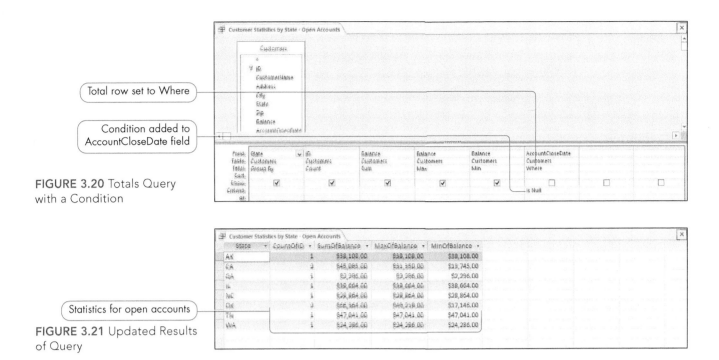

Total row set to Where

Condition added to AccountCloseDate field

FIGURE 3.20 Totals Query with a Condition

Statistics for open accounts

FIGURE 3.21 Updated Results of Query

## Create a Totals Query with Multiple Grouping Levels

At times, you may want to add multiple grouping fields. For example, instead of grouping by State, you might want to group by City. However, if you group by city, customers with the same city name in different states would be grouped together. For example, all 50 states have a location named Greenville. If you grouped by city, all customers with a city of Greenville, regardless of state, would appear as a group. This is probably not your intention. Instead, you probably would want to see results by City and State, and thus would want to add multiple grouping levels. Figure 3.22 shows a second grouping level, and Figure 3.23 shows the results of the query if we group by State and then by City. Notice the multiple Greenville results.

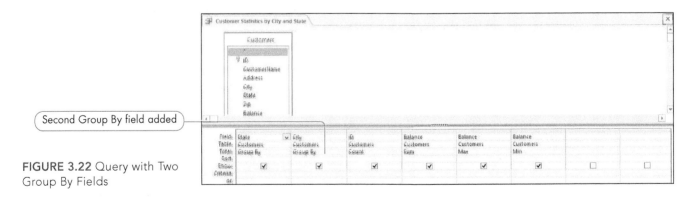

Second Group By field added

FIGURE 3.22 Query with Two Group By Fields

FIGURE 3.23 Results of Query with Two Group By Fields

## Add a Calculated Field to a Totals Query

**STEP 3 »** Once you have created a totals query, you can create calculated fields as you did earlier in the chapter. Often, you will want to apply an aggregate function to an existing field, such as summing up the values in a field. However, there may be times when you would prefer to apply an aggregate function to a calculation rather than a field.

We will use a customer purchases database to demonstrate this. When working with a customer order database, you may have a field for each order containing the total order cost and another field for each order containing the shipping cost. If you use the Sum aggregate function and group by the customer ID, you would have the total amount of their orders, and then as a separate column the total cost of the shipping they have paid. Instead of doing that, you may prefer to first create a calculated field that adds the total order cost and shipping cost for each order, and then group by a CustomerName. You will notice in Figure 3.24 we need to change the total row to Expression. After making that change, your results will resemble Figure 3.25.

FIGURE 3.24 Grouping Query Using a Calculation in a Purchases Database

| Total Bills | |
| --- | --- |
| CustomerName | TotalBill |
| Alice Ray | $588.99 |
| Alicia Byrd | $810.50 |
| Amber Ingram | $506.50 |
| Annette Gibson | $720.99 |
| Arthur Powell | $477.99 |
| Beth Vaughn | $208.99 |
| Carla Black | $478.50 |
| Crystal Delgado | $166.99 |
| Esther Bennett | $198.50 |
| Eva Turner | $673.99 |
| Florence Douglas | $833.99 |
| Frances Foster | $317.50 |
| Gina West | $629.99 |
| Gloria Medina | $615.99 |
| Harold Wolfe | $432.50 |
| Heather Davidson | $343.50 |
| Jamie Wheeler | $243.99 |
| Jeanette Griffin | $436.50 |
| Keith Strickland | $349.50 |
| Lawrence Payne | $390.50 |
| Leonard Delgado | $161.50 |
| Lynn Brooks | $363.50 |
| Marvin Santiago | $757.98 |
| Megan Wheeler | $720.99 |
| Phillip Medina | $676.50 |
| Steve Mills | $674.50 |
| Thelma Burgess | $529.99 |

**FIGURE 3.25** Results of Grouping Query with a Calculation in a Purchases Database

In the third Hands-On Exercise, you will add aggregate functions to datasheets, create a totals query, and add grouping, conditions, and calculated fields to totals queries.

*Quick* Concepts

1. What are the benefits of aggregate functions? Give an example. *p. 151*

2. How do you add a Total row to a datasheet? *p. 152*

3. What is a totals query? *p. 153*

4. What is the difference between a query with a Total row and a totals query? *p. 153*

# Hands-On Exercises

 Watch the Video for this Hands-On Exercise!

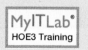 MyITLab® HOE3 Training

## 3 Aggregate Functions

The investors decide it would be helpful to analyze the property lists they purchased. Some of the lists do not have homes that match their target criteria. The investors will either need to purchase new lists or alter their criteria. You create several totals queries to evaluate the property lists.

**Skills covered:** Add Aggregate Functions to Datasheets • Create a Totals Query with Grouping and Conditions • Add a Calculated Field to a Totals Query

## STEP 1 ≫ ADD AGGREGATE FUNCTIONS TO DATASHEETS

You begin your property list analysis by creating a total row in the Datasheet view of the Mortgage Payments query. This will give you a variety of aggregate information for each column. Refer to Figure 3.26 as you complete Step 1.

Step g: Average of PricePerSqFt

Step f: Count of Listing

Step e: Average of ListPrice

Step c: Total row

**FIGURE 3.26** Total Row Added to Query Datasheet

a. Open *a03h2Property_LastFirst* if you closed it at the end of Hands-On Exercise 2 and save it as **a03h3Property_LastFirst**, changing *h2* to *h3*.

b. Right-click the **Mortgage Payments query** in the Navigation Pane and select **Design View**. Drag the **Listing field** from the Properties table to the fifth column.

   The Listing field is now in the fifth column, between the SqFeet and Sold fields. The other columns shift to the right.

> **TROUBLESHOOTING:** If you drag the Listing field to the wrong position, you can drag it again to the correct location.

c. Switch to Datasheet view. Click **Totals**, in the Records group on the HOME tab to display the Total row.

   The Total row displays as the last row of the query results.

d. Click in the cell that intersects the Total row and the List Price column.

e. Click the arrow and select **Average** to display the average value of all the properties that have not sold. Widen the List Price column if you can't see the entire total value.

   The average list price of all properties is $129,799.63.

f. Click the arrow in the Total row in the Listing column and select **Count** from the list.

   The count of properties in this datasheet is 8.

g. Click in the **Total row** in the Price Per Sq Ft column. Click the arrow and select **Average** to display the average price per square foot.

   The average price per square foot is $102.57.

h. Save and close the query.

You create a totals query to help Don and Matt evaluate the properties in groups. Refer to Figure 3.27 and Figure 3.28 as you complete Step 2.

**FIGURE 3.27** Overall Results Query

a. Click **Query Design** in the Queries group of the CREATE tab.

   You create a new query in Query Design; the Show Table dialog box opens.

b. Add the Properties table from the Show Table dialog box. Close the Show Table dialog box.

c. Add the SalePrice and Sold fields from the Properties table to the query design grid.

d. Click **Totals** in the Show/Hide group of the QUERY TOOLS DESIGN tab to show the Total row.

   A new row labeled Totals displays at the bottom of the screen in the design grid, between the Table and Sort rows. Each field will have Group By listed in the new row by default.

e. Click the **Group By arrow** in the SalePrice column Total row and select **Avg.**

f. Click the **Group By arrow** in the Sold column Total row and select **Where.** Type **Yes** in the Criteria row.

   This criterion will limit the results to sold houses only.

g. Click in the **SalePrice field** and click **Property Sheet** in the Show/Hide group. Change the SalePrice format to **Currency.** Close the Property Sheet. Run the query and compare your results to Figure 3.27.

   The results show an overall average of $273,588.34 for the sold properties in the database.

h. Click **Save** on the Quick Access Toolbar and type **Overall Results** as the Query Name in the Save As dialog box. Click **OK.** Close the query.

i. Click **Query Design** in the Query group of the HOME tab to create a new query.

j. Add the Properties table and the Lists table from the Show Table dialog box. Close the Show Table dialog box.

k. Add the NameOfList field from the Lists table and the SalePrice, Listing, and Sold fields from the Properties table to the query design grid.

l. Click **Totals** on the QUERY TOOLS DESIGN tab in the Show/Hide group to show the Total row.

   A new row labeled Total appears at the bottom of the screen in the design grid between the Table and Sort rows.

m. Change the Total row for *SalePrice* to **Avg.**

n. Change the Total row for *Listing* to **Count.**

o. Change the Total row for *Sold* to **Where.** Type **Yes** in the Criteria row.

   This criterion will limit the results to sold houses only.

p. Click in the **SalePrice field** and click **Property Sheet** in the Show/Hide group. Change the SalePrice format to **Currency.**

q. Change the caption of the Listing column to **Number Sold.** Run the query and widen the columns as shown in Figure 3.28.

   Notice Major Houses has the only average sale price under $200,000. As Don and Matt are hoping to focus on inexpensive properties, they will focus on properties offered by this source. Notice the query results show the number of properties sold in each source, in addition to the average sale price. This will help determine which sources have been more effective.

Steps n and q: Count of Listing, with caption of Number Sold

Step k: Grouped by NameOfList

Steps m and p: Average of SalePrice, formatted as Currency

**FIGURE 3.28** Totals Query Results

r. Click **Save** on the Quick Access Toolbar and type **Results By Realtor** as the Query Name in the Save As dialog box. Click **OK**. Keep the query open for the next step.

## STEP 3 ▶ ADD A CALCULATED FIELD TO A TOTALS QUERY

The previous query shows the average value of the properties by realtor. However, Don and Matt learned at the seminar they attended that the longer a property has been on the market, the better your chances of negotiating a better price. You will revise the query to include the average number of days on the market for each realtor. Refer to Figure 3.29 as you complete Step 3.

Step d: Formula entered

Step c: Total row

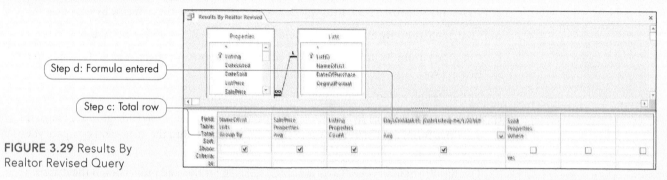

**FIGURE 3.29** Results By Realtor Revised Query

a. Click the **FILE tab**, click **Save As**, and then click **Save Object As**. Click **Save As**, and in the *Save 'Results By Realtor' to:* box, type **Results By Realtor Revised**.

b. Switch to the Datasheet view for the new Results By Realtor Revised query, if necessary.

c. Click **Totals** in the Records group of the HOME tab. Change the Total to **Sum** in the Number Sold column.

The total number of houses sold (90) now displays at the bottom of the Number Sold column.

d. Switch to Design view. In the first blank column, type **DaysOnMarket: [DateListed] – #4/1/2016#** to create a new calculated field. Change the Total row to **Avg**.

The DaysOnMarket field will show the average number of days on the market for each realtor's listings.

e. Display the Property Sheet for the DaysOnMarket field and change the Format property to **Fixed**. Change the Decimal Places property to **0**. Close the Property Sheet.

> **TROUBLESHOOTING:** If you do not see a Decimal Places property immediately beneath the Format property, change the format to Fixed, save and close the query, and then reopen the query. Refer to Figure 3.4 for the location of Decimal Places.

f. Run the query and examine the DaysOnMarket field.

Major Houses listings have an average of 117 days on the market. The combination of inexpensive prices and properties that do not sell quickly may help Don and Matt negotiate with the realtor.

g. Save and close the query.

h. Exit Access. Submit based on your instructor's directions.

# Chapter Objectives Review

After reading this chapter, you have accomplished the following objectives:

1. **Create a calculated field in a query.**
   - Calculations can be based on fields, constants, and/or functions.
   - Understand the order of operations: Calculated fields follow the same order of operations as mathematical equations—parentheses, then exponentiation, then multiplication and division, and finally addition and subtraction.
   - Build expressions with correct syntax: Expressions must be written using proper syntax—the rules governing the way you give instructions to Access.

2. **Format and save calculated results.**
   - Calculated results may not have the format you want; change the properties of a calculated field using the Property Sheet.
   - Recover from common errors: Common errors include forgetting the colon in the appropriate location, spelling errors, and misuse of the order of operations.
   - Verify calculated results: Always check the results of your equation; Access will check for syntax errors, but not logic errors.

3. **Create expressions with the Expression Builder.**
   - Expression Builder helps create complex expressions.
   - Create an expression: Expression Builder allows you to choose fields and built-in functions easily, and gives you a larger screen to view your expression.
   - Launch the Expression Builder: Clicking the Builder button will open the tool.

4. **Use built-in functions in Access.**
   - Access includes functions, or predefined computations that perform complex calculations.
   - There are almost 150 built-in functions in Access.

   - Some require arguments: inputs (often fields or constants) given to a function.
   - Calculate payments with the Pmt Function: The Pmt function accepts the rate per term, number of payments, and loan amount and calculates a loan payment.

5. **Add aggregate functions to datasheets.**
   - Aggregate functions perform calculations on an entire column of data and return a single value.
   - Include functions such as Sum, Avg, and Count.
   - Add a total row in a query or table: The total row displays at the bottom of a query or table; it can perform any aggregate function on each column.

6. **Create queries with aggregate functions.**
   - This gives you more control over application of your aggregate functions.
   - Create a basic totals query: Create a query as usual and click the Totals button in Design view.
   - Create a totals query with grouping: Grouping allows you to summarize your data by the values of a field; instead of showing overall averages, add state as a grouping field and see averages for each state.
   - Create a totals query with a condition: Conditions can be added to totals queries, such as only showing listings with the Sold field equal to No.
   - Create a totals query with multiple grouping levels: You can add multiple grouping levels; for example, you could group by State and then by City to get more detailed results.
   - Add a calculated field to a totals query: You can apply an aggregate function to the results of a calculation; for example, subtract a date from today's date to get the number of days a listing is active and calculate the overall average of days listings are active.

# Key Terms Matching

Match the key terms with their definitions. Write the key term letter by the appropriate numbered definition.

a. Aggregate Function          h. Order of Operations
b. Argument                    i. Pmt Function
c. Constant                    j. Property Sheet
d. Expression                  k. Syntax
e. Expression Builder          l. Total Row
f. Function                    m. Totals Query
g. Grouping

1. _____ A value that does not change. **p. 130**

2. _____ A formula used to calculate new fields from the values in existing fields. **p. 130**

3. _____ Determines the sequence by which operations are calculated in an expression. **p. 131**

4. _____ Dictates the structure and components required to perform the necessary calculations in an equation or evaluate expressions. **p. 131**

5. _____ Enables you to change settings such as number format, number of decimal places, and caption. **p. 133**

6. _____ An Access tool that helps you create more complicated expressions. **p. 141**

7. _____ A predefined computation that performs a complex calculation. Almost 150 are built into Access. **p. 143**

8. _____ Any data needed to produce output for a function. **p. 143**

9. _____ Calculates the periodic loan payment given the interest rate per period, term of the loan in months, and the original value of the loan. **p. 143**

10. _____ Performs calculations on an entire column of data and returns a single value. Includes functions such as Sum, Avg, and Count. **p. 151**

11. _____ Displays aggregate function results as the last row in the Datasheet view of a table or query. **p. 151**

12. _____ Makes an additional row available in the query design grid. Used to display aggregate data when the query is run. **p. 153**

13. _____ Allows you to summarize your data by the values of a field. **p. 153**

# Multiple Choice

1. Which of the following correctly identifies the rules for the order of operations?

   (a) Parentheses, exponentiation, addition, subtraction, multiplication, division

   (b) Exponentiation, parentheses, addition, subtraction, multiplication, division

   (c) Addition, subtraction, multiplication, division, exponentiation, parentheses

   (d) Parentheses, exponentiation, multiplication, division, addition, subtraction

2. What is the result of the following expression?
   $(3 * 5) + 7 - 2 - 6 / 2$

   (a) 17

   (b) 7

   (c) 14.5

   (d) 13

3. Which of the following *cannot* be adjusted in the Property Sheet?

   (a) Number of decimal places

   (b) Mathematical expression

   (c) Caption

   (d) Number format (for example, Currency)

4. Which of the following is *not* an aggregate function?

   (a) Pmt

   (b) Avg

   (c) Count

   (d) Min

5. Which of the following can be added to a totals query?

   (a) Conditions

   (b) Grouping fields

   (c) Aggregate functions

   (d) All of the above can be added to a totals query

6. Which statement about a totals query is *true*?

   (a) A totals query is created in Datasheet view.

   (b) A totals query may contain several grouping fields but only one aggregate field.

   (c) A totals query is limited to only two fields, one grouping field and one aggregate field.

   (d) A totals query may contain several grouping fields and several aggregate fields.

7. Which of the following statements is *true*?

   (a) A total order cost would be a common field to group by.

   (b) A last name would be a common field to group by.

   (c) For best results, add as many group by fields as possible.

   (d) None of the above statements is true.

8. After creating a calculated field, you run the query and a Parameter dialog box appears on your screen. How do you respond to the Parameter dialog box?

   (a) Click OK to make the parameter box go away.

   (b) Look for a possible typing error in the calculated expression.

   (c) Type numbers in the Parameter box and click OK.

   (d) Close the query without saving changes. Reopen it and try running the query again.

9. A query contains student names. You run the query and while in Datasheet view, you notice a spelling error on one of the student's names. You correct the error in Datasheet view. Which statement is *true*?

   (a) The name is correctly spelled in this query but will be misspelled in the table and all other queries based on the table.

   (b) The name is correctly spelled in this query and any other queries, but will remain misspelled in the table.

   (c) You cannot edit data in a query.

   (d) The name is correctly spelled in the table and in all queries based on the table.

10. Which of the following about the Total row in the query design grid is *false*?

    (a) The Total row enables you to apply aggregate functions to the fields.

    (b) The Total row does not display by default in all new queries.

    (c) The Total row is located between the Table and Sort rows.

    (d) The Total row cannot be applied to numeric fields.

# Practice Exercises

## 1 Comfort Insurance

The Comfort Insurance Agency is a mid-sized company with offices located across the country. Each employee receives a performance review annually. The review determines employee eligibility for salary increases and the annual performance bonus. The employee data is stored in an Access database, which is used by the human resources department to monitor and maintain employee records. Your task is to calculate the salary increase for each employee; you will also calculate the average salary for each position. This exercise follows the same set of skills as used in Hands-On Exercises 1 and 2 in the chapter. Refer to Figure 3.30 as you complete this exercise.

FIGURE 3.30 Raises and Bonuses Query

a. Open *a03p1Insurance*. Save the database as **a03p1Insurance_LastFirst**.

b. Examine the Relationships for the database. Notice the table structure, relationships, and fields. Once you are familiar with the database, close the Relationships window.

c. Create a new query in Design view. Add the Employees and Titles tables.

d. Add the LastName, FirstName, Performance, and Salary fields from the Employees table to the query. Add the 2016Increase field from the Titles table to the query.

e. Click the top row of the first blank column in the query design grid and type **NewSalary:[Salary]+[Salary]\*[2016Increase]** to create a calculated field that adds the existing salary to the increase. You may opt to use the Expression Builder if you prefer.

f. Click **Run** in the Results group to run the query. Look at the output in the Datasheet view. Verify that your answers are correct. Notice that the fourth column heading displays *2016 Increase*.

This is the caption for the 2016Increase field in the Titles table that was carried over to the query. When a caption exists for a field in the table Design view, the caption also displays in the Query Datasheet view instead of the field name in the query.

g. Switch back to Design view. Click in the **NewSalary calculated field**, display the Property Sheet, and then change the format to **Currency**. Type **New Salary** in the **Caption box**. Close the Property Sheet.

h. Save the query as **Raises and Bonuses**. Close the query.

i. Create a new query in Design view. Add the Employees and Titles tables.

You will create a query to show the average salary by position.

**j.** Add the TitleName field from the Titles table. From the Employees table, add the Salary field.

**k.** Display the Total row. Change the Total row for Salary to **Avg**. Leave the TitleName field set to **Group By**.

**l.** Click the **Salary field** and display the Property Sheet. Change the format for the field to **Currency**.

**m.** Run the query. Save the query as **Average Salary By Position** and close the query.

**n.** Exit Access and submit based on your instructor's directions.

## 2 Analyze Orders

You are the marketing manager of your company, and you must use the order information from an Access database to analyze sales trends. You need to determine the order revenue for all orders, grouped by Ship Country. The company would also like to check to see if there are order delays related to a specific employee. You must analyze shipping performance based on the number of days it takes to ship each order. This exercise follows the same set of skills as used in Hands-On Exercises 2 and 3 in the chapter. Refer to Figure 3.31 as you complete this exercise.

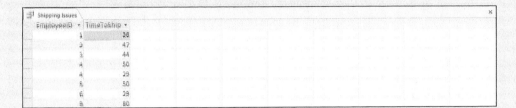

**FIGURE 3.31** Shipping Issues Query

**a.** Create a new blank desktop database named **a03p2Orders_LastFirst**.

You will be shown a blank table in Datasheet view.

**b.** Click **View** in the Views group to switch to Design view. Save the table as **Orders**.

**c.** Change the first Field Name to **OrderID** and change the Data Type to **Number**. Type **CustomerID** in the second row and press **Tab**. Accept **Short Text** as the Data Type. Type **EmployeeID** in the third row and press **Tab**. Select **Number** for the Data Type.

**d.** Type and format the remainder of the fields as follows:

| | |
|---|---|
| OrderDate | Date/Time |
| ShippedDate | Date/Time |
| ShipVia | Number |
| Revenue | Currency |
| ShipCountry | Short Text |

**e.** Click **View** in the Views group to switch to Datasheet view. Click **Yes** to save the table. Add the three records as shown in the following table. Press **Tab** to move to the next field.

| Order ID | Customer ID | Employee ID | Order Date | Shipped Date | Ship Via | Revenue | Ship Country |
|---|---|---|---|---|---|---|---|
| 10248 | WILMK | 5 | 1/6/2017 | 1/19/2017 | 1 | $142.86 | Belgium |
| 10249 | TRADH | 6 | 1/7/2017 | 1/10/2017 | 2 | $205.38 | Germany |
| 10250 | HANAR | 4 | 1/10/2017 | 1/30/2017 | 2 | $58.60 | Venezuela |

**f.** Open the *a03p2Orders* Excel file and click **Enable Editing**, if necessary. Click and hold **row 2** and drag through **row 828** so that all of the data rows are selected. Click **Copy** in the Clipboard group.

**g.** Return to Access and click on the **asterisk (*)** on the fourth row of the Orders table. Click **Paste** in the Clipboard group and click **Yes** to confirm that you want to paste all 827 rows into the Orders table. Save and close the table, and then close the spreadsheet and Excel. If prompted to save the data in the clipboard, click **No**.

**h.** Click the **CREATE tab** and click **Query Design** in the Queries group to start a new query. The Show Table dialog box opens. Add the Orders table and close the Show Table dialog box.

**i.** Add EmployeeID to the query and sort the table by EmployeeID in ascending order.

**j.** Use the Expression Builder to create a new calculated field. Type the following: **TimeToShip: [ShippedDate]-[OrderDate]**

Run the query and verify that TimeToShip is displaying valid values.

**k.** Switch back to Design view. Add the criteria **>21** to the TimeToShip field. Run the query and compare your results with Figure 3.31.

The results do not show a pattern of one employee's orders being delayed.

**l.** Save the query as **Shipping Issues**. Close the query.

**m.** Click the **CREATE tab** and click **Query Design** in the Queries group to start a new query. The Show Table dialog box opens. Add the Orders table and close the Show Table dialog box. Click **Totals** in the Show/Hide group.

**n.** Insert the ShipCountry and Revenue fields from the Orders table.

**o.** Verify the value for ShipCountry is set to **Group By** in the Totals row in Design view and verify that the value for the Revenue field is set to **Sum**.

**p.** Click in the **Revenue field**. Display the Property Sheet and change the caption to **Total Revenue**.

**q.** Click **Run** to see the results and save the query as **Revenue by Ship Country**. Close the query.

**r.** Exit Access and submit based on your instructor's directions.

## 1 Small Business Loans

You are the manager of the small business loan department for the U.S. government. You need to calculate the payments for the loans that are currently on the books. To do this, you will need to create a query and add the Pmt function to calculate the loan payments for each loan. You will also summarize each loan by loan type (M=Mortgage, C=Car, and O=Other). Refer to Figure 3.32 as you complete this exercise.

**FIGURE 3.32** Loan Payments Query Results

a. Open Access and create a new blank desktop database named **a03m1Loans_LastFirst**.

Access will display a table named Table1 with one field, ID.

b. Switch to Design view. Type **Customers** in the **Save As dialog box** and click **OK**.

c. Change the first Field Name to **CustomerID** and accept **AutoNumber** as the Data Type. Type **Company** in the second row and press **Tab**. Accept **Short Text** as the Data Type. Type **FirstName** in the third row and press **Tab**. Accept **Short Text** as the Data Type.

d. Type the remainder of the fields:

| | |
|---|---|
| LastName | Short Text |
| City | Short Text |
| State | Short Text |
| Zip | Short Text |

e. Verify the first field is set as the primary key.

f. Switch to Datasheet view. Click **Yes** to save the table. Add the records as shown in the following table. Note you will allow Access to assign an ID. Once you have entered the records, close the Customers table.

| Company | FirstName | LastName | City | State | Zip |
|---|---|---|---|---|---|
| Jones and Co | Robert | Paterson | Greensboro | NC | 27401 |
| Elements, Inc. | Merve | Kana | Paterson | NJ | 07505 |
| Godshall Meats, LLC | Francisco | De La Cruz | Beverly Hills | CA | 90210 |

g. Click the **External Data tab** and click **Excel** in the Import & Link group. Click **Browse** to locate the *a03m1Loans* spreadsheet. Select the database and click **Open** at the bottom of the dialog box.

h. Ensure the *Import the source data into a new table in the current database option* is selected and click **OK**. Click **Next** three times, until you are asked to add a primary key. From the *Choose my own Primary Key* menu, select **LoanID** (this should be the default option). Click **Next** once more and click **Finish**. Click **Close** in the Save Import Steps dialog box.

i. Open the Loans table in Design view. Select the **InterestRate field** and change the format to **Percent**. Change the field size for the CustomerID field to **Long Integer**. Click **Yes** when prompted that some data may be lost. Save and close the table.

j. Click the **Database Tools tab** and click **Relationships** in the Relationships group. Add both tables to the Relationships window and close the Show Table dialog box.

k. Drag the **CustomerID field** from the Customers table and drop it onto the CustomerID field in the Loans table. Check the **Enforce Referential Integrity check box** in the Edit Relationships dialog box and click **Create**. Save and close the Relationships window.

l. Create a query using the two tables that will calculate the payment amount for each loan. Add the following fields: **Company, LoanID, Amount, InterestRate, Term**, and **LoanClass**. Sort the query by LoanID in ascending order. Save the query as **Loan Payments**.

m. Add a calculated field named **Payment** in the first blank column to calculate the loan payment for each loan, using the Expression Builder. Use the Pmt function. Insert the appropriate field names in place of the placeholder arguments. Assume the loans have monthly payments (12 payments per year). Ensure the payment displays as a positive number. Run the query.

The first loan should have a value of approximately $243.15 (the extra decimal places will be removed shortly). Refer to Figure 3.32. If your number does not match up, reexamine your formula.

> **TROUBLESHOOTING:** If you cannot see the fields from your current query, ensure you have saved the query. Try closing and reopening the query.

n. Switch to Design view and change the display to **Currency format**. Run the query again to verify your changes. Compare your results to Figure 3.32.

o. Switch to Datasheet view and add a **Totals row**. Use it to calculate the sum of the amount column, the average interest rate, and the average term. Save and close the query.

p. Create a copy of Loan Payments. Save the new query as **Loan Payments Summary**.

q. Open the Loan Payments Summary query in Design view and rearrange the columns as follows: LoanClass, LoanID, Amount, and InterestRate. Delete columns CompanyName, Term, and Payment. Click **Totals** in the Show/Hide group. Change the Total row from left to right as follows: Group By, Count, Sum, and Avg. Run the query.

As we sorted the previous query by LoanID in Ascending order, this query will have the same sort by default.

r. Switch to Design view and display the Property Sheet. For the LoanID field, change the caption to **Loans**. For the Amount field, change the caption to **Total Amount** and change the format to **Currency**. For the InterestRate field, change the caption to **Avg Interest Rate** and change the format to **Percent**. Run the query. Save and close the query.

s. Exit Access, and submit based on your instructor's directions.

## 2 Investment Properties

You are in charge of LGS Investment's database, which contains all of the information on the properties your firm has listed and sold. Your task is to determine the length of time each property was on the market before it sold. You also need to calculate the sales commission from each property sold. Two agents will receive commission on each transaction: the listing agent and the selling agent. You also need to summarize the sales data by employee and calculate the average number of days each employee's sales were on the market prior to selling and the total commission earned by the employees. Refer to Figure 3.33 as you complete this exercise.

FIGURE 3.33 Sales Summary
Query

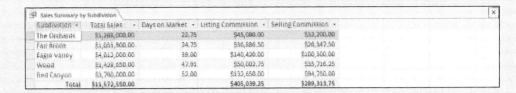

a. Open *a03m2Homes*. Save the database as **a03m2Homes_LastFirst**.

b. Create a new query, add the necessary tables, and then add the following fields: from the Agents table, add the LastName field; from the Properties table, the DateListed, DateSold, SalePrice, SellingAgent, and ListingAgent fields; and from the SubDivision table, the Subdivision field.

c. Add criteria to the table to ensure the DateSold field is not empty (in other words, properties that have not been sold). Format the SalePrice field as **Currency**. Save the query as **Sales Report**.

d. Create a calculated field using the Expression Builder named **DaysOnMarket** by subtracting DateListed from DateSold. This will calculate the number of days each sold property was on the market when it sold. Add a caption of **Days on Market**.

e. Calculate the commissions for the selling and listing agents using two calculated fields. The listing commission rate is **3.5%** of the sale price, and the selling commission rate is **2.5%** of the sale price. You can type these in directly or use the Expression Builder. Name the newly created fields **ListComm** and **SellComm**. These fields contain similar expressions. They need to be named differently so that the proper agent—the listing agent or the selling agent—gets paid. Add captions and format the fields as **Currency**.

f. Save the query after you verify that your calculations are correct. In Datasheet view, add the Total row. Calculate the average number of days on the market and the sum for the SalePrice and the two commission fields. Save and close the query.

g. Create a copy of the Sales Report query named **Sales Summary by Last Name**. Remove the DateListed, SellingAgent, ListingAgent, and Subdivision fields.

h. Display the Total row. Group by LastName and change the DateSold field Total row to **Where**, so the condition carries over. Show the sum of SalePrice, the average of DaysOnMarket, and the sum for both ListComm and SellComm. Change the caption for the SalePrice field to **Total Sales** and format the DaysOnMarket field as **Fixed**. Run the query. Adjust column widths as necessary.

i. Adjust the Total row in the Datasheet view so it shows the sum of TotalSales. Save the query.

j. Create a copy of the Sales Summary by Last Name query named **Sales Summary by Subdivision**. Modify the query so the grouping is based on the Subdivision field, not LastName. Sort the query results so the fewest Days on Market is first and the most Days on Market is last. Limit the results to the top five rows.

k. Exit Access and submit based on your instructor's directions.

## 3 Political Pollsters

You are working with a group that would like to analyze survey results. You are specifically looking for trends in the data based on gender, political affiliation, and income level. To demonstrate the power of Access, you and your group will perform a small survey, add the results to a database, and create some queries to demonstrate how grouping can help get results.

a. Individually, open the *a03t1Survey.docx* file. Collect 10 responses each (unless directed to do otherwise by your instructor). You should try to survey a diverse group of people. You can do this survey via e-mail, Facebook, or another appropriate method. Bring the collected data to your group.

b. Open the *a03t1Survey* database and save the database as **a03t1Survey_GroupName**. Use the Enter New Survey Result form to enter all of your information into the existing database. There are four records to start your database.

**c.** Open the Questions By Gender query. Notice your average for question 1 is a number between 1 and 3. As your survey document listed Agree as a 3, Neutral as 2, and Disagree as 1, the higher the value, the more strongly people agree with the question. Modify the query so that you display the average of Question2, Question3, Question4, and Question5. Change the format for the new fields to **Fixed**.

**d.** Create a query named **Questions By Party**, using the Questions By Gender query as a guide, grouping by the PoliticalAffiliation field rather than the Gender field.

**e.** Create a query named **Questions By Income Level**, using the Questions By Gender query as a guide, grouping by the IncomeLevel field rather than the Gender field.

**f.** Examine your results. Discuss the results with your group and type up your conclusions in a new Word document named **a03t1SurveyResults_GroupName**. You should be able to make around five conclusions. An example of a conclusion might be that people of lower income levels are less interested in being taxed to support free Internet than people of higher income.

**g.** Exit Access and Word and submit based on your instructor's directions.

# Beyond the Classroom

## Too Many Digits

RESEARCH CASE

This chapter introduced you to calculated fields. Open the database *a03b2Interest* and save the database as **a03b2Interest_LastFirst**. Open the Monthly Interest query in Datasheet view. Notice the multiple digits to the right of the decimal in the Monthly Interest column; there should only be two digits. Search the Internet to find a function that will resolve this rounding problem. You only want to display two digits to the right of the decimal (even when you click on a Monthly Interest value). Apply your changes to the Monthly Interest field, change the format to **Currency**, and then run the query to test your changes. Save the query as **Monthly Interest Revised**. If you manage to find a solution, add a second column named **MonthlyInterestRounded** that rounds to the nearest dollar. Close the query, close the database, and then exit Access. Submit your work based on your instructor's directions.

## Payroll Summary Needed

DISASTER RECOVERY

You were given an Excel spreadsheet that contains paycheck information for your company. Your task is to summarize this data by employee Social Security Number (SSN) and report your results to your supervisor. Open the spreadsheet *a03b3Paychecks* and examine the data. Select all the data and copy the data. You will use Access to summarize the data in this spreadsheet. Open the Access database named *a03b3Payroll* and save it as **a03b3Payroll_LastFirst**. Open the Payroll table, select the first row, and then paste the records. Create a new totals query that summarizes the data by SSN; include the count of pay periods (using the ID field) and the sum of each currency field. Do not include the PayDate field in this query. Create a calculated field named **Total Compensation**, which totals all assets the employees have, including pay, 401(k) retirement, and health benefits. Add appropriate captions to shorten the default captions. Run the query and save it as **Payroll Summary**. Close the query, close the database, and then exit Access. Submit the database based on your instructor's directions.

## Customer Service Dialog

SOFT SKILLS CASE

Passaic County Technology Services (PCTS) provides technical support for a number of local companies. Part of their customer service evaluation involves logging how calls are closed and a quick, one-question survey given to customers at the end of a call, asking them to rate their experience from 1 (poor) to 5 (excellent). To evaluate the effectiveness of their operation, they have asked you to create some queries to help evaluate the performance of the company. Open the database *a03b4PCTS* and save the database as **a03b4PCTS_LastFirst**.

1. Create a query to show each technician and his or her effectiveness.

   - List each technician's first and last names, the number of calls, and the average of the customer's satisfaction for all calls assigned to the rep.
   - Format the average in Standard format and sort by the average so the highest average customer satisfaction appears first.
   - Save the query as **Tech Effectiveness**.

2. Create a query to show how effective the company is by call type.

   - List the call type's description (for example, Hardware Support) and the number of calls and average customer satisfaction for all calls of that type.
   - Format the average in Standard format and sort by the average so the highest average customer satisfaction appears first.
   - Save the query as **Call Type Effectiveness**.

**3.** Create a query to show how satisfied each customer is.

- List the company name and the number of calls and average customer satisfaction for all calls.
- Format the average in Standard format and sort by the average so the highest average customer satisfaction appears first.
- Save the query as **Customer Happiness**.

Now that you have created these queries, your supervisor should be able to quickly determine which technicians have the happiest customers, which call types the company is most effective on, and which customers are less happy than others. Close the queries, close the database, and then exit Access. Submit the database based on your instructor's directions.

# Capstone Exercise

Northwind Traders, an international gourmet food distributor, is concerned about shipping delays over the past six months. Review the orders over the past six months and identify any order that was not shipped within 30 days. Each customer that falls within that time frame will be called to inquire about any problems the delay may have caused. In addition, you will create an order summary and an order summary by country.

## Database File Setup

Open the food database, use Save As to make a copy of the database, and then use the new database to complete this capstone exercise. You will add yourself to the employee database.

a. Locate and open *a03c1Food* and save the database as **a03c1Food_LastFirst**.

b. Open the Employees table. Add yourself as an employee. Fill in all information, with the hire date as today. Set your *Title* to **Technical Aide**, extension to **1144**, and the Reports To field to **Buchanan, Steven**. Leave the EmployeePicture field blank.

c. Close the Employees table.

## Shipping Efficiency Query

You need to create a query to calculate the number of days between the date an order was placed and the date the order was shipped for each order. As you create the query, run the query at several intervals so you can verify that the data look correct. The result of your work will be a list of orders that took more than three weeks to ship. The salespeople will be calling each customer to see if there was any problem with their order.

a. Create a query using Query Design. From the Customers table, include the fields CompanyName, ContactName, ContactTitle, and Phone. From the Orders table, include the fields OrderID, OrderDate, and ShippedDate.

b. Run the query and examine the records. Save the query as **Shipping Efficiency**.

c. Add a calculated field named **DaysToShip** to calculate the number of days taken to fill each order. (*Hint*: The expression will include the OrderDate and the ShippedDate; the results will not contain negative numbers.)

d. Run the query and examine the results. Does the data in the DaysToShip field look accurate? Save the query.

e. Add criteria to limit the query results to include any order that took more than 30 days to ship.

f. Add the Quantity field from the Order Details table and the ProductName field from the Products table to the query. Sort the query by ascending OrderID. When the sales reps contact these customers, these two fields will provide useful information about the orders.

g. Switch to Datasheet view to view the final results. This list will be distributed to the sales reps so they can contact the customers. In Design view, add the caption **Days to Ship** to the DaysToShip field.

h. Save and close the query.

## Order Summary Query

You need to create an Order Summary that will show the total amount of each order in one column and the total discount amount in another column. This query will require four tables: Orders, Order Details, Products, and Customers. Query to determine if employees are following the employee discount policy. You will group the data by employee name, count the orders, show the total dollars, and show the total discount amount. You will then determine which employees are following the company guidelines.

a. Create a query using Query Design and add the four tables above. Add the fields OrderID and OrderDate. Set both fields' Total row to **Group By**.

b. Add a calculated field in the third column. Name the field **ExtendedAmount**. This field should multiply the number of items ordered by the price per item. This will calculate the total amount for each order. Format the calculated field as **Currency** and change the caption to **Total Dollars**. Change the Total row to **Sum**.

c. Add a calculated field in the fourth column. Name the field **DiscountAmount**. The field should multiply the number of items ordered, the price per item, and the discount field. This will calculate the total discount for each order. Format the calculated field as **Currency** and add a caption of **Discount Amt**. Change the Total row to **Sum**.

d. Run the query. Save the query as **Order Summary**. Return to Design view.

e. Add criteria to the OrderDate field so only orders made between 1/1/2016 and 12/31/2016 are displayed. Change the Total row to **Where**. This expression will display only orders that were created in 2016.

f. Run the query and view the results. Save and close the query.

## Order Financing Query

Northwind is considering offering financing options to their customers with 5% interest, to be paid over 12 months.

a. Create a copy of the Order Summary query named **Order Financing**.

b. Switch to Design view of the new query and remove the DiscountAmount field.

c. Add a new field using the Expression Builder named **SamplePayment**. Insert the Pmt function with the following parameters:

- Use **.05/12** for the rate argument (5% interest, paid monthly)

- Use the number **12** for the num_periods argument (12 months)

- Use the calculated field **ExtendedAmount** for the present_value

**d.** Change the Total row to **Expression** for the SamplePayment field.

**e.** Change the Format for the SamplePayment field to **Currency**.

**f.** Save and close the query.

## Order Summary by Country Query

You need to create one additional query based on the Order Summary query you created in a previous step. This new query will enable you to analyze the orders by country.

**a.** Create a copy of the Order Summary query named **Order Summary by Country**.

**b.** Replace the OrderID field with the Country field in Design view of the new query.

**c.** Run the query and examine the summary records; there should be 21 countries listed.

**d.** Switch to Design view and change the sort order so that the country with the highest ExtendedAmount is first and the country with the lowest ExtendedAmount is last.

**e.** Run the query and verify the results.

**f.** Save and close the query.

**g.** Exit Access and submit based on your instructor's directions.

# Creating and Using Professional Forms and Reports

CHAPTER 4

## Moving Beyond Tables and Queries

Yuri Arcurs/Shutterstock

## OBJECTIVES    AFTER YOU READ THIS CHAPTER, YOU WILL BE ABLE TO:

1. Create forms using form tools p. 176
2. Use form views p. 183
3. Work with a form layout control p. 186
4. Sort records in a form p. 188

5. Create reports using report tools p. 196
6. Use report views p. 203
7. Modify a report p. 205
8. Sort records in a report p. 208

## CASE STUDY | Coffee Shop Starts New Business

The La Vida Mocha coffee shop in Paterson, New Jersey, once was an ordinary coffee shop selling retail coffee, tea, and pastries to its loyal customers in northern New Jersey. Then, in 2012, owner Ryung Park decided to use her knowledge of the coffee industry to sell coffee products to businesses in her area. This new venture grew quickly and soon became 25% of her annual revenue. Realizing that this new business would need more of her time each day, she decided to create an Access database to help track her customer, product, and order information.

With the help of a student from Passaic County Community College, she created a database with tables to hold data for customers, products, sales reps, and orders. She is currently using these tables to enter and retrieve information.

Ryung wants to have one of her employees, Nabil, manage the database. However, she does not want him to work in the tables; she wants him to work with forms. Ryung heard that forms have an advantage over tables because they can be designed to show one record at a time—this will reduce data-entry errors. Ryung would also like to create several reports for her own benefit so she can stay on top of the business by reviewing the reports each week.

You have been hired to help Ryung create the new forms and reports that she needs for the business. She will describe the forms and reports to you in detail and also provide written instructions. You will be expected to work independently to create the forms and reports.

# Form Basics

A *form* is a database object that is used to add data into or edit data in a table. Most Access database applications use forms rather than tables for data entry and for looking up information. Three main reasons exist for using forms rather than tables for adding, updating, and deleting data. They are:

- You are less likely to edit the wrong record by mistake.
- You can create a form that shows data from more than one table simultaneously.
- You can create Access forms to match paper forms.

If you are adding data using a table with many columns, you could jump to the wrong record in the middle of a column accidentally. For example, you could enter the data for one record correctly for the first 10 fields but then jump to the row above and overwrite existing data for the remaining field values unintentionally. In this case, two records would have incorrect or incomplete data. A form will not allow this type of error because most forms restrict entry to one record at a time.

Many forms require two tables as their record source. For example, you may want to view a customer's details (name, address, e-mail, phone, etc.) as well as all of the orders he or she has placed. This would require using data from both the Customers and the Orders tables in one form. Similarly, you may want to view the header information for an order while also viewing the detail line items for the order. This would require data from both the Orders and Order Details tables. Both of these examples enable a user to view two record sources at the same time and make changes—additions, edits, or deletions—to one or both sources of data.

Finally, when paper forms are used to collect information, it is a good idea to design the electronic forms to match the paper forms. This will make data entry more efficient and reliable and ease the transition from paper form to computer form. Access forms can be designed to emulate the paper documents already in use in an organization. This facilitates the simultaneous use of both paper forms and electronic data. Databases do not necessarily eliminate paper forms; they supplement and coexist with them.

In this section, you will learn the basics of form design. You will discover multiple methods to create and modify Access forms.

# Creating Forms Using Form Tools

Access provides a variety of options for creating forms. There are a number of built-in layouts that you can choose from. Database designers may eventually develop a preference for one or two types of form layouts, but keep in mind you have a lot of options if needed. You will want to find a balance between creating a form that is simple while still powerful enough to be of use.

Access provides 14 different tools for creating forms. You can find these options in the Forms group on the Create tab. The Forms group contains four of the most common form tools (Form, Form Design, Blank Form, and Form Wizard), a list of Navigation forms, and More Forms, as shown in Figure 4.1. Navigation forms provides a list of six templates to create a user interface for a database; the More Forms command lists four additional form tools (Multiple Items, Datasheet, Split Form, and Modal Dialog). Select a table or query, click one of the tools, and Access will create a form using the selected table or query. The most common of these tools, the *Form tool*, is used to create data-entry forms for customers, employees, products, and other primary tables.

**FIGURE 4.1** Forms Group on Create Tab

A complete list of all the Form tools available in Access is found in the Form Tools Reference at the end of this section. Many of the tools will be covered in this chapter. Some tools will not be covered, however, because they are not commonly used or because they are beyond the scope of this chapter (e.g., Form Design, Blank Form, Navigation forms, and Modal Dialog form). Use Microsoft Access Help to find more information about Form tools not covered in this chapter.

## TIP  Usability Testing

After a database object (such as a form) is finalized, it should be tested by both the database designer and the end users. The designer should be certain the report meets any criteria the users have given him or her. The designer should also browse through the records to make sure the values in all records (and not just the first record) display correctly. Likewise, the end users should have the opportunity to test the form and provide feedback. After all, they will be the ones using it, so the database designer has a responsibility to ensure the end users are comfortable with the object.

Ideally, a form should simplify data entry. Creating a form is a collaborative process between the form designer and the form users. This process continues throughout the life of the form, because the data needs of an organization may change. Forms designed long ago to collect information for a new customer account may not have an e-mail field; the form would have to be modified to include an e-mail field. The form designer needs to strike a balance between collecting the information users need to do their jobs and cluttering the form with extraneous fields. The users of the data know what they need and usually offer good feedback about which fields should be on a form. If you listen to their suggestions, your forms will function more effectively, the users' work will be easier, and your data will contain fewer data-entry errors.

After discussing the form with the users, it will help you to create the form in Access if you sketch the form first. After sketching the form, you will have a better idea of which form tool to use to create the form. After the form is created, use the sketch to determine which fields are required and in what the order of fields should be.

## Identify a Record Source

Before you create a form, you must identify the record source. A **record source** is the table or query that supplies the records for a form or report. You may also see the record source referred to as a data source in certain help files and instructions. Use a table if you want to include all the records from a single table. Use a query if you need to filter the records in a table, if you need to combine records from two or more related tables, or if you do not want to display all fields.

For example, if a sales rep wants to create a form that displays customers from a single state only—where his customers reside—he should base the form on a query. Or, if a parts manager needs to review only parts with a zero on-hand quantity, he could create a form based on a query that includes only records with on-hand equal to zero.

## Use the Form Tool

STEP 1 ≫  As noted earlier, the Form tool is the most common tool for creating forms. To use the Form tool:

1. Select a table or query from the Navigation Pane
2. On the CREATE tab, in the Forms group, click Form.

Based on that table or query, Access automatically creates a new form. You may need to modify the form slightly, but you can create a stacked layout form in a just one click. A *stacked layout* displays fields in a vertical column. Because this is a form, it will display one record at a time, as shown in Figure 4.2. The other type of layout you may use is a *tabular layout*, which displays data horizontally across the page.

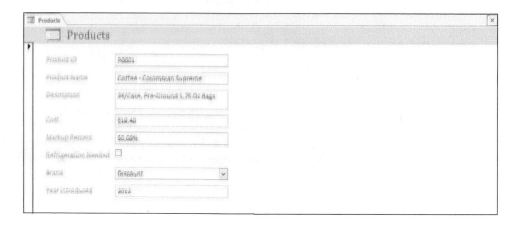

**FIGURE 4.2** Form with a Stacked Layout

## Understand Controls

Notice in Figure 4.3 that each field has a label on the left and a text box on the right. These are referred to as controls. *Controls* are the text boxes, buttons, boxes, and other tools you use to add, edit, and display the data in a form or report. In Figure 4.3, Product ID, Product Name, Description, and the rest of the field labels are controls. In addition, the boxes containing the values for each field (P0001, Coffee–Colombian Supreme, etc.) are all controls. More specifically, the form locations that hold data are generally text box controls, and the text in front of those, marking what the field means, are label controls.

**FIGURE 4.3** Form Controls

A *layout control* provides guides to help keep controls aligned horizontally and vertically and give your form a uniform appearance. The fields are all aligned in Figure 4.3 because a layout control keeps them that way. Picture the layout control as a bookcase, with each field being a shelf on the bookcase.

## Work with Form Views

There are three different views of a form available. The first, *Form view*, is a simplified interface primarily used for data entry. This view does not enable you to make changes to the layout. As such, the Form view is an excellent way for users to interact with the form. This ensures they do not accidentally change the form layout. Figure 4.4 shows a form in Form view. Notice forms can include features such as drop-down lists.

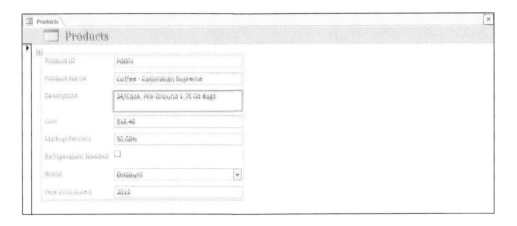

Forms may include drop-down lists

**FIGURE 4.4** Form in Form View

The second view, *Layout view,* enables users to make changes to the layout while viewing the data on the form. Reports have a similar view with the same name. This will be discussed later in the chapter. Layout view is useful for testing the functionality of the form and adjusting sizes of fields as needed. In the previous section, you were shown how to create a form using the Form Tool. When you do this, Access opens the form in Layout view ready for customizing. Figure 4.5 shows a form in Layout view.

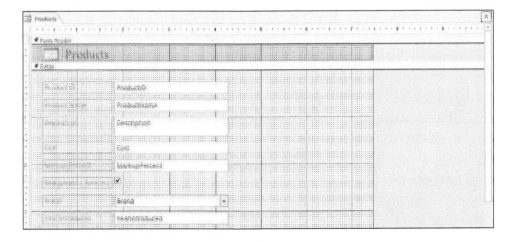

**FIGURE 4.5** Form in Layout View

The third view, *Design view,* allows you to change advanced design settings you cannot see in the Layout view, such as a background image. Reports also have a Design view, which will also be discussed later in this chapter. Design view is a much more powerful way of changing the form layout. It is more complex than Layout view, so you would likely use Design view only when you need to perform advanced form layout adjustments. Figure 4.6 shows a form in Design view.

**FIGURE 4.6** Form in Design View

These three views will be described in more detail later in this chapter.

## Work with a Subform

When you use the Form tool to create a form, Access analyzes the table relationships you created in the database. If the table that the main form is based upon is related to another table through a relationship, then Access automatically adds a subform to the main form. The subform displays records in the related table, generally laid out in a table, similar to an Excel spreadsheet. For example, assume you have sales representatives stored in a SalesReps table and customer information stored in a Customers table. Also assume a relationship exists between the two tables. If you create a new form based on SalesReps using the Form tool, Access will add a Customers subform to the bottom of the main form, showing all customers assigned to each sales representative (see Figure 4.7).

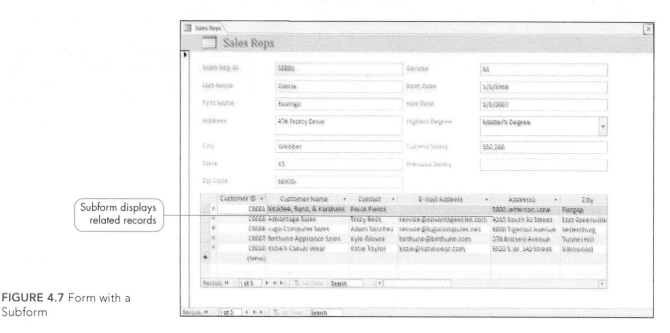

Subform displays related records

**FIGURE 4.7** Form with a Subform

At times, you may want the subform as part of your form; at other times, you may want to remove it. To remove a subform from a form:

1. Switch to Design view.
2. Click anywhere inside the subform.
3. Press Delete.

## Create a Split Form

A **split form** combines two views of the same record source—one section is displayed in a stacked layout (form view) and the other section is displayed in a tabular layout (datasheet view). By default, the form view is positioned on the top and the datasheet view is displayed on the bottom; however, the form's page orientation can be changed from horizontal to vertical in Layout view. If you select a record in the top half of the form, the same record will be selected in the bottom half of the form and vice versa. For example, if you create a split form based on an Orders table, you can select an Order in the datasheet section and then see the order's information in the *Form view* section (see Figure 4.8). This gives you the option to enter data in the Form view while being able to navigate between orders more quickly. The top and bottom halves are synchronized at all times.

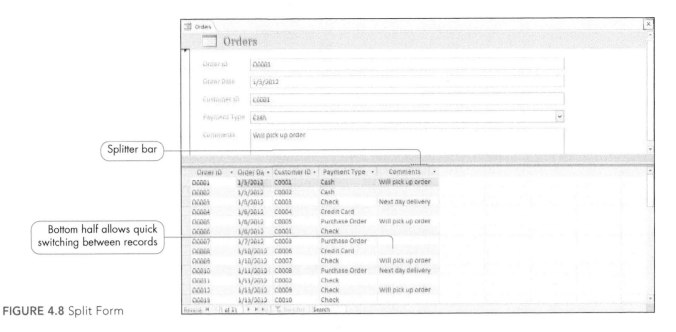

Splitter bar

Bottom half allows quick switching between records

**FIGURE 4.8** Split Form

To create a split form, do the following:

1. Select a table or query in the Navigation Pane.
2. Click the CREATE tab.
3. Click More Forms in the Forms group.
4. Select Split Form.

Once you have completed those steps, a new split form displays. You can add, edit, or delete records in either section. The *splitter bar* divides the form into two halves. Users can adjust the splitter bar up or down unless the form designer disables this option.

## Create a Multiple Items Form

A *Multiple Items form* displays multiple records in a tabular layout similar to a table's Datasheet view. However, a Multiple Items form gives you more customization options than a datasheet, such as the ability to add graphical elements, buttons, and other controls. Figure 4.9 shows a Multiple Items form created from the Employees table.

**FIGURE 4.9** Multiple Items Form

To create a Multiple Items form, do the following:

1. Select a table or query from the Navigation Pane.
2. Click the CREATE tab.
3. Click More Forms in the Forms group.
4. Select Multiple Items from the list of options.

## Create Forms Using the Other Form Tools

A Datasheet form is a replica of a table or query's Datasheet view except that it still retains some of the form properties. Database designers can also use the Datasheet form to display data in a table-like format but change the form properties to not allow a record to be deleted. This would protect the data from accidental damage while still providing the users with the familiar Datasheet view.

The Form Design tool and the Blank Form tools can be used to create a form manually. Click one of these tools and Access will open a completely blank form. Click Add Existing Fields in the Tools group on the Design tab and add the necessary fields.

The Navigation option in the Forms group enables you to create user interface forms that have the look and feel of a Web-based form and enable users to open and close the objects of a database. In other words, you could set up a form that allows users to click on the forms you want them to view. This is an excellent option to simplify the database for data-entry personnel who may not understand the program. These forms are also useful for setting up an Access database on the Internet.

The Modal Dialog Form tool can be used to create a dialog box. This feature is useful when you need to gather information from the user before working with another object. Dialog boxes are common in all Microsoft Office applications.

## REFERENCE | Form Tools

| Form Tool | Location | Use |
|---|---|---|
| Form | Create tab, Forms group | Creates a form with a stacked layout displaying all of the fields in the record source. |
| Form Design | Create tab, Forms group | Create a new blank form in Design view. |
| Blank Form | Create tab, Forms group | Create a new blank form in Layout view. |
| Form Wizard | Create tab, Forms group | Answer a series of questions and Access will create a custom form for you. |
| Navigation | Create tab, Forms group, Navigation button | Create user-interface forms that can also be used on the Internet. Six different Navigation form layouts are available from the drop-down list. |
| Split Form | Create tab, Forms group, More Forms button | Creates a two-part form with a stacked layout in one section and a tabular layout in the other. |
| Multiple Items | Create tab, Forms group, More Forms button | Creates a tabular layout form that includes all of the fields from the record source. |
| Datasheet | Create tab, Forms group, More Forms button | Creates a form that resembles the datasheet of a table or query. |
| Modal Dialog | Create tab, Forms group, More Forms button | Creates a custom dialog box that forces the user to respond before working with another object. |

 **TIP | Print with Caution!**

Users can print a form by clicking the File tab and selecting the Print option. However, printing from a form should be done with caution. Forms are not generally designed for printing, so you may end up with hundreds of pages of printouts. A form with a stacked layout of 1,000 records could print thousands of pages unless you choose the Selected Record(s) option in the Print dialog box. The Selected Record(s) option, as shown in Figure 4.10, will only print the current record (or selected records).

Selected Record(s) option

**FIGURE 4.10** Printing Selected Records

# Using Form Views

Access provides different views for a form, similar to the different views in tables and queries. Tables and queries have Design view and Datasheet view. Most forms have Layout view, Form view, and Design view.

As you work with the form tools to create and modify forms, you will often need to switch between the three form views in Access: Layout view, Form view, and Design view. Most of your design work will be done in Layout view; occasionally, you will switch to Design view to add a more advanced feature, such as a background, or to use a layout option that is otherwise unavailable. Users of the form will only work in Form view. There should be no reason for a user to switch to Layout or Design view. Modifications to the form should be done by the designated form designer.

After a form is generated by a Form tool, you may need to modify it. Commonly, you may add a field, remove a field, change the order of fields, change the width of a field, modify the theme, or modify label text. These changes can be made in a form's Layout view. Advanced changes, such as changing headers or footers or adding a background image, can be made in a form's Design view.

## Edit Data in Form View

**STEP 2 »** Use Form view to add, edit, and delete data in a form; the layout and design of the form cannot be changed in this view. Recall from a previous chapter that you can move from one field to another field by pressing Tab on your keyboard or clicking the desired field with your mouse.

## Alter a Form in Layout View

Use Layout view to alter the form design while still viewing the data. You use Layout view to add or delete fields in a form, modify field properties, change the column widths, and enhance a form by adding a color scheme or styling. While you are working in Layout view, you can see the data as it would appear in Form view, but you cannot edit the data in Layout view. Seeing the data in Layout view makes it easier to size controls, for example, to ensure the data is visible. It is good practice to test a form in Form view after making changes in Layout view.

## Use the Form Layout Tools Tabs

Forms have a number of options you can use to format. Once you are in Layout or Design view, you will have access to the report layout tools. You have three tabs available:

- Design: Use this tab to make changes to the design of the form, such as adding sorting, changing themes, and inserting additional controls.
- Arrange: Use this tab to change the layout of a form, to move fields, or to insert space.
- Format: Use this tab to change the font; add or remove bolding, italics, or underlining; change font size; change font color or background; adjust text alignment; or add a background image.

## Add a Field to a Form

STEP 3 » To add a field to a form, do the following:

1. Open the form in Layout view.
2. Click Add Existing Fields in the Tools group on the DESIGN tab to reveal the available fields from the form's record source. A Field List pane appears at the right of your screen.
3. For a single-table form, you will be presented with a list of fields. For a multiple-table form, you will first need to click the + (plus) next to the appropriate table to locate the desired field.
4. Drag the new field to the precise location on the form, using the shaded line (the color may vary, based on your Office configuration) as a guide for the position of the new field. The other fields will automatically adjust to make room for the new field.

Depending on the layout of the form, the shaded line will appear vertically (tabular layouts) or horizontally (stacked).

## Delete a Field from a Form

To delete a field, do the following:

1. Switch to Layout view.
2. Click the text box control of the field to be deleted (note the shaded border around the control).
3. Click the Select Row option on the Layout tab in the Rows & Columns group.
4. Press Delete. The other fields will automatically adjust to close the gap around the deleted field.

## Adjust Column Widths in a Form

When column widths are adjusted in a form with a stacked layout, all columns will increase and decrease together. Therefore, it is best to make sure that field columns are wide enough to accommodate the widest value in the table. For example, if a form contains information such as a customer's first name, last name, address, city, state, ZIP, phone, and e-mail address, you will need to make sure the longest address and the longest e-mail address are completely visible (because those fields are likely to contain the longest data values).

To decrease column widths in a form with a stacked layout, do the following:

1. Open the form in Layout view.
2. Click the text box control of the first field to select it.
3. Move the mouse over the right border of the field until the mouse pointer turns into a double arrow.
4. Drag the right edge to the left or right until you arrive at the desired width.

You will notice that all the fields change as you change the width of the first field. All fields that are part of the layout will have a standard width. If you wanted to resize one specific field, you would need to remove that field from the layout control. Note that "removing a field from the layout control" does not mean "removing a field from the form." Recall that the layout control keeps each field in place. If you remove a field from the layout control, it stays on the form but can be moved more freely.

## Modify Form Controls using the Format Tab

When you view a form in Layout view, the Form Layout Tools tab displays the Design tab, Arrange tab, and Format tab. The Format tab, shown in Figure 4.11, contains a series of commands that enable you change the font, display, and alignment of the controls on a form. This is useful if you need to quickly change the look of one cell. For example, if you have a form that shows the information about the sale of a vehicle, you might want to emphasize the net profit of each transaction.

FIGURE 4.11 Format Tab

From this tab, you can change a number of properties. For example, you can perform these tasks, and more:

- Change the font size: Click the Font Size arrow in the Font group.
- Change emphasis: In the Font group, add bold, italics, or underlining.
- Change alignment: In the Font group, choose left, center, or right align.
- Change a control's background color: Click the Background Color arrow (refer to Figure 4.11) and select a color for the background.
- Change a control's font color: Click the Font Color arrow (refer to Figure 4.11) and select a color for the cell's font.
- Change number format: In the Number group, change to currency, percentage, or add commas; increase or decrease decimal places.

## Selecting Controls

Controls, as mentioned, include both the labels identifying a field and the text box displaying field values. There may be times you want to select multiple controls. You will notice when you click on one control and click on another that the original control is deselected. If you need to select multiple controls, click on the first control you wish to select, hold down CTRL on your keyboard, and then click on the other controls you wish to select. Once they are selected, you can perform many tasks, such as formatting or deletion.

## Add a Theme to a Form

You can apply a theme to a form in order to give the form a more professional finish. A ***theme*** is a defined set of colors, fonts, and graphics that can be applied to a form (or report). Click Themes in the Themes group on the Design tab, select a theme from the Themes Gallery, and Access will apply the theme to the form. Each theme has a name; you can determine the name of a theme by pointing the mouse to a theme and waiting for the tip to pop up, showing the name.

You can apply a theme to a single form or to all the forms in your database that share a common theme. Applying the same theme to all forms will provide a consistent look to your database; most users prefer a consistent theme when using Access forms. The same themes found in Access are also available in Excel, Word, and PowerPoint. Therefore, you can achieve a uniform look across all Office applications. Themes can be customized and saved so that the theme you create can be used again. Click the Save Current Theme command as shown in Figure 4.12 to do so.

Save Current Theme

FIGURE 4.12 Themes

## Add Styling to a Form

Modifying the font size of labels, changing the font color of labels, and adding a background color can enhance a form and also make it more usable. It is best to choose a familiar font family, such as Arial or Calibri, for both the form label controls and the text box controls. Apply bold to the labels in order to help the user distinguish labels from the text boxes. You should also consider right-aligning the labels and left-aligning the text box controls to reduce distance between the label and field, as illustrated in Figure 4.13. You may also want to separate the primary key field from the rest of the form by providing a sufficient visual boundary.

One note of caution: Try to avoid what graphic artists refer to as the "ransom note effect." Using too many font families, font sizes, colors, and other effects can take away from your design.

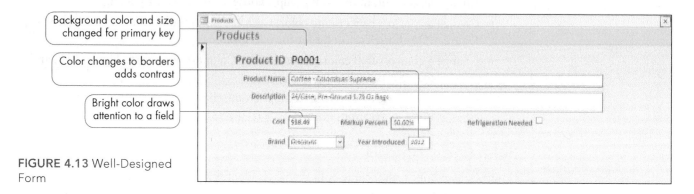

Background color and size changed for primary key

Color changes to borders adds contrast

Bright color draws attention to a field

**FIGURE 4.13** Well-Designed Form

# Working with a Form Layout Control

Whenever you use one of the form tools to create a new form, Access will add a layout control to help align the fields. Recall that the layout control helps keep controls aligned in order to give your form a uniform appearance. The layout control provides structure for the fields but is restrictive. If you wish to have more control over the location of your fields, you can remove the layout control and position the controls manually on the grid.

## Modify a Form Using the Arrange Tab

The Arrange tab appears in both Layout view and Design view. Use this tab to change the layout of a form, to move fields up and down, to insert a space above or below your current position, or to insert a space to the left or the right of the current field. To use these commands, first open a form in Layout view or Design view and click the Arrange tab. Next, select a field or fields and click the appropriate command.

The Table group contains commands that enable you to add gridlines to a form's layout, to change a form's layout from stacked to tabular (and vice versa), or to remove a form's layout. The Remove Layout command is only available in Design view.

**STEP 4 ▶**
To change the arrangement of a form, do the following:

1. Open the form in Layout view.
2. Click any of the field text boxes.
3. Click the ARRANGE tab.
4. Click Select Layout in the Rows & Columns group.
5. Click Tabular or Stacked in the Table group.

To remove a form layout control, do the following:

1. Switch to Design view (if you are not in Design view, you will not see the Remove Layout option).
2. Click on one of the fields that is currently part of the layout.
3. On the ARRANGE tab, click Select Layout in the Rows & Columns group.
4. Click Remove Layout in the Table group.
5. Switch to Layout view to arrange fields.

If you have removed the layout control or have a form that never had one, you can add one if you do the following:

1. Switch to Layout view or Design view (you can switch in either view).
2. Select all the controls you would like added back to the layout control, such as the field labels and text boxes. Hold down CTRL on your keyboard and click on each control, or click the FORMAT tab and in the Selection group, click Select All if you want to add everything to a layout.
3. On the ARRANGE tab, in the Table group, click Tabular or Stacked

The Rows & Columns group contains commands that enable you to insert rows and columns inside a form's layout. For example, in a form with a stacked layout, you may want to separate some fields from the rest of the fields. To do this, you could select a text box and click Insert Below. This will create a space after the selected field. This group also contains the Select Layout, Select Column, and Select Row commands. In Figure 4.14, three rows have been inserted above the Cost field.

**FIGURE 4.14** Rows Inserted Using the Arrange Tab

The Move group contains two commands that enable you to move a field up or down in a stacked layout. For example, if you want to move the second field in a stacked layout to the first position, select the second field's text box and label and click Move Up in the Move group. Moving fields up or down in a form may cause unexpected results; you can always use the Undo command if you need to revert back to a previous layout.

The Position group contains commands that enable you to modify the margins and the padding of controls in a form. This group also contains the Anchoring command, which enables you to change where the form's controls appear on the screen. By default, forms are anchored at the top left; however, you can change this to any of the nine options using the anchoring command.

## TIP | Apply a Background Image to a Form

To apply a Background Image to a form, open the form in Design view, click the Format tab, and then click Background Image in the Background group. Next, click Browse to locate the image you want to apply to the form. Once the image has been applied to the form, you can change the properties of the image so that the image is anchored and sized correctly.

# Sorting Records in a Form

When a form is created using a Form tool, the sort order of the records in the form is dependent on the sort order of the record source—a table or a query. Tables are usually sorted by the primary key, whereas queries can be sorted in a variety of ways. Adding and removing sorts are shown in Figure 4.15.

**FIGURE 4.15** Home Tab
Sort & Filter Group

## Sorting by a Single Field

You can easily sort on a single field, in ascending or descending order.

To sort by a single field, do the following:

1. Open the form in Form view.
2. Select the field you want to use for sorting.
3. On the HOME tab, in the Sort & Filter group, click Ascending or Descending.

If the form is based on a query, you can instead modify the underlying query's sort order. This method enables you to create a more advanced sort order based on multiple fields. Open the query in Design view, add the sorting you want, and then save and close the query.

## Remove Sorting in a Form

To remove the sort order in a form, do the following:

1. Switch to Form view.
2. On the HOME tab, in the Sort & Filter group, click Remove Sort.

---

### TIP  Inconsistent Sorting Due to Spaces

Including extra spaces when you enter values into fields can cause issues with sorting. To Access, the following values are not the same:

Little Falls, NJ 07424

Little  Falls, NJ 07424

Notice the extra space after the word *Little*. If you attempt to sort, these cities will end up in different places in the sort. The first Little Falls (without the extra space) would appear between Little Egg Harbor Township and Little Ferry. However, the second version would end up above Little Egg Harbor Township, because Access treats the space as a different character.

Inconsistent spacing can cause inconsistent sorting. Try to remember that when performing data entry. If you inherit a database with this issue, you might consider performing a Replace, replacing two spaces with one.

---

1. How does a form simplify data entry (when compared to entering data into a table)? *p. 176*

2. What is the record source of a form? *p. 177*

3. What is the difference between Layout view and Design view? *p. 179*

4. What is the difference between a form with a subform and a split form? *p. 180*

5. What is a layout control? What are the pros and cons of a layout control? *p. 186*

# Hands-On Exercises

Watch the Video for this Hands-On Exercise!

MyITLab®
HOE1 Training

## 1 Form Basics

It is your first day on the job at La Vida Mocha. After talking with Ryung about her data-entry needs, you decide to create several sample forms with different formats. You will show each form to Ryung and Nabil to get feedback and see if they have a preference.

**Skills covered:** Create Forms Using Form Tools • Use Form Views • Work with a Form Layout Control • Sort Records in a Form

### STEP 1 ▶ CREATE FORMS USING FORM TOOLS

You will create some forms to help Ryung and Nabil with their data entry process. After discussing their needs, you created some sketches that you will implement. Refer to Figure 4.16 as you complete Step 1.

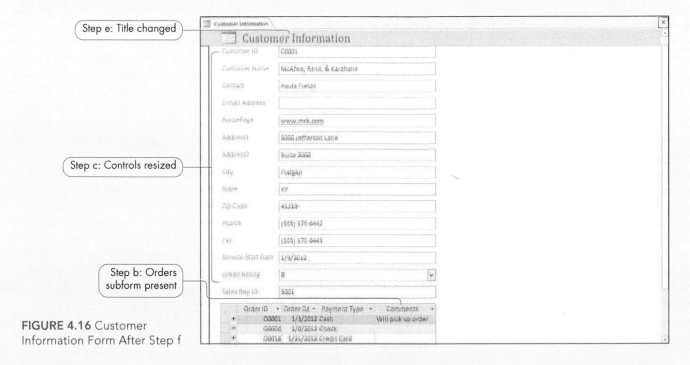

**FIGURE 4.16** Customer Information Form After Step f

a. Open *a04h1Coffee*. Click the **FILE tab**, select **Save As**, and click **Save As**. Type **a04h1Coffee_LastFirst** as the file name. Click **Save**.

> **TROUBLESHOOTING:** Throughout the remainder of this chapter and textbook, click Enable Content whenever you are working with student files.

> **TROUBLESHOOTING:** If you make any major mistakes in this exercise, you can close the file, repeat step a above, and then start over.

b. Click the **Customers table** in the Navigation Pane. Click the **CREATE tab** and click **Form** in the Forms group.

Access creates a new form with two record sources—Customers (with stacked layout, on top) and Orders (with datasheet layout, below). Access found a one-to-many relationship between the Customers and Orders tables. The form opens in Layout view.

**c.** Click the top text box containing *C0001* if it is not already selected. The text box is outlined with a shaded border. Move the mouse to the right edge of the shaded border until the mouse pointer changes to a double-headed arrow. Drag the right edge to the left until the text box is approximately half of its original size.

All the text boxes and the subform at the bottom adjust in size when you adjust the top text box. This is a characteristic of Layout view—enabling you to easily modify all controls at once.

> **TROUBLESHOOTING:** You may need to maximize the Access window or close the Navigation Pane if the right edge of the text box is not visible.

**d.** Ensure the labels at the left all appear without being cut off. If they are cut off, adjust the size of the labels like you did in step c.

**e.** Click **Save** in the Quick Access Toolbar, and then type **Customer Information** as the form name in the **Save As dialog box**. Click **OK**.

**f.** Click the **Customers title** at the top of the form to select it, click again, and then change the title to **Customer Information**. Press **Enter** to accept the change. Your form should now look like Figure 4.16. Close the form.

> **TROUBLESHOOTING:** If you make a mistake that you cannot easily recover from, consider deleting the form and starting over. The Form tool makes it easy to start over again.

**g.** Verify the Customers table is selected in the Navigation Pane. Click the **CREATE tab** and click **More Forms** in the Forms group. Select **Split Form**.

Access creates a new form with a split view, one view in stacked layout and one view laid out like a datasheet.

**h.** Click anywhere on the Coulter Office Supplies customer record in the bottom portion of the form (record 14). Note: You may need to scroll down to see this record.

The top portion shows all the information for this customer.

**i.** Click the **Customers title** at the top of the form to select it, click **Customers** again, and then change the title to **Customers - Split View**. Press **Enter** to accept the change.

**j.** Click **Save** on the Quick Access Toolbar and type **Customers - Split View** in the **Form Name box**. Click **OK**. Close the form.

**k.** Click the **Products table** in the Navigation Pane. Click the **CREATE tab**, click **More Forms** in the Forms group, and then select **Multiple Items**.

Access creates a new multiple-item form based on the Products table. The form resembles a table's Datasheet view.

**l.** Click the **Products title** at the top of the form to select it, click again on **Products**, and then change the title to **Products - Multiple Items**. Press **Enter** to save the title.

**m.** Save the form as **Products - Multiple Items** and close the form.

**n.** Click the **Orders table** in the Navigation Pane. Click **Form** in the Forms group on the CREATE tab.

A form with a subform showing each line of the order is created.

**o.** Switch to Design view. Click anywhere inside the subform and press **Delete** on your keyboard.

The subform is removed.

**p.** Save the form as **Order Information**. Close all open objects.

## STEP 2 ≫ USE FORM VIEW TO CHANGE DATA

Now that you have created three forms, you will show Nabil how to use the forms to perform data entry.

**a.** Right-click the **Customer Information** form in the Navigation Pane and click **Open**. Advance to the sixth customer, *Lugo Computer Sales*, using the **Next Record button** on the Navigation Bar at the bottom of the form.

> **TROUBLESHOOTING:** Two Navigation bars exist, one for the main form and one for the subform. Make sure you use the bottom-most one that shows 14 records.

**b.** Double-click the **Customers table** in the Navigation Pane.

Two tabs now display in the main window. You will compare the table data and the form data while you make changes to both.

**c.** Verify the sixth record of the Customers table is *Lugo Computer Sales*, which corresponds to the sixth record in the Customer Information form. Click the tabs to switch between the table and the form.

**d.** Click the **Customer Information tab** and replace *Adam Sanchez*, the contact for Lugo Computer Sales, with your name. Advance to the next record to save the changes. Click the **Customers tab** to see that the contact name changed in the table as well.

The contact field and the other fields on the Customer Information form automatically change the data in the underlying table.

> **TROUBLESHOOTING:** If the change to Adam Sanchez does not display in the Customers table, check the Customer Information form to see if the pencil displays in the left margin. If it does, save the record by advancing to the next customer and recheck to see if the name has changed.

**e.** Close the Customer Information form and the Customers table.

**f.** Open the Customers – Split View form. In the bottom portion of the split form, click **Lugo Computer Sales**, the sixth record. Notice the top portion now displays the information for Lugo Computer Sales. Notice there is an error in the e-mail address—*service* is misspelled. In the top portion of the form, change the e-mail address to **service@lugocomputer.net**.

**g.** Click another record in the bottom pane and click back on **Lugo Computer Sales**.

The pencil disappears from the record selector box and the changes are saved to the table.

## STEP 3 ≫ USE LAYOUT VIEW TO MODIFY A FORM LAYOUT

You will make some changes to the layouts based on recommendations Nabil gave you after seeing the forms in action. You will also add a missing field to the main table and add it to the form. Refer to Figure 4.17 as you complete Step 3.

Step d: Refrig? column resized

**FIGURE 4.17** Final Version of Products—Multiple Items Report

a. Switch the Customers – Split View form to Layout view. Move your mouse over the splitter bar, the border between the top and bottom portions of the window. When the pointer shape changes to a double-headed arrow, drag the **splitter bar** up until it almost touches the Sales Rep ID field. Save and close the form.

b. Open the Products – Multiple Items form in Layout view. Move the mouse over the bottom edge of cell P0001 until the pointer shape changes to a two-headed arrow. Drag the bottom edge up to reduce the height of the rows so they are as tall as they need to be to accommodate the information.

Changing the height of one row affects the height of all the rows.

c. Click anywhere on the Cost column and click **Select Column** in the Rows & Columns group on the ARRANGE tab. Press **Delete** to remove the column. Repeat the process to delete *MarkupPercent*.

d. Click the **Refrigeration Needed label** to select it. Change the label to the abbreviation **Refrig?**. Shrink the field so it is as wide as necessary. Save and close the form.

You removed fields from the Products – Multiple Items form and the other fields adjust to maintain an even distribution (after you remove the blank space).

e. Open the Customer Information form in Layout view.

f. Click **Themes** in the Themes group on the DESIGN tab. Right-click the **Slice theme** and click **Apply Theme to This Object Only**.

The font and color scheme adjust to match this theme.

> **TROUBLESHOOTING:** Recall that you can determine which theme is named Slice by pointing the mouse to a theme and waiting for a tip to display. Themes are displayed in alphabetical order.

g. Click **Shape Fill** in the Control Formatting group on the FORMAT tab. Click **Light Turquoise, Background 2**.

The background color of the CustomerID field changes to light turquoise.

> **TROUBLESHOOTING:** If you do not see a Light Turquoise, Background 2 in the first row, ensure you have selected the Slice theme.

**h.** Select the **Customer Name field** (which should be *McAfee, Rand, & Karahalis*). Change the font size to **16**.

The customer name appears in a larger font, setting it apart from the other fields.

**i.** Save and close the form.

**j.** Right-click the **Customers table** in the Navigation Pane and click **Design View**.

You will add the HomePage field to the Customers table.

**k.** Click the **Address1 field** and click **Insert Rows** in the Tools group.

A new row is inserted above the Address1 field.

**l.** Type **HomePage** in the blank **Field Name box** and choose **Hyperlink** as the Data Type.

**m.** Save and close the Customers table.

**n.** Right-click the **Customer Information form** in the Navigation Pane and click **Layout View**.

You will add the HomePage field to the Customer Information form.

**o.** Click **Add Existing Fields** in the Tools group on the DESIGN tab to display the Field List pane (if necessary).

**p.** Click the **HomePage field**. Drag the field from the Field List pane to the form, below the E-mail Address field, until a shaded line displays between *E-mail Address* and *Address1*, and release the mouse. Close the Field List pane.

Access shows a shaded line to help you place the field in the correct location.

**q.** Switch to Form view. Press **Tab** until you reach the HomePage field and type www.mrk.com into the field. Save and close the form.

**r.** Click the **Revenue query** in the Navigation Pane. Click **Form** in the Forms group on the CREATE tab to create a new form based on this query.

**s.** Display the form in Design view. Select all text box field controls (from *Last Name* down to *Revenue*) by clicking on the first field (Last Name), holding down **CTRL** on your keyboard, and clicking on each of the other controls. Click **Remove Layout** in the Table group on the ARRANGE tab. Switch to Layout view.

**t.** Resize the controls individually so they are approximately the same size as shown in Figure 4.18.

**u.** Click the **Price control**. Hold down **CTRL** and click the **Revenue control**, the **Price label**, and the **Revenue label**. Drag the fields to the locations shown in Figure 4.18. Switch to Form view.

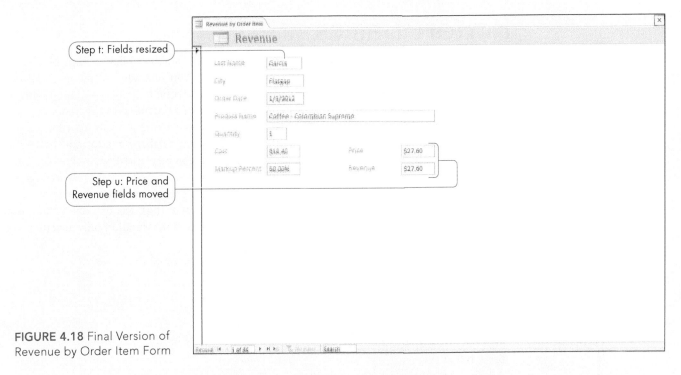

Step t: Fields resized

Step u: Price and Revenue fields moved

**FIGURE 4.18** Final Version of Revenue by Order Item Form

v. Save the form as **Revenue by Order Item**. Close the form.

## STEP 4 ≫ USE A CONTROL LAYOUT AND SORT RECORDS IN A FORM

Ryung tested the Customer Information form and likes the way it is working. She asks you to change the sorting to make it easier to find customers with a similar customer name. She also has an old form that she hopes you can make easier to read but keep in the vertical format.

a. Open the Sales Reps form in Layout view. Notice the form is not laid out well.

b. Click **Select All** in the Selection group on the FORMAT tab.

All 14 controls are outlined.

c. Click **Tabular** in the Table group on the ARRANGE tab.

The controls are lined up horizontally.

d. Click **Stacked** in the Table group on the ARRANGE tab. Switch to Form view.

Ryung wanted the form laid out vertically. The controls are lined up vertically and are much easier to read.

e. Save and close the form.

f. Open the Customer Information form in Form view. Click **Next record** in the Navigation bar at the bottom several times to advance through the records.

Take note that the customers are in Customer ID order.

g. Click **First record** in the Navigation bar to return to customer *McAfee, Rand, & Karahalis*.

h. Click the **Customer Name field** and click **Ascending** in the Sort & Filter group on the HOME tab.

Advantage Sales displays, as they are the first customer name in alphabetical order.

i. Click **Next record** in the Navigation bar at the bottom to advance through the records.

The records are in Customer Name order.

j. Save and close the Customer Information form.

k. Keep the database open if you plan to continue with the next Hands-On Exercise. If not, close the database and exit Access.

# Report Basics

By now, you know how to plan a database, create a table, establish relationships between tables, enter data into tables, and extract data using queries. You generated output by printing table and query datasheets. You also learned how to create several types of data-entry forms. These forms can also be used for inquiries about the data in a database. In this section, you will learn how to create professional reports using the report-writing tools in Access.

A *report* is a document that displays information from a database in a format that outputs meaningful information to its readers. Access reports can be printed, viewed on screen, or even saved as a file. Much like a report you might do for a class, Access does research (gets information from the tables or queries) and organizes and presents it in a meaningful way (the final report, formatted for on-screen viewing or for printing). Reports are unable to change data in your database; a report is designed for output of information only, whether to the screen, to the printer, or to a file.

The following are all examples of reports that might be created in Access:

1. A telephone directory sorted by last name
2. A customer list grouped by sales rep
3. An employee list sorted by most years of service
4. A financial statement
5. A bill or invoice
6. A bar chart showing sales over the past 12 months
7. A shipping label
8. A letter to customers reminding them about a past due payment

Although you can print information from forms, information printed may not be easily understood or economical in terms of paper use. Most of the printed documents generated by Access will come from reports. Reports can be enhanced to help the reader understand and analyze the data. For example, if you print the Datasheet view from the Customers table, you will be able to locate the key information about each customer. However, using report tools, you can group the customers by sales rep and highlight the customers who have not placed an order in six months. This is an example of converting a list of customers into an effective business tool. To increase business, the sales reps could contact their customers who have not ordered in six months and review the findings with the sales manager. A sales report could be run each month to see if the strategy has helped produce any new business.

In this section, you will create reports in Access by first identifying a record source, then sketching the report, and finally choosing a Report tool. You will learn how to modify a report by adding and deleting fields, resizing columns, and adding a color scheme. You will also learn about the report sections, the report views, and controls on reports. After having worked through forms in the earlier section on forms, you will discover that there are many similarities between forms and reports.

## Creating Reports Using Report Tools

Access provides five different report tools for creating reports. The report tools are found on the Create tab, in the Reports group, as shown in Figure 4.19. Click one of these tools and Access will base the report using the table or query that is currently selected. The most common of the tools, the *Report tool*, is used to instantly create a tabular report based on the table or query currently selected. The Report Design tool is used to create a new blank report in Design view. This tool is used by advanced users who want to create a blank report with no help from Access. The Blank Report tool is used to create a new blank report so that you can insert fields and controls manually and design the report. The Report Wizard tool will ask a series of questions and help you create a report based on your answers. The Labels tool is used to create a page of labels using one of the preformatted templates provided by Access. Table 4.1 provides a summary of the five report tools and their usage.

FIGURE 4.19 Create Tab Reports Group

After you create a report using one of the report tools, you can perform modifications in Layout view or Design view.

TABLE 4.1 Report Tools and Their Usage

| Report Tool | Usage |
| --- | --- |
| Report | Create a tabular report showing all of the fields in the record source. |
| Report Design | Create a new blank report in Design view. Add fields and controls manually. |
| Blank Report | Create a new blank report in Layout view. Add fields and controls manually. |
| Report Wizard | Answer a series of questions and Access will design a custom report for you. |
| Labels | Choose a preformatted label template and create a sheet of labels. |

Before you create a report in Access, you should ask these questions:

- What is the purpose of the report?
- Who will use the report?
- Which tables are needed for the report?
- What information needs to be included?
- How will the report be distributed? Will users pull the information directly from Access, or will they receive it through e-mail, fax, or the Internet?
- Will the results be converted to Word, Excel, HTML, or another format?

In the *Forms* section of this chapter, you learned that it is helpful to talk to users and sketch an Access form before you launch Access. The same holds true for creating an Access report. Users can give you solid feedback, and creating a sketch will help you determine which report tool to use to create the report.

The first step in planning your report is to identify the record source. You may use one or more tables, queries, or a combination of tables and queries as the report's record source. Sometimes, a single table contains all of the records you need for the report. Other times, you will need to incorporate several tables. When multiple tables are needed to create a report, you can add all the necessary tables into a single query and then base the report on that query. (As stated earlier, multiple tables in a query must be related, as indicated with join lines. Tables with no join lines usually indicate an incorrect record source.)

Reports can also contain graphics as well as text and numeric data. For example, you can add a company logo. After you identify the record source, you also need to specify which graphic images are needed (and the location of the images).

## Use the Report Tool

STEP 1 » After you sketch the report, you can decide which report tool is appropriate to produce the desired report. Access provides several tools that you can use to create a report (refer to Figure 4.20). Which one you select depends on the layout of the report, the record source, and the complexity of the report design.

The easiest way to create a report is with the Report tool. The Report tool is used to instantly create a tabular report based on the table or query currently selected. To create a report using the Report tool, do the following:

1. Select a table or query in the Navigation Pane.
2. Click the CREATE tab and click Report in the Reports group. Access creates a tabular layout report instantly. Notice, this type of report displays data horizontally across the page in a landscape view, as shown in Figure 4.20.

Table form allows for printing

**FIGURE 4.20** Tabular Report

If you prefer, you can display a report using a stacked layout, which displays fields in a vertical column. This type of report is less common, as it would result in longer printouts. The number of records on one page depends on the number of records in the record source. You can also force a new page at the start of each record.

## Use the Report Wizard to Create a Basic Report

You can also create a professional report with the Report Wizard. The **Report Wizard** asks you questions and then uses your answers to generate a customized report. The wizard uses six dialog boxes to collect information about your report. After thinking through the structure, the layout, and the record source, you are ready to launch the Report Wizard.

1. Select the report's record source in the Navigation Pane and click Report Wizard in the Reports group on the CREATE tab.

   The wizard opens with the table or query (the record source) displayed in the first dialog box. Although you chose the record source before you started, the first dialog box enables you to select fields from additional tables or queries.

2. Choose the fields you want to include in the report. Click the Tables/Queries drop-down list to display a list of available tables or queries. As with the query wizard you used in a previous chapter, you can click > to choose a single field, >> to choose all fields, < to remove a field, and << to remove all fields from the report. See Figure 4.21. Set the desired fields and click Next.

Fields in the report

Choose Tables/Queries from which to add fields

Add or remove fields

**FIGURE 4.21** Selecting Fields for a Report

3. The next dialog box, shown in Figure 4.22, asks, "Do you want to add any grouping levels?" As you learned in a previous chapter, grouping lets you organize and summarize your data, based on values in a field. For a basic report, you will not select any grouping fields and instead just click Next.

**FIGURE 4.22** Grouping Options

4. The next dialog box, shown in Figure 4.23, asks "What sort order do you want for your records?" For the sort options, specify which field you want to sort by first and optionally add a second, third, and fourth sort. For each field, choose ascending order and/or descending order. Click on the word Ascending and it will toggle to Descending; clicking again will switch back to Ascending. Set the desired sort options and click Next.

**FIGURE 4.23** Sort Options for a Basic Report

5. The next dialog box will determine the report's appearance. You will be given the option to select Columnar, Tabular, or Justified as the layout.

   - Columnar will display the information in a column. This leads to reports that are easier to read, but long printouts.
   - Tabular will display the data in a table format. This is good for saving space, but it may be difficult to fit all fields on one printed page.
   - Justified will display the information in a column as well. If you have Long Text fields, this is a good option to ensure all your data fits.

   Tabular is the option you choose to fit the report on as few pages as possible. Clicking an option will give you a general preview in the preview area. You can also select the orientation for the report, either Portrait or Landscape (see Figure 4.24). Select an appropriate format for the report. Set the desired options and click Next.

**FIGURE 4.24** Layout Options for a Basic Report

6. Decide on an appropriate name for the report. Type a descriptive report name so you can easily determine what information is in the report based on the title. This step, shown in Figure 4.25, is the last step in the Report Wizard. Name the report and click Finish.

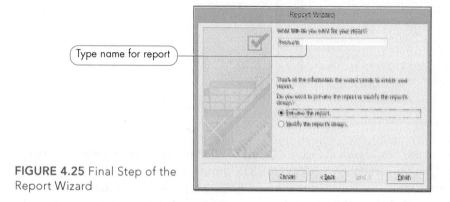

Type name for report

Now that you have stepped through the wizard, you will get a report incorporating all the options you chose, as shown in Figure 4.26. You may need to adjust the size of fields, as some may not be fully displayed.

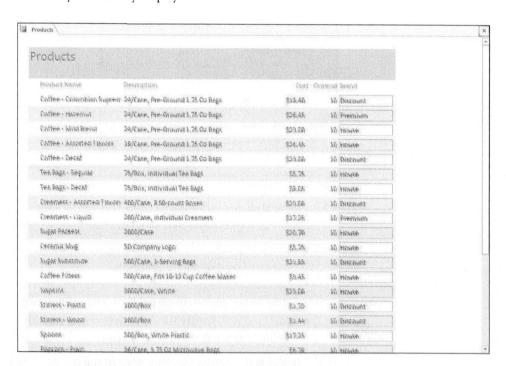

**FIGURE 4.26** Results of Report Wizard

## Use the Report Wizard with Grouping

In the previous example, we created a basic report using the Report Wizard. However, we can use grouping if we want to summarize our report by a certain field. We can also display overall totals and percentages based on a predefined format. The Report Wizard still has six dialog boxes when you add grouping, but two dialog boxes will change.

1. Select the report's record source in the Navigation Pane and click Report Wizard in the Reports group on the CREATE tab.
2. Choose the fields you want to appear in the report and click Next.
3. The next dialog box asks, "Do you want to add any grouping levels?" In the previous example, we just clicked Next. Here is where you add grouping. As we learned in a previous chapter, grouping lets you organize and summarize your data based on values in a field. Select the field you want to group by and click the > button to add the new

group. If you need a second or third grouping level, add those field names in order. The order in which you select the groups dictates the order of display in the report. Figure 4.27 shows the sort options for a grouped report. In this specific example, records are being grouped by the Brand. Once you have selected the appropriate options, click Next.

4. Because we have specified grouping, the next dialog box asks, "What sort order and summary information do you want for detail records?" Here, you can click Summary Options if you want to add aggregate functions (e.g., sum, average, minimum, and maximum) and to specify whether you want to see detail records on the report or only the aggregate results (see Figure 4.28). You can also choose to calculate percentages, so if you had one group that made up half your sales, you would see 50%. Click OK to return to the Report Wizard. The sort options are the same as before. Set the appropriate options and click Next.

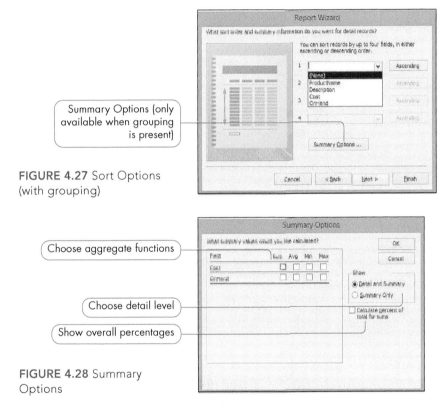

Summary Options (only available when grouping is present)

**FIGURE 4.27** Sort Options (with grouping)

Choose aggregate functions

Choose detail level

Show overall percentages

**FIGURE 4.28** Summary Options

5. The next dialog box, shown in Figure 4.29, will determine the report's appearance. If you have selected grouping, you will be prompted to select the layout from three options:

- Stepped Layout will display column headings at the top of the page and keep the grouping field(s) in their own row.
- Block Layout will include the grouping field(s) inline with the data, saving some space when printing. It has one set of column headings at the top of each page.
- Outline Layout will display the grouping field(s) on their own separate rows and has column headings inside each group. This leads to a longer report when printing but may help make the report easier to read.

Clicking any of these layouts will give you a general preview in the preview area. The option to choose Portrait or Landscape is still available. Click Next.

**Layout (options)**

**FIGURE 4.29** Layout Options (with grouping)

6. Decide on an appropriate name for the report. Type a descriptive report name. Click Finish. Your grouped report will resemble Figure 4.30.

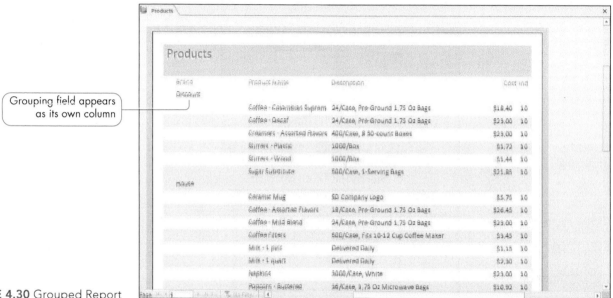

**Grouping field appears as its own column**

**FIGURE 4.30** Grouped Report

## Use the Label Wizard

The *Label Wizard* enables you to easily create mailing labels, name tags, and other specialized tags. A *mailing label report* is a specialized report that comes preformatted to coordinate with name-brand labels, such as Avery. Access includes most common labels built into the program. Even if you purchase a store brand from an office supply store, they will generally state the comparable Avery label number.

To use the Label Wizard, do the following:

1. Select the table or query that will serve as the record source for the report.
2. Click Labels in the Reports group on the CREATE tab.
3. Select the manufacturer, the product number, and the label type and click Next.
4. Choose the font type and size and click Next.
5. Add the fields to the label template, as shown in Figure 4.31. You will need to place the fields exactly as you wish them to appear, including adding a comma between City and State and pressing Enter after the CustomerName.
6. Add any sort fields and click Next.
7. Name the report and click Finish to generate your labels. The results are shown in Figure 4.32.

Select from Available fields

Label fields should be exactly as you want them to appear

FIGURE 4.31 Setting up Labels

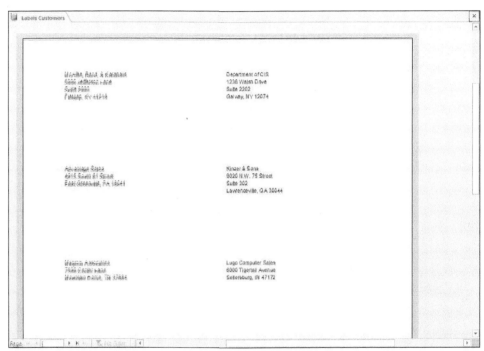

FIGURE 4.32 Output of Label Wizard

# Using Report Views

As you work with the report tools to create and modify reports, you will find the need to frequently switch between the four report views in Access—Layout view, Print Preview, Design view, and Report view. Most of your design work will be done in Layout view, but occasionally, you will need to switch to Design view to apply a more advanced feature, such as a calculated field. Users of the report will use Print Preview or Report view. There should be no reason for a user to switch to Layout view or Design view. Modifications to the report should be done by the designated report designer. To switch between the four views, click the View arrow in the Views group and select the desired view.

## View a Report in Report View

**Report view** enables you to view a report onscreen in a continuous page layout. Report view is similar to Form view for forms. However, because the data shown in a report cannot be changed, it is simply a way of viewing the information without having to worry about accidentally moving a control. In addition, using report view allows quick access to filtering options.

## Alter a Report in Layout View

Use Layout view to alter the report design while still viewing the data. You should use Layout view to add or delete fields in the report, modify field properties, change the column widths, sort, and filter data by excluding certain records. Although Layout view appears similar to Print

Preview, you will find sufficient variations between the two views, so that you will still always need to verify the report in Print Preview to evaluate all the changes made in Layout view.

## Print or Save a Report in Print Preview

STEP 2 ▶▶ *Print Preview* enables you to see exactly what the report will look like when it is printed. Most users prefer to use Print Preview prior to printing the report. This enables you to intercept errors in reports before you send the report to the printer. You cannot modify the design in this view; switch to Layout view or Design view to modify the design. To switch to Print Preview, you can click View and select Print Preview. By default, Print Preview will display all the pages in the report. Figure 4.33 shows an Access report in Print Preview.

Once you are in Print Preview, you have the option to save the report to a file as well. This is a useful option if you plan on distributing some of your information electronically but do not want to distribute the entire database. On the Print Preview tab in the Data group, you will find a number of different data types. See Figure 4.33. Simply choose the type of file you wish to create, and choose the directory and file name.

**FIGURE 4.33** Data Group on Print Preview Tab

Commonly used formats include Excel, Word, or Portable Document Format (PDF). *Portable Document Format (PDF)* is a file type that was created for exchanging documents independent of software applications and operating system environment. In other words, you can e-mail files in this format to users running Mac operating system or a Linux operating system, and they can open it, even if they do not have Microsoft Office. Acrobat files often open in a program called Adobe Reader, a free tool that displays PDF files.

Because databases contain a great deal of information, Access reports may become very long, requiring many pages to print. Experienced Access users always use Print Preview prior to printing their reports. Some reports may require hundreds of pages to print. Other reports may be formatted incorrectly, and a blank page may print after each page of information. It would be better to correct this problem prior to sending it to the printer.

# Modifying a Report

After a report is generated by one of the report tools, you may need to modify it. Similar to forms, the common changes to a report are add a field, remove a field, change the order of fields, change the width of a field, and modify the title. Much like a form, the Report has many options you can use to format a report. Once you are in Layout or Design view, you will have access to the report layout tools. You have four tabs available:

- Design: Use this tab to make changes to the design of the report, such as adding sorting, changing themes, and inserting additional controls.
- Arrange: Use this tab to change the layout of a report, to move fields up and down, to insert a space above or below your current position, or to insert a space to the left or the right of the current field.
- Format: Use this tab to change the font; add or remove bolding, italics, or underlining; change font size; change font color or background; adjust text alignment; or add a background image.
- Page Setup: Use this tab to change paper size, margins, page orientation, or to add columns.

## Modify a Report Using the Arrange Tab

The Arrange tab displays in both Layout view and Design view. To use these commands, first open a report in Layout view or Design view and click the Format tab. Next, select a field or fields and click the appropriate command. Some key commands are highlighted in Figure 4.34.

**FIGURE 4.34** Arrange Tab

The Table group contains commands that enable you to add gridlines to a report's layout, to change a report's layout from stacked to tabular (and vice versa), or to remove a report's layout. The Remove Layout command is available in Design view only. For example, if a report was created with a tabular layout, you could change it to a stacked layout by doing the following:

**STEP 3 »**

1. Open the report in Layout view.
2. Click the ARRANGE tab.
3. Click on any text box in the *Detail* section.
4. Click Select Layout in the Rows & Columns group.
5. Click Stacked in the Table group.

The Rows & Columns group contains commands that enable you to insert rows and columns inside a report's layout. For example, in a report with a stacked layout, you may want to separate the first three fields from the rest of the fields. To do this, you could select the third text box and click Insert Below. This will create a space after the third field. This group also contains the Select Layout, Select Column, and Select Row commands.

The Merge/Split group contains commands that enable you to merge and split the cells on a report. There are times when you may want to deviate from the basic row and column formats that the Access Report Wizards create. In this case, you can change the layout of the report using the merge cells and split cell commands. These commands do not change the actual controls, only the layout of the controls.

The Move group contains two commands that enable you to move a field up or down in a stacked layout. For example, if you want to move the second field in a stacked layout to the first position, select the second field's text box and label, and then click Move Up in the Move group. Moving fields up or down in a report may cause unexpected results; you can always use the undo command if you need to revert back to the beginning.

The Position group contains commands that enable you to modify the margins and the padding of controls in a report. This group also contains the Anchoring command, which enables you to change where the report's controls appear on the screen. By default, reports are anchored at the top left; however, you can change this to any of the nine options using the anchoring command.

## Modify Report Controls using the Format Tab

The Format tab contains a series of commands that enable you change the font, display, and alignment of the controls on a report, as shown in Figure 4.35. This is useful if you need to quickly change the look of one cell. For example, you may have an important field you want to emphasize. To do so, do the following:

1. Switch to Layout view (or Design view).
2. Select the field you wish to format.
3. Click the FORMAT tab.
4. Change the format as desired. You can format the text as you would in Microsoft Word.

**FIGURE 4.35** Format Tab

> ### TIP Apply a Background Image to a Report
>
> To apply a Background Image to a report, open the report in Layout view (or Design view), click the Format tab, and then click Background Image in the Background group. Next, click Browse to locate the image you want to apply to the report. Once the image has been applied to the report, you can change the properties of the image so that the image is anchored and sized correctly.

## Add a Field to a Report

Adding a field to a report with a tabular layout is similar to adding a field to a form with a tabular layout. To add a field to a report, do the following:

1. Switch to Layout view.
2. On the DESIGN tab, in the Tools group, click Add Existing Fields to reveal the available fields in the report's record source. The Field List pane will display on the right-hand side of your screen.
3. For a single-table report, you will be presented with a list of fields. For a multiple-table report, you will first need to click the + (plus) next to the appropriate table to locate the desired field.
4. Drag the new field to a precise location on the report, using the vertical shaded line as a guide for the position of the new field, and release the mouse. The other fields will automatically adjust to make room for the new field.

The process of adding a field to a report with a stacked layout is the same as a tabular layout. The only difference is the shaded line will appear horizontally.

## Delete a Field from a Report

To delete a field from the *Detail* section of a tabular report, do the following:

1. Switch to the Layout view (or Design view) of the report.
2. Click the text box of the field to be deleted. Click Select Column in the Rows & Columns group on the ARRANGE tab. Note the shaded border appears around the field and the label for the field.
3. With the shaded border visible, press Delete on your keyboard. The field disappears and the other fields fill in the gap.

## Adjust Column Widths in a Report

You can adjust the width of each column in a tabular report individually so that each column is wide enough to accommodate the widest value. For example, if a report contains first name, last name, address and city, and email address, you will need to make sure the longest value in each field is completely visible. Scroll through the records to make sure this is the case.

To modify column widths in a tabular report, do the following:

1. Switch to the Layout view (or Design view) of the report.
2. Click the text box of the field you want to adjust. The field will have a shaded border around it, indicating it is selected.
3. Move the mouse to the right border of the selected field; when the mouse pointer turns to a double arrow, drag the edge to the right (to increase) or the left (to decrease) until you arrive at the desired width.

## Changing Margins and Orientation

Sometimes, you may wish to print a page in Landscape or adjust the margins rather than adjusting widths. You will notice the Page Setup tab has these options. In the Page Size group, you can change the margins, and in the Page Layout group, you can choose Portrait or Landscape. See Figure 4.36 for locations of commonly used tools on this tab.

**FIGURE 4.36** Report Layout Tools Page Setup Tab

## Add a Theme to the Report

You can enhance the report's appearance by applying one of the themes provided by Access. To apply a theme, do the following:

1. Switch to Layout view (or Design view).
2. Click Themes in the Themes group on the DESIGN tab. Scroll through the themes until you find a theme you like; hover over one of the options to see a quick preview of the current report using the current theme. (This is easier to preview in Layout view.)
3. Right-click a theme and select *Apply Theme to This Object Only*. You can also apply the theme to all objects.

## Work with a Report Layout Control

Whenever you use one of the report tools to create a new report, Access will add a layout control to help align the fields. Layout controls in reports work the same as layout controls in forms. As discussed earlier in this chapter, the layout control provides guides to help keep controls aligned horizontally and vertically and give your report a uniform appearance.

There are times when you may want to remove the layout control from a report in order to position the fields without aligning them to each other. If you want to remove the layout control from a report, do the following:

1. Switch to Design view (this is not available in Layout view).
2. Click anywhere inside the layout control you want to remove.
3. Click Select Layout in the Rows & Columns group on the ARRANGE tab.
4. In the Table group, click Remove Layout and the layout control is gone. All of the controls are still on the report, but the rectangle binding them together is gone.

You can add a layout control to a report by first selecting all the controls you want to keep together. Then, click Stacked or Tabular in the Table group and the layout control appears.

## Sorting Records in a Report

When a report is created using the Report tool, the sort order of the records in the report is initially dependent on the sort order of the record source—similar to the way records are sorted in a form. The primary key of the record source usually dictates the sort order. However, a report has an additional feature for sorting. While in Layout view or Design view, click Group & Sort in the Grouping & Totals group on the Design tab. The Group, Sort, and Total pane displays at the bottom of the report. This section enables you to set the sort order for the report and override the sorting in the report's record source. Note that if you did not use the Report Wizard, this is how you would add grouping and totals to a report.

Sorting is important because sorting by a primary key may not be intuitive. For example, sorting by a field like LastName might be a better choice than a primary key so users see the records are in alphabetical order by LastName.

### Change the Sorting in a Report

STEP 4 ≫ If you want to change the sorting in the report, do the following:

1. Switch to Layout view.
2. On the DESIGN tab, in the Grouping & Totals group, click Group & Sort to display the *Group, Sort, and Total* section, as shown in Figure 4.37. This will appear at the bottom of the report.

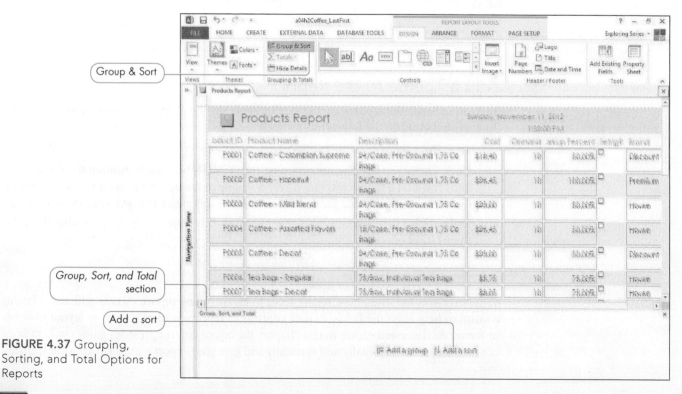

**FIGURE 4.37** Grouping, Sorting, and Total Options for Reports

3. Click *Add a sort* and select the field you wish to sort by, which you can change as shown in Figure 4.38. The default sort order is ascending.

Select sort field

FIGURE 4.38 Adding a Sort to a Report

4. If you wish to add a second sort, click *Add a Sort* again. For example, you could sort first by Brand and then by ProductName, as shown in Figure 4.39.

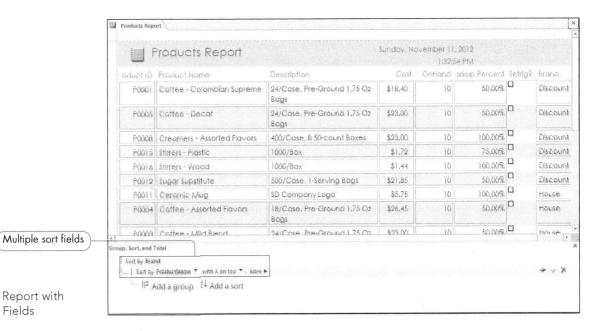

Multiple sort fields

FIGURE 4.39 Report with Multiple Sort Fields

Quick Concepts

1. Compare controls in forms and controls in reports. *p. 196*

2. What are the benefits of using the report wizard? *p. 198*

3. What is the difference between Print Preview and Report view? *pp. 203–204*

4. What are the benefits of a report layout control when modifying a report? *pp. 207–208*

5. Why is sorting the records in a report important? *p. 208*

Watch the Video
for this Hands-
On Exercise!

MyITLab®
HOE2 Training

## 2 Report Basics

You create a Products report using the Access Report tool to help Ryung stay on top of the key data for her business. After Access creates the report, you modify the column widths so the entire report fits on one page (portrait or landscape, depending on the report). You also use the Report Wizard tool to create other reports for Ryung.

**Skills covered:** Create Reports Using Report Tools • Use Report Views • Modify a Report • Sort Records in a Report

---

## STEP 1 >> CREATING REPORTS USING REPORT TOOLS

You use the Report tool to create an Access report to help Ryung manage her product information. This report is especially useful for determining which products she needs to order to fill upcoming orders. Refer to Figure 4.40 as you complete Step 1.

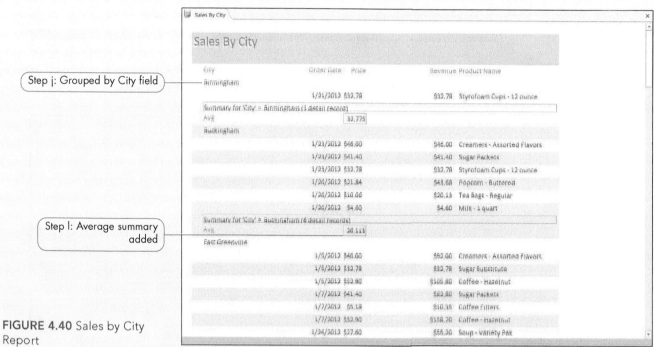

Step j: Grouped by City field

Step l: Average summary added

**FIGURE 4.40** Sales by City Report

a. Open *a04h1Coffee_LastFirst* if you closed it at the end of Hands-On Exercise 1. Click the **FILE tab**, select **Save As**, and then click **Save As**. Type **a04h2Coffee_LastFirst** as the file name, changing *h1* to *h2*. Click **Save**.

b. Select the **Products table** in the Navigation Pane. Click the **CREATE tab** and click **Report** in the Reports group.

   Access creates a new tabular layout report based on the Products table. The report opens in Layout view ready to edit.

c. Click the **Products title** at the top of the report to select it, click again on **Products**, and then change the title to **Products Report**. Press **Enter** to accept the change.

d. Right-click the **Products report tab** and select **Print Preview**.

   The report is too wide for the page; you will exit Print Preview and change the orientation to Landscape.

**e.** Click **Close Print Preview**.

**f.** Click the **PAGE SETUP tab** and click **Landscape** in the Page Layout group.

The report changes to Landscape orientation. Most of the columns now fit onto one page. You will make further revisions to the report later on so that it fits on one page.

**g.** Save the report as **Products Report**. Close the report.

**h.** Select the **Revenue query** in the Navigation Pane. Click the **CREATE tab** and click **Report Wizard** in the Reports group.

The Report Wizard launches.

**i.** Click the **City field** and click the > **button** to add the City field to the report. Repeat the same process for the **OrderDate**, **Price**, **Revenue**, and **ProductName fields**. Click **Next**.

**j.** Select **City** and click the > **button** to add grouping by city. Click **Next**.

**k.** Select **OrderDate** for the sort order and leave the order as **Ascending**. Click **Summary Options**.

**l.** Click the **Avg check box** on the Price row to summarize the Price field. Click **OK**.

**m.** Click **Next**. Click **Next** again to accept the default layout.

**n.** Type **Sales by City** for the title of the report. Click **Finish**.

The report is displayed in Print Preview mode. Some of the data values and labels cannot be seen. Next, you will adjust the controls.

**o.** Click **Close Print Preview**.

**p.** Switch to Layout view if necessary and adjust the controls so all the field values are visible as shown in Figure 4.40.

**q.** Display the report in Print Preview to verify your changes.

**r.** Save and close the report.

## STEP 2 ≫ USING REPORT VIEWS

The Products report you created for La Vida Mocha looks very good, according to Ryung. However, she does not have Access at home and would like to have a copy of the report saved so she can bring it home. You will save a copy of the report for her.

**a.** Open the **Products Report** and switch to **Print Preview**. Click **PDF or XPS** in the Data group on the PRINT PREVIEW tab. Enter the file name **a04h2Products_LastFirst** and click **Publish**.

Windows will open the report in your system's default PDF viewer, which may be Adobe Reader or the Windows 8 Reader app.

**b.** Switch back to Access, if necessary. Click **Close** when asked if you want to save the export steps.

**c.** Click **Close Print Preview** and close the report.

## STEP 3 ≫ MODIFYING A REPORT

Ryung realized the Products table is missing a field. She would like you to add this to the table and update the report to reflect the new field. She would also like to make sure the report fits nicely onto one landscape page. She has also asked you to show her some sample color schemes.

**a.** Right-click the **Products table** and select **Design view**.

You need to add the OnHand field to the Products table.

**b.** Click the **MarkupPercent field** and click **Insert Rows** in the Tools group on the DESIGN tab.

A new blank row displays above the MarkupPercent field.

**c.** Type **OnHand** in the **Field Name box** and select **Number** as the Data Type.

**d.** Save the table. Click **View** to change to Datasheet view.

The new OnHand column appears empty in each row. Next, you will add sample data to the new field.

**e.** Fill in the number **10** for each item's OnHand field.

**f.** Close the Products table.

**g.** Right-click the **Products Report** and select **Layout view**.

**h.** Click **Add Existing Fields** in the Tools group on the DESIGN tab unless the Field List already appears on the right of your screen.

**i.** Drag the **OnHand field** from the Field List pane between the Cost and MarkupPercent fields. Close the Field List pane.

Because of the tabular layout control, Access adjusts all the columns to make room for the new OnHand field.

**j.** Display the report in Print Preview.

The report is still too wide for a single page.

**k.** Click **Close Print Preview**. Switch to Layout view if necessary.

**l.** Click anywhere on the **Year Introduced column**. Click the **ARRANGE tab** and click **Select Column** in the Rows & Columns group. Press **Delete** to remove the column.

The Year Introduced column is removed from the report and the other fields fill the empty space.

> **TROUBLESHOOTING:** If you cannot see the Year Introduced column, try scrolling to the right.

**m.** Click the **ProductID column heading** and drag the right border to the left until the Product ID heading still fits, but any extra white space is removed.

**n.** Click the **Refrigeration Needed column heading** and rename the column **Refrig?**. Adjust the column width of the Refrig? column so any extra white space is removed.

**o.** Click **Themes** in the Themes group on the DESIGN tab.

The available predefined themes display.

**p.** Right-click the **Organic theme** and choose **Apply Theme to This Object Only**. Display the report in Print Preview.

Access reformats the report using the Organic theme.

> **TROUBLESHOOTING:** If you cannot figure out which theme is which, you can hover the mouse over each theme and a ScreenTip will display the theme name.

**q.** Click **Close Print Preview**. Click the **FILE tab**, select **Save As**, select **Save Object As**, and then click **Save As**. Type **Products Organic** as the report name and click **OK**.

You saved the report with one theme. Now, you will apply a second theme to the report and save it with a different name.

**r.** Switch to Layout view and click **Themes** in the Themes group to apply a different theme.

**s.** Right-click the **Retrospect theme** and choose **Apply Theme to This Object Only**. Display the report in Print Preview.

If we do not tell Access to apply the theme to this object only, all objects will change.

**t.** Click **Close Print Preview**. Click the **FILE tab**, select **Save As**, select **Save Object As**, and then click **Save As**. Type **Products Retrospect** as the report name and click **OK**. Close the report.

You will be able to show Ryung two different themes.

## STEP 4 ≫ SORTING RECORDS IN A REPORT

Ryung would like the Products Report report to be sorted by Product Name order (rather than ProductID order). You change the sort order and preview again to see the results.

**a.** Open **Products Report** in Layout view.

> **TROUBLESHOOTING:** If you cannot see the Products Report, click the Shutter Bar to maximize the Navigation Pane.

**b.** Click **Group & Sort** in the Grouping & Totals group on the DESIGN tab.

The *Add a group* and *Add a sort* options appear at the bottom of the report.

> **TROUBLESHOOTING:** If the options do not appear, they may have been showing. Try clicking Group & Sort again.

**c.** Click **Add a sort**.

A new Sort bar displays at the bottom of the report.

**d.** Select **Brand** from the list.

The report is now sorted by Brand in Ascending order (with Discount on top).

**e.** Click **Add a group**.

**f.** Select **Brand** from the list.

The report is now grouped by Brand.

**g.** Display the report in Print Preview.

**h.** Close Print Preview and save and close the report.

**i.** Close the database. Submit the database and the PDF file *a04h2Products_LastFirst* based on your instructor's directions.

# Chapter Objectives Review

After reading this chapter, you have accomplished the following objectives:

## 1. Create forms using form tools.

- A form is used to add data to or edit data in a table.
- Access provides 14 different tools for creating forms.
- If you use a form, you are less likely to edit the wrong record.
- Forms can show data from multiple tables at once.
- Forms can be customized to match a paper form.
- Identify a record source: A record source is the table or query that supplies the records.
- Use the Form tool: The Form tool creates a basic form.
- Understand controls: Controls are the text boxes, buttons, boxes, and other tools you use to add, edit, and display data in a form or report.
- Work with form views: Form view is a simplified interface used for data entry, but it allows no changes. Layout view allows users to make changes to the layout while viewing the data on the form. Design view allows you to change advanced design settings you cannot see in the Layout view.
- Work with a subform: A subform displays data from a related table for each record in the main table.

## 2. Create a split form: A split form combines two views of the same record source—one section is displayed in a stacked layout and the other section is displayed in a tabular layout.

- Create a multiple-item form: This form displays multiple records in a tabular layout similar to a table's Datasheet view, with more customization options.
- Create forms using the other form tools: A Datasheet form is a replica of a table or query's Datasheet view except that it still retains some of the form properties. The Form Design tool and the Blank Form tools can be used to create a form manually. The Navigation option in the Forms group enables you to create user interface forms that have the look and feel of a Web-based form and enable users to open and close the objects of a database. The Modal Dialog Form tool can be used to create a dialog box.

## 3. Use form views.

- Edit data in Form view: Most users will work in Form view. This allows changes to data but not to design elements.
- Alter a form in Layout view: Layout view allows you to change the design of a form while viewing data.
- Add a field to a form: Fields can be added to an existing form using the Field List.
- Delete a field from a form: Fields can be removed, but you may need to select the entire control to avoid leaving empty space in the form.
- Adjust column widths in a form: Column widths often need to be adjusted. Numeric fields may show up as #### if the value cannot be displayed in the box.
- Use the Form Layout tools tabs: There are three Form Layout tabs that allow you to manipulate the design of a form.

- Modify form controls using the Format tab: The Format tab allows changes to the font, including bold, italic, underlining, font size, font color, font background, and alignment.
- Select controls: Controls can be selected manually or by using the Arrange tab.
- Add a theme to a form: Themes can be applied to a single form or to all objects in the database.
- Add styling to a form: Forms can have many types of styles applied. Take care to avoid too many styles on a single form, as it can distract from the form.

## 4. Work with a form layout control.

- Modify a form using the Arrange tab: The Arrange tab appears in both Layout view and Design view and allows you to change form layout, field order, and spacing options.
- The Table group lets you add gridlines, change from stacked to tabular layout (and vice versa), or remove a form's layout.
- The Move group contains lets you move fields.
- The Position group lets you modify the margins and the padding of controls in a form.

## 5. Sort records in form.

- Default sort order is the sort order of the data source (table, query, etc.).
- Sort by a single field: Forms can be sorted by a single field in either ascending or descending order.
- Remove sorting in a form: Sorts can be removed from a form at any point.

## 6. Create reports using report tools.

- A report is a document that displays information from a database in a format that outputs meaningful information to its readers.
- Access reports can be printed, viewed on screen, or saved as files.
- Reports cannot change data in your database.
- Use the Report tool: Access has five report tools: The Report tool instantly creates a tabular report based on the table or query currently selected. The Report Design tool creates a new blank report in Design view. The Blank Report tool creates a new blank report so that you can insert fields and controls manually and design the report. The Report Wizard tool helps you create a report. The Labels tool creates a page of mailing labels using a template.
- Use the Report Wizard to create a report: The Report Wizard will guide you step by step through creating a report, asking questions and generating output.
- Use the Report Wizard with grouping: The Report Wizard options will change when you add grouping. It will also allow summary options such as creating a sum of a field for each grouping level.
- Use the Label Wizard: The Label Wizard can produce printable labels. Access includes predefined standard formats for common labels.

7. **Use report views.**
   - View a report in Report view: Report view is ideal for viewing data onscreen. Neither data nor design can be changed.
   - Alter a report in Layout view: Layout view allows you to change the design of a report while viewing data.
   - Print or save a report in Print Preview: Print Preview shows the way the report will display when printed. It also allows you to save the report as a file in a number of formats.

8. **Modify a report.**
   - Modify a report using the Design tab: The Design tab allows you to add or change sorting, change report theme, and insert additional controls.
   - Modify a report using the Arrange tab: The Arrange tab allows you to change the report layout, move fields, and insert spaces.
   - Modify report controls using the Format tab: The Format tab allows changes to the font, including bold, italic, underlining, font size, font color, font background, and alignment.
   - Add a field to a report: Fields can be added to an existing report using the Field List.
   - Delete a field from a report: Fields can be removed, but you may need to select the entire control to avoid leaving empty space in the report.
   - Adjust column widths in a report: Column widths often need to be adjusted. Numeric fields may show up as #### if the value cannot be displayed in the box.
   - Change margins and orientation: You can display the report in portrait or landscape format and increase or decrease margin size.
   - Add a theme to the report: Themes can be applied to a single report or to all objects in the database.
   - Work with a Report Layout control: The Layout control keeps the fields neatly spaced, making it harder to place fields in an exact location but keeping a standard format.

9. **Sort records in a report.**
   - Default sort order for reports is the sort order of the record source.
   - Change the sorting in a report: Sorting can be done by a single or by multiple fields.

# Key Terms Matching

Match the key terms with their definitions. Write the key term letter by the appropriate numbered definition.

a. Controls
b. Design view
c. Form
d. Form tool
e. Form view
f. Label Wizard
g. Layout control
h. Layout view
i. Multiple Items form
j. Portable Document Format (PDF)
k. Print Preview
l. Record source
m. Report
n. Report tool
o. Report view
p. Report Wizard
q. Split form
r. Stacked layout
s. Tabular layout
t. Theme

1. _____ A database object that is used to add data into or edit data in a table. **p. 176**

2. _____ Used to create data entry forms for customers, employees, products, and other primary tables. **p. 176**

3. _____ The table or query that supplies the records for a form or report. **p. 177**

4. _____ Displays fields in a vertical column. **p. 178**

5. _____ Displays data horizontally. **p. 178**

6. _____ The text boxes, buttons, boxes, and other tools you use to add, edit, and display the data in a form or report. **p. 178**

7. _____ Provides guides to help keep controls aligned horizontally and vertically and give your form a uniform appearance. **p. 178**

8. _____ A simplified interface primarily used for data entry; does not allow you to make changes to the layout. **p. 178**

9. _____ Enables users to make changes to a layout while viewing the data on the form or report. **p. 179**

10. _____ Enables you to change advanced design settings you cannot see in the Layout view, such as a background image. **p. 179**

11. _____ Combines two views of the same record source—one section is displayed in a stacked layout and the other section is displayed in a tabular layout. **p. 180**

12. _____ Displays multiple records in a tabular layout similar to a table's Datasheet view, with more customization options. **p. 181**

13. _____ A defined set of colors, fonts, and graphics that can be applied to a form or report. **p. 185**

14. _____ A document that displays information from a database in a format that outputs meaningful information to its readers. **p. 196**

15. _____ Used to instantly create a tabular report based on the table or query currently selected. **p. 196**

16. _____ Asks you questions and then uses your answers to generate a customized report. **p. 198**

17. _____ Enables you to easily create mailing labels, name tags, and other specialized tags. **p. 202**

18. _____ Enables you to see what a printed report will look like in a continuous page layout. **p. 203**

19. _____ Enables you to see exactly what the report will look like when it is printed. **p. 204**

20. _____ A file type that was created for exchanging documents independent of software applications and operating system environment. **p. 204**

# Multiple Choice

1. The table or query that supplies the records for a form or report is also known as the:

   (a) Control.

   (b) Record Source.

   (c) Theme.

   (d) Tabular Layout.

2. Which of the following statements is *false*?

   (a) Both forms and reports can use tabular and stacked layouts.

   (b) A stacked layout displays data in a vertical column.

   (c) A tabular layout displays data horizontally.

   (d) Stacked layouts are more common for reports because they will use less paper when printed.

3. Which of the following is *not* an example of a control?

   (a) A text box on a form

   (b) Buttons on a report

   (c) A report

   (d) A box on a report

4. The simplest interface you can use to modify control widths in a form is in:

   (a) Layout view.

   (b) Form view.

   (c) Design view.

   (d) Report view.

5. Which of the following views is the most powerful, but also the most complicated?

   (a) Design view.

   (b) Layout view.

   (c) Form view/Report view.

   (d) Print Preview.

6. Which of the following statements about reports are *false*?

   (a) Reports can be saved to a file on your computer.

   (b) Reports are primarily used to modify data.

   (c) Reports can produce output in a number of ways, including mailing labels.

   (d) Reports can be created simply using the Report tool.

7. Use the _____ to see exactly what the printed report will look like before printing.

   (a) Report tool

   (b) Report Wizard

   (c) Report view

   (d) Print Preview

8. If you have a client working on a Mac system, which of the following file formats would be the best choice to use to ensure the client can open it?

   (a) Microsoft Word

   (b) Microsoft Excel

   (c) Microsoft Access

   (d) Portable Document Format (PDF)

9. Which of the following statements is *false*?

   (a) Reports are generally used for printing, emailing, or viewing data on the screen.

   (b) Layout controls for forms and reports are the defined sets of colors, fonts, and graphics.

   (c) Forms are often used for inputting data.

   (d) Forms and reports both include controls, such as text boxes, that can be resized.

10. Which of the following statements is *false*?

    (a) You can use grouping to show a list of properties by state.

    (b) Sorting can be done on both forms and reports.

    (c) Sorting can be done in ascending or descending order.

    (d) You can either group or sort (but not both).

# Practice Exercises

## 1 | Financial Management

You are working as a customer service representative for a financial management firm. Your task is to contact a list of prospective customers and introduce yourself and the services of your company. You will create a form to help you view one customer at a time while also helping add and update the data. After creating the form, you will customize it and add sorting. You will also create a report to show you all the data on one screen, for viewing purposes. This exercise follows the same set of skills as used in Hands-On Exercises 1 and 2 in the chapter. Refer to Figure 4.41 as you complete this exercise.

Step d: Title changed to New Leads

Step g: NetWorth field moved above FirstName

Step f: Font size changed to 14 for NetWorth

Step j: Sort added; Farrah Aaron is the first record

**FIGURE 4.41** Form After Moving Net Worth Control

a. Start Access and open **a04p1Prospects**. Save the database as **a04p1Prospects_LastFirst**.

b. Click the **Leads table**. Click the **CREATE tab** and click **Form** in the Forms group.

   A new form based on the Leads table displays in Layout view.

c. Click the **ID text box** and drag the right border of the first field to the left to shrink the column by approximately half of its original size.

   The other columns will shrink as well.

d. Change the title of the form to **New Leads**.

e. Click **Themes** in the Themes group of the DESIGN tab. Select the **Integral theme** (first row, third column).

f. Change the font size to **14** for the NetWorth text box control.

g. Click **Select Row** in the Rows & Columns group on the ARRANGE tab. Click **Move Up** in the Move group on the ARRANGE tab until *NetWorth* appears above *First*.

> **TROUBLESHOOTING:** If both items do not move together, undo, ensure both are selected, and then follow the instructions in step g.

NetWorth should now appear above the FirstName. See Figure 4.41.

h. Save the form as **Leads Form**. Switch to Form view.

i. Navigate to record 63. Enter your first and last names in the appropriate fields. Leave the e-mail address blank.

j. Click in the **Last field** (if necessary) and click **Ascending** in the Sort & Filter group of the HOME tab Farrah Aaron should be the first record displayed unless your last name appears before hers alphabetically.

k. Save and close the form.

l. Click the **Leads table**. Click **Report** in the Reports group on the CREATE tab.
A new report is created based on the Leads table.

m. Make fields as small as possible to remove extra white space. Do not try to fit the entire report all on one page, as you will be using this for on-screen viewing only.

n. Save the report as **Leads Report**. Close the report.

o. Exit Access. Submit the database based on your instructor's directions.

## 2 Comfort Insurance

The Human Resources department of the Comfort Insurance Agency has initiated its annual employee performance reviews. You will create a form for them to help organize input and a report showing employee salary increases and bonuses. The employee data, along with forms and reports, are stored in an Access database. You need to prepare a report showing employee raises and bonuses by city. This exercise follows the same set of skills as used in Hands-On Exercises 1 and 2 in this chapter. Refer to Figure 4.42 as you complete this exercise.

FIGURE 4.42 Final Employee Compensation Report

a. Open *a04p2Insurance*. Save the database as **a04p2Insurance_LastFirst**.

b. Select the **Locations table**. Click the **CREATE tab** and click **Form** in the Forms group.
A new form based on the Locations table opens in Layout view.

c. Click the **LocationID text box** containing *L01*. Move the mouse to the right edge of the shaded border until the mouse pointer changes to a double-headed arrow. Drag the right edge to the left to reduce the size of the text box to approximately half of its original size.

The LocationID field and all the other fields should become smaller.

d. Click the subform at the bottom of the form. Press **Delete** to delete the subform.

e. Click **Themes** in the Themes group on the DESIGN tab. Right-click the **Wisp theme** (third row, first column) and select **Apply Theme to This Object Only**.

f. Save the form as **Locations**. Close the form.

g. Select the **Locations table**. Click the **CREATE tab** and click **Report** in the Reports group.

A new tabular layout report based on the Locations table opens in Layout view.

h. Click the **LocationID label** and drag the right border of the label to the left to reduce the size of the control to approximately half of its original size.

i. Repeat the sizing process with the **Zipcode label** and the **OfficePhone label**. Adjust the other columns if necessary until there are no controls on the right side of the vertical dashed line.

j. Display the report in Print Preview. Verify that the report is only one page wide. Save the report as **Locations** and close the report.

k. Select the **Employees Query**. Click the **CREATE tab** and click **Report Wizard** in the Reports group to launch the Report Wizard. Respond to the questions as follows:
   - Click (≫) to add all the fields to the Selected Fields box. Click **Next**.
   - Accept grouping by Location. Click **Next**.
   - Select **LastName** for the first sort order and **FirstName** for the second. Click **Summary Options**.

> **TROUBLESHOOTING:** If you do not see summary options, click Back and click Summary Options at the bottom of the dialog box.

   - Click **Sum** for Salary, **Avg** for 2012Increase, and **Avg** for YearsWorked. Accept all other defaults. Click **OK**. Click **Next**.
   - Accept the Stepped layout. Change Orientation to **Landscape**. Click **Next**.
   - Type **Employee Compensation** for the title of the report. Click **Finish**.

The report is displayed in Print Preview mode. Some of the columns are too narrow. Next, you will adjust the columns.

l. Click **Close Print Preview**. Switch to Layout view.

m. Adjust the column widths so that all the data values are showing and the report appears on one page. Some of the columns will need to be reduced, and some will need to be widened.

n. Click **Themes** in the Themes group on the DESIGN tab. Right-click the **Slice theme** and choose **Apply Theme to This Object Only**.

o. Display the report in Print Preview. Close the Navigation Pane and verify that the report is still one page wide. Compare your report to Figure 4.42. Adjust column widths to display all values.

p. Save and close the Employee Compensation report. Close the database.

q. Exit Access. Submit based on your instructor's directions.

## 1 Hotel Chain

ANALYSIS
CASE

You are the general manager of a large hotel chain. You track revenue by categories, such as conference room rentals and weddings. You need to create a report that shows which locations are earning the most revenue in each category. You will also create a report to show you details of your three newest areas: St. Paul, St. Louis, and Seattle.

a. Open *a04m1Rewards*. Save the database as **a04m1Rewards_LastFirst**.

b. Select the **Members table** and create a Multiple Items form. Save the form as **Maintain Members**.

c. Modify the form in Layout view as follows:
   - Change the MemNumber label to **MemID** and reduce the MemNumber column width.
   - Adjust the column widths to eliminate extra white space.
   - Delete the form icon (the picture next to the title of the form) in the Form Header.

d. Change the sorting on the MemberSince control so that the members who joined most recently are displayed first.

 **DISCOVER**

e. Click on the **LastName field**. Change the Control Padding to **Wide**. Hint: Search **Control Padding Wide** in Access Help.

   The controls have some extra space between them.

f. Save and close the form.

g. Select the **Revenue query** and create a report using the Report Wizard. Answer the wizard prompts as follows:
   - Include all fields.
   - Add grouping by City and by ServiceName.
   - Add a Sum to the Revenue field and check the **Summary Only option**.
   - Choose **Outline Layout**.
   - Name the report **Revenue by City and Service**.

h. Scroll through all the pages to check the layout of the report while in Print Preview mode.

i. Exit Print Preview. Switch to Layout view and delete the NumInParty and PerPersonCharge controls.

j. Change the font size, font color, and/or background color of the Sum control (not the Revenue control) so the control stands out from the other controls.

k. Change the font size, font color, and/or background color of the Grand Total control (found at the end of the report) so the control stands out as well.

l. Change the sort on the report, so that it sorts by city in descending order—that is, so that the last city alphabetically (St. Paul) is displayed first.

 m. Examine the data in the report to determine which city of St. Paul, St. Louis, and Seattle has the highest Sum of event revenue. You will use this information to modify a query.

 n. Modify the Totals by Service query so the criteria for the City field is the city you determined had the highest sum from St. Paul, St. Louis, or Seattle. Save and close the query.

o. Create a report using the Report tool based on the Totals by Service query. Name the report **Targeted City**.

p. Close the report. Close the database.

q. Exit Access. Submit based on your instructor's directions.

## 2 Benefit Auction

FROM
SCRATCH

You are helping to organize a benefit auction to raise money for families who lost their homes in a natural disaster. The information for the auction is currently stored in an Excel spreadsheet, but you have volunteered to migrate this to Access. You will create a database that will store the data from Excel in an Access database. You will create a form to manage the data-entry process. You also need to create two reports: one that lists the items collected in each category and one for labels so you can send the donors a thank-you letter after the auction.

a. Open Access and create a new database named **a04m2Auction_LastFirst**. A new table appears with an ID column.

b. Switch to Design view. Type **Items** in the **Save As dialog box** and click **OK**.

c. Change the ID Field Name to **ItemID**. Type **Description** in the second row and press **Tab**. Accept **Short Text** as the Data Type. Type **50** in the **Field Size property** in Field Properties.

d. Type the remainder of the fields and adjust the data types as shown:

| Field Name | Data Type |
|---|---|
| DateOfDonation | Date/Time |
| Category | Short Text |
| Price | Currency |
| DonorName | Short Text |
| DonorAddress1 | Short Text |
| DonorAddress2 | Short Text |

e. Open Excel. Open the **a04m2_Items** file. Examine the length of the Category, DonorName, DonorAddress1, and DonorAddress2 columns. Determine how many characters are needed for each field, and round to the nearest 5. For example, if a field needs 23 characters, you would round up to 25. You will use this to change field sizes in the table.

f. Change the field size for the Category, DonorName, DonorAddress1, and DonorAddress2 to the sizes you chose in step e. Save the table.

g. Copy and paste the rows from the Excel file into the table. Resize the columns so all data is visible. Close the table.

> **TROUBLESHOOTING:** Recall that you must click the Record Selector (pencil icon, to the left of a blank row) to paste data.

> **TROUBLESHOOTING:** Once you have pasted the data, ensure your chosen field sizes did not cause you to lose data. If so, update the field size, delete the records you pasted in, and then repeat step g.

h. Verify that the Items table is selected. Create a new form using the Form tool.

i. Change the layout of the form to a **Tabular Layout**. Resize field widths to reduce extra space. It is acceptable for field values to appear on two lines.

j. Change the title of the form to **Items for Auction**.

k. Add conditional formatting so that each Price that is greater than 90 has a text color of **Green**. Use the Green color in the first row of the options.

l. Save the form as **Auction Items Form**.

m. Switch to Form view. Create a new record with the following information. Note it will automatically assign an ItemID of 27 for you.

| Description | DateOfDonation | Category | Price | DonorName | DonorAddress1 | DonorAddress2 |
|---|---|---|---|---|---|---|
| iPad | 12/31/2016 | House | $400 | Staples | 500 Market St | Brick, NJ 08723 |

n. Add a sort to the form, so the lowest priced items appear first. Close the form.

o. Select the **Items table** in the Navigation Pane and create a report using the Report Wizard. Include all fields except the donor address fields, group by Category, include the Sum of Price as a Summary Option, accept the default layout, and then save the report **Auction Items by Category**.

p. Switch to Layout view and adjust the controls so all data is visible. Preview the report to verify the column widths are correct.

q. Sort the report so the least expensive items are shown first. Save and close the report.

r. Create mailing labels based on the Avery 5660 template. Place the donor name on the first line, address on the second, and city, state, and ZIP on the third line. Sort the labels by DonorName. Name the report **Donor Labels**. After you create the labels, display them in Print Preview mode verify everything will fit onto the label template. Close the label report.

s. Exit Access. Submit the database based on your instructor's directions.

## 3 Used Cell Phones for Sale

COLLABORATION CASE

You and a few of your classmates started a new business selling used cell phones, MP3 players, and accessories. You have been using an Access database to track your inventory. You need to create several forms and reports to increase database efficiency and analysis. You have used Access forms and reports as part of your classwork, but you would like to experiment with them as they apply to you in a real-world scenario.

a. Choose one unique type of form and one unique type of report each. Based on your experience in class, you saw there were a number of different types of forms and reports that can be created. Choose one each from the following:

Forms: Form tool, Form Wizard, Multiple Items Form, Split Form

Reports: Report Tool, Report Wizard, Label Wizard

b. Open Access and open the *a04t1Phones* database individually. Save the file as **a04t1Phones_LastFirst**. Each of you will create your forms and reports in an individual database.

c. Create a form and a report based on the Inventory table, using the type of form and report you chose in step a, unless you chose Label Wizard. If you chose Label Wizard, you should create a report based on the Mailing List table, using Avery 8660 as your destination label.

d. Save the form and report as **LastFirst**, replacing Last and First with your last and first names.

e. Make the report as attractive and useful as possible. You may want to change sorting, add grouping (to reports), remove or add a layout control, change formatting options, and/or change the background color. Modify the form and report, save the changes, and exit Access.

f. Meet as a group. Open the *a04t1Phones* database and save the file as **a04t1Phones_GroupName**.

g. Import the form and report from each of your databases.

Your *a04t1Phones_GroupName* file will now have one form and one report for each student.

h. Examine the forms and reports each of you created.

i. Examine your results. Determine which forms and reports you would keep, if this were the real world. Rename the forms and reports you would keep as **Keep_LastFirst** and rename the ones you would discard as **Discard_LastFirst**. Do not delete the forms and reports you will not use.

j. Modify the forms and reports you plan to keep as a group, if necessary. Save the changes and close all forms and reports. Ensure each student has a copy of the final *a04t1Phones_GroupName* database.

k. Exit Access and submit both the *a04t1Phones_GroupName* and *a04t1Phones_LastFirst* databases based on your instructor's directions.

# Beyond the Classroom

## Create a Split Form

This chapter introduced you to Access forms, including the split form. It is possible to turn an existing form into a split form if you modify a few form properties. Perform an Internet search to find the steps to convert a form to a split form. First, create a new database and name the file **a04b2Split_LastFirst**. Next, import *only* the Books table and Books form from the *a04b2BooksImport* database. To import the objects, click the **External Data tab** and click **Access** in the Import & Link group. After the new objects have been imported, use the information from the Internet to convert the Books form into a split form. Make sure the datasheet is on the bottom half. Change the form so it sorts by Title in ascending order. Save the form as **Split Form Books**. Close Access. Submit the database based on your instructor's directions.

## Properties by City

Munesh, a co-worker, is having difficulty with an Access report and asked you for your assistance. He was trying to fix the report and seems to have made things worse. Open the *a04b3Sales* database and save the file as **a04b3Sales_LastFirst**. In the new database, open Properties Report in Report View. Notice Munesh moved fields around and the report does not fit on one page. In addition, there is a big gap between two fields and he moved the Bed and Bath fields so they are basically on top of one another. Add all of the fields to a Tabular Layout. Add grouping by City. Sort the report by Year Built in descending order. Change the report to Landscape orientation and adjust the column widths so they all fit onto one page. Save the new report as **Properties by City**. Close Access. Submit the database based on your instructor's directions.

## Performance Reviews

Passaic County Medical Monitoring provides visiting nurse care for patients in and around Passaic County, New Jersey. They have recently moved their records into an Access database. The director of Human Resources, Farrah Hassan, brings the nurses in yearly for a performance review. Employees are rated by a survey given to patients, asking them to rate the nurses on a scale of 1 (poor) to 5 (superb). You have been asked to create a one-page summary report to show the average of each employee's ratings. You will open her *a04b4Perform* database and save it as **a04b4Perform_LastFirst**. Use the Report Wizard to create a report based on the Performance and Nurses tables, group by the nurse, and add summary options to average the results for Promptness, Attitude, Knowledge, and Gentleness. The final report should display the NurseID, NurseFirst, and NurseLast fields and the averages for each of the four columns. You will also want to format each of the columns in the final report so they show two decimal places. You calculated the results by hand for nurse 1, Lan Wang, and her averages were 3.00 for Promptness, 3.11 for Attitude, 3.67 for Knowledge, and 3.67 for Gentleness, so when you create your report, you can check that it shows the correct data. Save the report as **Overall Ratings**, close Access, and submit the database based on your instructor's directions.

# Capstone Exercise

Your boss asked you to prepare a schedule for each speaker for the national conference being hosted next year on your campus. She wants to mail the schedules to the speakers so that they can provide feedback on the schedule prior to its publication. You assure her that you can accomplish this task with Access.

## Database File Setup

You need to copy an original database file, rename the copied file, and then open the copied database to complete this capstone exercise. After you open the copied database, you replace an existing employee's name with your name.

a. Open *a04c1_NatConf*.

b. Save the database as **a04c1NatConf_LastFirst**.

c. Open the Speakers table.

d. Find and replace *YourName* with your name. Close the table.

## Create and Customize a Form

You need to create a form to add and update Speakers. Use the Form tool to create the form and modify the form as explained. You will also add a layout to an existing form.

a. Select the **Speakers table** as the record source for the form.

b. Use the Form tool to create a new stacked form.

c. Change the title to **Enter/Edit Speakers**.

d. Reduce the width of the text box controls to approximately half of their original size.

e. Delete the Sessions subform.

f. View the form and data in Form view. Sort the records by LastName in ascending order.

g. Save the form as **Edit Speakers**. Close the form.

h. Open the Room Information form in Layout view. The form does not have a Form Layout. Select all controls and apply the **Stacked Layout**.

i. Save and close the form.

## Create a Report

You need to create a report based on the Speaker and Room Schedule query. You decide to use the Report Wizard to accomplish this task. You will also need to email the schedule to the presenters, so you will save the report as a PDF.

a. Select the **Speaker and Room Schedule query** as the record source for the report.

b. Activate the **Report Wizard** and use the following options as you go through the Wizard:

- Select all of the available fields for the report.
- View the data by Speakers.
- Accept LastName and FirstName as grouping levels.
- Use **Date** as the primary sort field in ascending order.
- Accept the Stepped and Portrait options.
- Save the report as **Speaker Schedule**.
- Switch to Layout view and apply the **Organic theme** to only this report.

c. Preview the report. Switch to Layout view. Adjust the column widths if necessary.

d. Switch to Print Preview and save the report as a PDF named **a04c1Speaker_LastFirst**.

e. When the PDF displays, close the program that displays it and return to Access. Exit Print Preview. Close the report.

## Add an Additional Field

You realize the session times were not included in the query. You add the field to the query and then start over with the Report Wizard.

a. Open the Speaker and Room Schedule query in Design view.

b. Add the **StartingTime field** in the Sessions table to the design grid, after the Date field. Run the query.

c. Save and close the query.

d. Click the **Speaker and Room Schedule query**. Start the Report Wizard again and use the following options:

- Select all of the available fields for the report.
- View the data by Speakers.
- Use the LastName, FirstName fields as the primary grouping level.
- Use Date as the primary sort field in ascending order.
- Use StartingTime as the secondary sort field in Ascending order.
- Select the **Stepped** and **Portrait options**.
- Name the report **Speaker Schedule Revised**.
- Switch to Layout view and apply the **Facet theme** (first row, second column) to only this report.

e. Adjust the column widths in Layout view so that all the data is visible.

f. Add a space to the column heading labels as needed. For example, the column LastName should read Last Name.

g. Save and close the report. Close the database.

h. Exit Access. Submit the database and PDF based on your instructor's directions.

# Access Application Capstone Exercise

**FROM SCRATCH**

You were recently hired by your local college to help with registering all transfer students. The college's Transfer Counseling Department is a one-stop location for transfer students to come with questions. They have been working with Excel spreadsheets generated by the Information Technology department, but they are hoping to do more with an Access database. They have had a number of problems, including employees putting information in the wrong fields, putting information in the wrong format, and creating incorrect formulas. They are also hoping for more consistent ways of finding information, as well as being able to generate reports. Your tasks include importing an existing Excel worksheet as a table into your Access database; modifying the table; creating a relationship between two tables; creating queries with calculated fields, functions, and totals; creating a form for input; and creating a report.

## Set Up the Database File and Import an Excel Worksheet

To start, you have been provided with a database the Information Technology department created. The database has one table and one form. You will be importing an Excel spreadsheet into a table and creating a primary key.

a. Start Access. Open *a00c1College* and save the database as **a00c1College_LastFirst**.

b. Import the *a00c1Transfer* Excel workbook into a table named **Transfer Schools**. While importing the data, choose **StudentID** as the primary key field. Ensure *StudentID* has a data type of Short Text.

## Modify a Table

Now that you have imported the data from the spreadsheet, you will modify the field properties in the Transfer Schools table and demonstrate sorting.

a. Set the StudentID field size to **10**.

b. Remove the @ symbol from the StudentID format property.

c. Change the AdmittingSchool field size to **75**.

d. Change the RegistrationFee and TuitionDue fields to have **0** decimal places.

e. Switch to Datasheet View. Resize all columns so all data are displayed.

f. Sort the Transfer Schools table on the CreditsTransferred field in ascending order.

g. Save and close the table.

## Create Relationships

Now that the table is imported and modified, you will create a relationship between the two tables.

a. Add the Transfer Schools and Transfer Students tables to the Relationships window.

b. Create a one-to-one relationship between the StudentID field in the Transfer Students (primary) table and the StudentID field in the Transfer Schools (related) table. Enforce referential integrity between the two tables.

c. Save the changes and close the Relationships window.

## Modify Data in a Form

You will demonstrate changing information in a form.

a. Open the Transfer Students Data Entry form.

b. Change the major for *Cornelius Kavanaugh* to **Elementary Education**. Close the form.

## Create a Query

Rey Rivera, a counselor in the center, would like your assistance in helping him find certain information. You will create a query for him and demonstrate how he can change information.

a. Create a new query using Design view. This query will access fields from both the Transfer Schools and Transfer Students tables. From the Transfer Students table, add the FirstName, LastName, Major, Class, and GPA fields. From the Transfer Schools table, add the AdmissionDate, TuitionDue, CreditsEarned, and CreditsTransferred fields.

b. Save the query as **Transfer Credits**.

c. Set the criteria in the AdmissionDate field to **8/1/2015**. Run the query (144 records will display).

d. Enter the TuitionDue for Diana Sullivan as **$1500** and the GPA for Audrey Owen as **3.51**.

e. Save the query.

## Create Calculated Fields

Now that you have created the query, you will create a second query for Rey that will calculate the number of credits students lost upon transfer, the tuition payments for which they will be responsible (assuming three payments per semester), and the payment due date.

a. Switch to Design view of the Transfer Credits query. Save the query as **Transfer Credit Calculations**.

b. Remove the criteria from the AdmissionDate field.

c. Create a calculated field in the first empty field cell of the query named **LostCredits** that subtracts CreditsTransferred from CreditsEarned.

d. Create another calculated field named **TuitionPayments** that determines tuition paid in three installments. Using the Pmt function, replace the rate argument with **0.025/3**, the num_periods argument with **3**, and the present_value argument with the student's tuition payment. Use **0** for the future_value and type arguments. Ensure the payment appears as a positive number.

e. Format the TuitionPayments calculated field as **Currency**.

f. Create another calculated field named **DueDate** after the TuitionPayments field. To calculate the due date, add **30** to their AdmissionDate. Run the query and verify that the three calculated fields have valid data.

g. Add a total row to the query. Average the GPA column and sum the LostCredits column. Save and close the query.

## Create a Totals Query

Cala Hajjar, the director of the center, needs to summarize information about the transfer students for the 2015–2016 academic year to present to the College's Board of Trustees. You will create a totals query for her to summarize the number of transfer students, average number of credits earned and transferred, and total tuition earned by transfer institution.

a. Create a new query in Design view. Add the Transfer Schools table.

b. Add the AdmittingSchool, StudentID, CreditsEarned, CreditsTransferred, and TuitionDue fields.

c. Sort the query by AdmittingSchool in ascending order.

d. Show the Total row. Group by AdmittingSchool and show the count of StudentID, the average CreditsEarned, the average of CreditsTransferred, and the sum of TuitionDue.

e. Format both average fields as **Standard**.

f. Change the caption for the StudentID field to **NumStudents**, the caption for the CreditsEarned average to **AvgCreditsEarned**, the caption for the CreditsTransferred average to **AvgCredits Transferred**, and the caption for SumOfTuitionDue to **TotalTuition**.

g. Run the query. Resize columns so all data are shown.

h. Save the query as **Transfer Summary**.

i. Close the query.

## Create a Form

Hideo Sasaki, the department's administrative assistant, will handle data entry. He has asked you to simplify the way he inputs information into the new table. You will create a form based on the new Transfer Schools table.

a. Create a Split Form using the Transfer Schools table as the source.

b. Change the height of the AdmittingSchool field to reduce extra space.

c. Remove the layout. Shrink each field so it is only as large as it needs to be.

d. Click on record 123455 in the bottom half of the split form. Make sure all fields are still visible. If not, adjust the controls so all values are visible.

e. Move the CreditsTransferred field so it is to the right of the CreditsEarned field on the same row.

f. Change the format of the TuitionDue field so the font size is **18** and the font color is **Red** (last row, second column in the *Standard Colors* section).

g. Change the fill color of the StudentID field to be **Yellow** (last row, fourth column in the *Standard Colors* section).

h. Save the form as **Transfer Schools Form**. Save and close the form.

## Create a Report

Cala Hajjar, the director of the center, saw the query you created for Rey. She is hoping you can create a more print-friendly version for her to distribute to the Board of Trustees. You will create a report based on the Transfer Credits Calculations query.

a. Create a report using the Report Wizard. Add the Class, FirstName, LastName, Major, GPA, and LostCredits fields from the Transfer Credit Calculations query. Do not add any grouping or sorting. Ensure the report is in Landscape orientation.

b. Save the report as **Transfer Students Report** and view the report in Layout view.

## Format a Report

Now that you have included the fields Cala has asked for, you will work to format the report to make the information more obvious.

a. Apply the **Wisp theme** (third row, first column) to this object only.

b. Group the report by the Class field. Sort the records within each group by LastName then by FirstName, both in ascending order.

c. Change the font size of the Class field to **16.**

d. Adjust the text boxes so the values are completely visible.

e. Switch to Print Preview mode and verify the report is only one page wide (note: it may be a number of pages long).

f. Export the results as a PDF document using the file name **a00c1Transfer_LastFirst**.

g. Save and close the report.

## Close and Submit Database

a. Compact and repair the database.

b. Create a backup of the database. Accept the default name for the backup.

c. Close all database objects and exit Access.

d. Submit the database, backup, and PDF based on your instructor's directions.

# Glossary

**Access** (Office Fundamentals) Relational database management software that enables you to record and link data, query databases, and create forms and reports. (Access) A database management system included in the Microsoft Office 2013 Professional suite.

**Aggregate function** Performs calculations on an entire column of data and returns a single value. Includes functions such as Sum, Avg, and Count.

**AND logical operator** Returns only records that meet all criteria.

**Argument** Any data needed to produce output for a function.

**Ascending** A sort that lists text data in alphabetical order or a numeric list in lowest to highest order.

**AutoNumber** A number data type that is generated by Access and is incremented each time a record is added.

**Back Up Database** An Access utility that creates a duplicate copy of the database.

**Backstage view** A component of Office 2013 that provides a concise collection of commands related to common file activities and provides information on an open file.

**Backup** A copy of a file or folder on another drive.

**Calculated field** Produces a value from an expression or function that references one or more existing fields.

**CamelCase notation** Uses no spaces in multiword field names but uses uppercase letters to distinguish the first letter of each new word.

**CAPTCHA** A scrambled code used with online forms to prevent mass sign-ups. It helps to ensure that an actual person is requesting the account.

**Caption property** Used to create a more readable label that appears in the top row in Datasheet view and in forms and reports.

**Cascade Delete Related Records** An option that directs Access to automatically delete all records in related tables that match the primary key that is deleted from a primary table.

**Cascade Update Related Fields** An option that directs Access to automatically update all foreign key values in a related table when the primary key value table is modified in a primary table.

**Charms** A toolbar for Windows 8 made up of five icons (Search, Share, Start, Devices, and Settings) that enables you to search for files and applications, share information with others within an application that is running, return to the Start screen, control devices that are connected to your computer, or modify various settings depending on which application is running when accessing the Setting icon.

**Clip art** An electronic illustration that can be inserted into an Office project.

**Clipboard** An Office feature that temporarily holds selections that have been cut or copied and allows you to paste the selections.

**Cloud storage** A technology used to store files and to work with programs that are stored in a central location on the Internet.

**Command** A button or area within a group that you click to perform tasks.

**Compact and Repair** An Access utility that reduces the size of the database and can repair a corrupt database.

**Comparison operator** An operator used to evaluate the relationship between two quantities.

**Constant** A value that does not change.

**Contextual tab** A Ribbon tab that displays when an object, such as a picture or table, is selected. A contextual tab contains groups and commands specific to the selected object.

**Controls** The text boxes, buttons, boxes, and other tools you use to add, edit, and display the data in a form or report.

**Copy** To duplicate an item from the original location and place the copy in the Office Clipboard.

**Criteria row** A row in the Query Design view that determines which records will be selected.

**Criterion** A number, text phrase, or an expression used to select records.

**Custom Web app** A database that can be built, used, and shared with others through the use of a host server (e.g., SharePoint or Office 365).

**Cut** To remove an item from the original location and place it in the Office Clipboard.

**Data redundancy** The unnecessary storing of duplicate data in two or more tables.

**Data type** Determines the type of data that can be entered and the operations that can be performed on that data.

**Database** A collection of data organized as meaningful information that can be accessed, managed, stored, queried, sorted, and reported.

**Database management system (DBMS)** A software system that provides the tools needed to create, maintain, and use a database.

**Datasheet view** A view that enables you to add, edit, and delete the records of a table.

**Date arithmetic** The process of adding or subtracting one date from another, or adding or subtracting a constant from a date.

**Default** Office settings that remain in effect unless you specify otherwise.

**Delimiter** A special character that surrounds the criterion's value.

**Descending** A sort that lists text data in reverse alphabetical order or a numeric list in highest to lowest order.

**Design view** A view that enables you to create tables, add and delete fields, and modify field properties; or to change advanced design settings not seen in Layout view, such as a background image.

**Dialog box** A window that displays when a program requires interaction with you, such as inputting information, before completing a procedure. This window typically provides access to more precise, but less frequently used, commands.

**Dialog Box Launcher**   An icon in a Ribbon group that you can click to open a related dialog box. It is not found in all groups.

**Enforce referential integrity**   A relationship option that ensures that data cannot be entered into a related table unless it first exists in a primary table.

**Enhanced ScreenTip**   A feature that provides a brief summary of a command when you point to the command button.

**Excel**   A software application used to organize records, financial transactions, and business information in the form of worksheets.

**Expression**   A formula used to calculate new fields from the values in existing fields.

**Expression Builder**   An Access tool that helps you create more complicated expressions.

**Field**   The smallest data element in a table, such as first name, last name, address, or phone number.

**Field property**   A characteristic of a field that determines how a field looks and behaves.

**Field row**   A row in the Query Design view that displays the field name.

**Field selector**   The column heading of a datasheet used to select a column.

**File**   Electronic data such as documents, databases, slide shows, worksheets, digital photographs, music, videos, and Web pages.

**File Explorer**   A component of the Windows operating system that can be used to create and manage folders.

**Filter**   Displays a subset of records based on a specified criterion.

**Filter by Form**   A filtering method that displays records based on multiple criteria.

**Filter by Selection**   A filtering method that displays only records that match selected criteria.

**Find**   An Office feature that locates a word or phrase that you indicate in a document.

**Folder**   A directory into which you place data files in order to organize them for easier retrieval.

**Font**   A combination of typeface and type style.

**Foreign key**   A field in one table that is also a primary key of another table.

**Form**   A database object that is used to add, edit, or delete table data.

**Form tool**   Used to create data entry forms for customers, employees, products, and other primary tables.

**Form view**   A simplified interface primarily used for data entry. Does not allow you to make changes to the layout.

**Format Painter**   A command that copies the formatting of text from one location to another.

**Function**   A predefined computation that simplifies creating a complex calculation and produces a result based on inputs known as arguments.

**Gallery**   A set of selections that displays when you click a More button, or in some cases when you click a command, in a Ribbon group.

**Group**   A subset of a tab that organizes similar tasks together; to combine two or more objects.

**Grouping**   Allows you to summarize your data by the values of a field.

**Homegroup**   A Windows 8 feature that enables you to share resources on a home network.

**Indexed property**   Setting that enables quick sorting in primary key order and quick retrieval based on the primary key.

**Join line**   A line used to create a relationship between two tables using a common field.

**Key Tip**   The letter or number for the associated keyboard shortcut that displays over features on the Ribbon or Quick Access Toolbar.

**Label Wizard**   Enables you to easily create mailing labels, name tags, and other specialized tags.

**Landscape**   An orientation for a displayed page or worksheet that is wider than it is tall.

**Layout control**   Provides guides to help keep controls aligned horizontally and vertically and give your form a uniform appearance.

**Library**   A collection of files from different locations that is displayed as a single unit.

**Live Preview**   An Office feature that provides a preview of the results of a selection when you point to an option in a list or gallery. Using Live Preview, you can experiment with settings before making a final choice.

**Macro**   A stored series of commands that carry out an action.

**Mailing label report**   A specialized report that comes preformatted to coordinate with name-brand labels.

**Margin**   The area of blank space that displays to the left, right, top, and bottom of a document or worksheet.

**Microsoft Office**   A productivity software suite including four primary software components, each one specializing in a particular type of output.

**Mini toolbar**   The feature that provides access to common formatting commands, displayed when text is selected.

**Module**   An object that is written using Visual Basic for Applications (VBA) and adds functionality to a database.

**Multiple Items form**   Displays multiple records in a tabular layout similar to a table's Datasheet view, with more customization options such as the ability to add graphical elements, buttons, and other controls.

**Multitable query**   Contains two or more tables. It enables you to take advantage of the relationships that have been set in your database.

**Navigation bar**   Bar located at the bottom of a table, query, or form that is used to move through records.

**Navigation Pane**   (Office Fundamentals) A section of the File Explorer interface that provides ready access to computer resources, folders, files, and networked peripherals. (Access) An interface element that organizes and lists database objects.

**Normalization**   The practice of good database design involving grouping data into the correct tables.

**NOT logical operator**   Returns all records except the specified criteria.

**Null**   The term Access uses to describe a blank field.

**Number data type**   A data type that can store only numerical data.

**Object**   A main component that is created and used to make a database function.

**One-to-many relationship** A relationship established when the primary key value in the primary table can match many of the foreign key values in the related table.

**Operating system** Software that directs computer activities such as checking all components, managing system resources, and communicating with application software.

**OR logical operator** Returns records meeting any of the specified criteria.

**Order of operations (order of precedence)** Determines the sequence by which operations are calculated in an expression.

**Paste** To place a cut or copied item in another location.

**Picture** A graphic file that is retrieved from storage media or the Internet and placed in an Office project.

**Pmt function** A predefined formula in Access that calculates the periodic loan payment.

**Portable Document Format (PDF)** A file type that was created for exchanging documents independent of software applications and operating system environment.

**Portrait** An orientation for a displayed page or worksheet that is taller than it is wide.

**PowerPoint** A software application used to create dynamic presentations to inform groups and persuade audiences.

**Primary key** The field (or combination of fields) that uniquely identifies each record in a table.

**Print Preview** Enables you to see exactly what the report will look like when it is printed.

**Property sheet** Enables you to change settings such as number format, number of decimal places, and caption, among many others.

**Query** Enables you to ask questions about the data stored in a database and then provides the answers to the questions by providing subsets or summaries of data.

**Query Design view** Enables you to create queries; the Design view is divided into two parts—the top portion displays the tables and the bottom portion (known as the *query design grid*) displays the fields and the criteria.

**Query sort order** Determines the order of records in the query's Datasheet view.

**Quick Access Toolbar** A component of Office 2013, located at the top-left corner of the Office window, that provides handy access to commonly executed tasks such as saving a file and undoing recent actions.

**Record** A group of related fields representing one entity, such as data for one person, place, event, or concept.

**Record selector** A small box at the beginning of a row used to select a record.

**Record source** The table or query that supplies the records for a form or report.

**Referential integrity** Rules in a database that are used to preserve relationships between tables when records are changed.

**Related tables** Tables that are joined in a relationship using a common field.

**Relational database management system (RDBMS)** A database management system that uses the relational model to manage groups of data (tables) and rules (relationships) between tables.

**Relationship** A connection between two tables using a common field.

**Replace** An Office feature that finds text and replaces it with a word or phrase that you indicate.

**Report** An object that contains professional-looking formatted information from underlying tables or queries.

**Report tool** Used to instantly create a tabular report based on the table or query currently selected.

**Report view** Enables you to see what a printed report will look like in a continuous page layout.

**Report Wizard** Asks you questions and uses your answers to generate a customized report.

**Ribbon** The long bar of tabs, groups, and commands located just beneath the Title bar.

**Run command** Used to produce query results (the red exclamation point).

**Select query** A type of query that displays only the records that match criteria entered in Query Design view.

**Short text data type** A text field that can store up to 255 characters but has a default field size of 50 characters.

**Shortcut menu** Provides choices related to the selection or area at which you right-click.

**Show row** A row in the Query Design view that controls whether the field will be displayed in the query results.

**Simply Query Wizard** Provides dialog boxes to guide you through the query design process.

**SkyDrive** An application used to store, access, and share files and folders.

**SmartArt** A diagram that presents information visually to effectively communicate a message.

**Snip** The output of using the Snipping Tool.

**Snipping Tool** A Windows 8 accessory program that provides users the ability to capture an image of all (or part of) their computer's screen.

**Sort** The process of listing records or text in a specific sequence, such as alphabetically by last name.

**Sort row** A row in the Query Design view that enables you to sort in ascending or descending order.

**Split form** Combines two views of the same record source—one section is displayed in a stacked layout, and the other section is displayed in a tabular layout.

**Splitter bar** Divides a form into two halves.

**Stacked layout** Displays fields in a vertical column.

**Start screen** The display that you see after you turn on your computer and respond to any username and password prompts.

**Status bar** A horizontal bar found at the bottom of the program window that contains information relative to the open file.

**Subfolder** A folder that is housed within another folder.

**Syntax** The rules that dictate the structure and components required to perform the necessary calculations in an equation or to evaluate expressions.

**Tab** A component of the Ribbon that is designed to appear much like a tab on a file folder, with the active tab highlighted, that is used to organize groups by function.

**Table**   An object used to store and organize data in a series of records (rows) with each record made up of a number of fields (columns) and is the foundation of every database.

**Table row**   A row in Query Design view that displays the data source.

**Tabular layout**   Displays data horizontally.

**Template**   A predesigned file that incorporates formatting elements, such as theme and layouts, and may include content that can be modified.

**Theme**   A collection of design choices that includes colors, fonts, and special effects used to give a consistent look to a document, workbook, database form or report, or presentation.

**Tile**   A colorful block on the Start screen that when clicked will launch a program, file, folder, or other Windows 8 app.

**Title bar**   A component of Microsoft Office that identifies the current file name and the application in which you are working and includes control buttons that enable you to minimize, maximize, restore down, or close the application window.

**Toggle**   The action of switching from one setting to another. Several Home tab tasks, such as Bold and Italic, are actually toggle commands.

**Total row**   A table row that displays below the last row of records in an Excel table, or in Datasheet view of a table or query, and displays summary or aggregate statistics, such as a sum or an average.

**User interface**   The screen display through which you communicate with the software.

**Validation rule**   Prevents invalid data from being entered into a field.

**View**   The way a file appears onscreen.

**Wildcard**   A special character that can represent one or more characters in the criterion of a query.

**Windows 8**   A Microsoft operating system released in 2012 that can operate on touch-screen devices as well as laptops and desktops because it has been designed to accept multiple methods of input.

**Windows 8 app**   An application specifically designed to run in the Start screen interface of Windows 8 that is either already installed and ready to use or can be downloaded from the Windows Store.

**Word**   A word processing software application used to produce all sorts of documents, including memos, newsletters, forms, tables, and brochures.

**Zoom slider**   A horizontal bar on the far right side of the status bar that enables you to increase or decrease the size of file contents onscreen.

# Index

calculated results, exercises, 136–140
calculated results, formatting, 133–135
calculated results, recovery from common errors, 134
calculated results, saving, 133–135
calculated results, verifying, 135
CamelCase notation, 64
caption property, 67
Cascade Delete Related Records, 80
Cascade Update Related Fields, 80
common errors, 134
Compact and Repair utility, 11
comparison operator, 22, 92–93
constant, 63
constants, 130
controls, 178. *see also* layout control
controls, modifying, 184–185
controls, selecting, 185
correct syntax, 131–133
Create tab, 5
criteria row, 90
criterion, 21
custom Web app, 37

data arithmetic, 63
database management system (DBMS), 2
databases, 2
data redundancy, 64
datasheet view, 6, 68–69
delimiter, 91
descending sorts, 20
Design view, 8, 179, 188, 205
desktop database, creating using template, 38–40, 42–44
Desktop task management template, 39

Enable Content button, 9
enforce referential integrity, 31–32
enforce referential integrity, exercises, 35–36
Excel, managing data with, 30
Excel, *vs* Access, 29
Excel, *vs* Access, exercises, 33
expression, 130
Expression Builder, expressions with, 141–143
Expression Builder, launching, 142–143

field, 3
field properties, 8, 67
field row, 90
field selector, 6

File tab, 5
Filter by Form, 22–23
Filter by Selection, 21, 23
filters, 21–23
filters, exercises, 24–26
Find command, 7
foreign key, 31, 67
form, 4
Format tab, 184–185, 206
formatting calculated results, 133–135
Form Design tool, 182
Form Layout Tools Tabs, 183
forms, 176
forms, adding field to, 184
forms, adding styling to, 186
forms, adding theme to, 185
forms, adjusting column width in, 184
forms, applying background image to, 187
forms, deleting field from, 184
forms, exercises, 190–195
forms, modifying controls, 184–185
forms, sorting records in, 188
forms, using form tools, 176–183
Form tools, 176–177, 182
Form view, 178–179
Form view, edit data in, 183
function, 143

Home tab, 5, 20, 38

join lines, 30

keyboard shortcuts, 10

Label Wizard, 202–203
Launch App, 38
layout control, form, 178, 186–187
layout control, report, 207–208
Layout view, 179, 183, 203–205

macro object, 4
many-to-many relationships, 81
Merge/Split group, 205
module, 4
Move group, 187, 206
Multiple Items form, 181
multiple-table databases, establishing table relationships, 78–82

## A

Access database, 2–3
Access database, adding a record, 10
Access database, Built-In Functions, 143–145
Access database, built-in tools, 29
Access database, content security, 8–9
Access database, Create tab, 5
Access database, creating a, 37–44
Access database, deleting records, 10–11
Access database, editing a record, 10
Access database, exercises, 13–19
Access database, using existing, 9–12
Access database, File tab, 5
Access database, filters, 21–23
Access database, Home tab, 5
Access database, interface of, 4–6
Access database, managing data with, 30
Access database, Navigation Pane, 5
Access database, object types in, 3–4
Access database, organizing information in, 3–4
Access database, Ribbon, 5
Access database, sorting of data, 20
Access database, tables, 60–69
Access database, title bar, 5
Access database, using existing, 9–12
Access database, views, 6–8
Access Report Wizards, 205
Access template, 37
aggregate functions, adding to datasheets, 151–152
aggregate functions, common, 151
aggregate functions, creating queries, 152–157
aggregate functions, exercises, 158–160
AND operator, 22, 93–94
argument, 143
arithmetic operators, 132
ascending sorts, 20
AutoNumber data type, 8, 66

## B

Back Up Database utility, 11–12
blank desktop database, 37
blank desktop database, creating a, 38
Blank Form tool, 182
Blank Report tool, 196
Built-In Functions, 143–145
Built-In Functions, exercises, 146–150

## C

calculated field in a query, 130, 132, 156–157